PURSUIT
OF LIGHT

An Extraordinary Journey

SANDY BREWER

PTH
Peach
Tree
House

Carlsbad, California

Cover photo by Andreas Koessler

ISBN hardcover: 978-0-9796554-4-9
ISBN paperback: 978-0-9796554-3-2
LCCN 2007928723

ATTENTION CORPORATIONS, UNIVERSITIES, COLLEGES, AND PROFESSIONAL ORGANIZATIONS: Quantity discounts are available on bulk purchases of this book for educational, gift purposes, or as premiums for increasing magazine subscriptions or renewals. Special books or book excerpts can also be created to fit specific needs. For information, please contact PeachTreeHouse, Inc, P.O. Box 1008, Carlsbad, CA 92008; Phone: (760) 230-8123.

www.PeachTreeHouse.com

ACKNOWLEDGMENTS

My deepest thanks to Dr. Mary Lou Rane, whose constant support, encouragement, and belief both in my writing and the value of this story made all the difference. Heartfelt thanks to Thomas Sharkey for always championing this book, for his infallible good taste, wise words, and amazing loyalty. Thanks to Charles Pearson for his creative vision, brilliant design ideas, and for just being him. Thank you to Dillard Ellis for his insight, the angels, and all that he adds. A warm shout-out to public relations pro extraordinaire, Carol Zahorsky, for her generosity and constant willingness to offer the next idea. And to Patti Green for working for us with such love, long into the night.

I have always had a natural ability to speak well, but without the gifted coaching and guidance I received from Devorah Cutler-Rubenstein at The Script Broker, I shudder to think what might have ended up on the page. Thanks, Devo.

Early readers made such a difference, and I am grateful to all of you, especially Gary Seidler, who went the extra mile for me. It lifted my spirit greatly. To the many people who gave me encouragement and informed feedback, thank you so much. To all my wonderful clients through these many years, it has been a privilege to work with you and to learn from you.

My kids and grandkids are fabulous. I thank all of you. A special salute to Kelly, who became a part of our business family this year.

And finally to John, my extraordinary husband and partner in all things: Thank you for never getting bored with all the rewrites—or at least pretending that you didn't. You're the best of everything.

For John

and

For Kelly, Keith, and Nick
who took the bumpy ride with me

With love and gratitude

"The black moment is the moment when the real message of transformation is going to come. At the darkest moment comes the light."

—Joseph Campbell

CONTENTS

INTRODUCTION

Life is about choice.

Victor Frankl lost his family and freedom in the Holocaust. Yet, in the midst of that horror, he discovered within himself an emotional perspective—an attitude or core awareness—that sustained him through his darkest hours. He chose that new attitude and managed to survive both physically and emotionally. He changed the way he viewed what was happening to him and with that shift created a new emotional reality. He saw and experienced himself as something greater than his circumstance. So great was his internal change—the way he viewed his reality—that when he emerged from the hell of a concentration camp, he established a second family and founded the branch of psychiatry known today as existentialism. Now that's an attitudinal shift!

Like Victor Frankl, we all must choose. Choice requires picking a point of view and understanding that one inherently has the capacity to do so. It is a birthright that we all need to claim. In fact, consciously choosing is imperative because once any individual changes a point of view, that person also changes his or her reality. Contrary to popular opinion, reality is not carved in stone. It's based on personal opinion. That's how three people can be in the same room at the same time, dialoguing on the same subject, and yet be experiencing three different realities all based on the exact same factual data. Simply put, personal reality—or how one experiences what we call reality—is not limited to a narrow definition of the facts, but rather depends on the way one emotionally experiences them.

Choice impacts every area of our lives. Being a victim is a choice. Living life in the constant melodrama of a tedious soap opera—not that there's anything wrong with that—is a choice. Happiness is a choice.

The secret to establishing a sense of joy, possibility, and freedom is pretty basic: Dissolve the attachment to pain and suffering—that knee-jerk reaction to think "but I've been hurt, and I'm entitled to feel this way." Of course you are. Yet, heartless as this may sound, it really doesn't matter how difficult personal backgrounds and situations may have been or may still be. The facts surrounding us don't have to change in order for us to embrace the peace that "surpasses all understanding," the peace that transcends circumstances, the peace that is inherent within us.

No, the facts don't have to change, but the way we identify with them does.

Personal reality is created by personal attitude. Bottom line? Attitude—the way we frame the conversations in our head—is everything.

Attitudes notwithstanding, however, let me warn you ahead of time that in terms of detail my story gets worse before it gets better. For mine is the tale of a little girl who was disenfranchised in so many ways—a tortured, abused child who found a way to survive and grow into a woman with humor, joy, and a love of life.

The moral of this story is not about man's inhumanity to man or some parents' inhumanity to children or even how the light at the end of the tunnel can make things even out—sort of. If it were, then this historic tale would have little value except to those who like to suffer by association.

So, if the focus is attitude, why even go into stories of abuse? I struggled with that a lot while debating what I wanted to write. It is not my desire or intention to relate personal dramas for the purpose of evoking pain or emotional responses in others, although I am well aware it is a risk I take.

"Then why do it?" I asked myself and others who were mentoring me.

"Because if you don't share the journey—or at least parts of it—on an openly personal level," came the answer from both within and without, "how can you inspire the recognition that no matter what transpired yesterday, it is insignificant when compared to what lies within the core of one's being today?"

I love this story for the potential it can serve and the light it might help to rekindle. So, I made my choice to share some stories of trauma, with the intention of using them to promote the attitudes of hope and change. I'm not saying that the whole process of choosing a new attitude over popularly accepted interpretations of drama and trauma—like good guys/bad guys, "he done me wrong," and other sad tales of victimization—doesn't require a bit of swimming upstream. Going against the mainstream is always an upriver battle. But think of it as a nice river on a sunny day.

This is about choosing to change core and culturally accepted belief systems. No one is limited to genetics or chronological history.

What if it is true that we are not what happened to us? What if it's also true that we are one with an ever-ongoing universe that is constantly birthing and rebirthing its essence in us?

As Albert Einstein said, "Once you can accept the universe as matter expanding into nothing that is something, wearing stripes with plaid comes easy."

PROLOGUE

"Don't do it!" I said to myself. It was difficult to resist. The hate in me was so great. It oozed through my veins like lava flowing out of an active volcano. It torched my skin. It incinerated my now. I wanted to scream. I wanted to throw something. To take the glass of water I was holding and slam it into the wall.

I set the glass down.

*"Don't do it," I repeated. I was drowning in fatigue. I couldn't hold on any longer. I was a swamp of contradiction. The fight had been pounded out of me and yet someplace inside of me it still existed. Or so I hoped. But on that night I knew only one thing for sure: I could **not** face another night.*

"Don't..." I started again. But before I could get the rest of the sentence out, I did. I opened my hand and slapped it across my face with all of my might. Then I did it again and again and again. The words "I hate you" exploded out of my mouth.

I was the "you" I hated.

1

IN THE BEGINNING...

Darkness fell hard and cold in early December of 1929 in rural Tennessee. While the country plunged like falling dominoes into the Great Depression, in sixteen-year-old Zona Patterson's world, nothing had changed. For her, 1929 wasn't much different than the year before and the year before that. Zona, a dark-haired, dark-eyed beauty who topped 5'2" only if she practically stretched her slender neck right out of her shoulders, was still stranded on the impoverished dirt-farm where she lived with her daddy and mama and her brother, Tom, who was almost two years her junior. A hundred over-worked acres, a few hogs and chickens for slaughter, two broken down plow horses, one cow, and the meanest goddamn rooster in the county surrounded the primitive four-room house that anchored the middle Tennessee farm on which she lived. School was out of the question. Even if Zona had been able to hitch a ride, her family couldn't afford for her to go. Until she got married off, her mind belonged on how to keep the chickens plump and the cow milked, and her hands belonged in the finger-chapping, soapy water of the washboard. So saith her mother, Evangeline, who just happened to be one of the great gospel manglers of her time.

Zona was stuck—stuck without any reasonable prospects—stuck daily in the quagmire of her mother's never-ending demands and put downs. On that cold winter night she lay staring into the darkness of her bedroom still smarting from mama's latest assault. Her face, exposed to the frigid night air, held a tear that seemed to freeze on her cheek. Forlornly, she scrunched deeper under the layer of hand-me-down quilts that was keeping the rest of her small-framed body reasonably warm. Lost in her own desolation, Zona wasn't aware of anyone else in the room until she felt the movement of her bedding.

Her fourteen-and-a-half-year-old brother, Tom, pulled his lanky 5'7" frame, made strong by years of farm chores and hunting, into her bed. His nightclothes lay in a pile on the floor. "Hey, Sissy," he said toying with her hair. Zona pushed his hand away. "Aw, come on now," he cajoled as he began to explore the rest of her. Lamely, she tried pushing him away again, but soon her loneliness gave way to his insistence and his raging hormones.

Nine months later almost to the day, Zona gave out-of-wedlock birth to a son, thereby validating mama's declaration that Zona never was, nor would ever be, anything better than the rutting pigs who lived in the sty out yonder. Her daddy shook his head, clucked his tongue, but, as usual, demurred to Evangeline and said nothing.

A world away on a Saturday afternoon in December of 1929 in the still thriving metropolis of Chicago, eight-year-old Virginia Vivian Johansen, more commonly known as Ginny, was having her own version of a bad day. She burst in the door of her house in full throttle sobs, racing to her daddy who was lounging in his favorite chair sipping on something the adults in hushed tones laughingly referred to as "moonshine." She and her two older sisters, Beth Ann and Clara, had just returned with their mother from a shopping trip to the local Goldblatt's Department Store. "Oh, Daddy," Ginny wailed, tossing her long reddish-brown hair. "There's the most beautiful dress at Goldblatt's. It's red with a green belt and a full circle skirt. It's just what I've always wanted, and Ma…." Ginny paused to hiccup another deep sob. "Ma wouldn't let me get it. She said you couldn't afford it anymore. And then Beth Ann and Clara started making fun of me for crying in the store. Daddy, please, please, please…."

Sidney Johansen patted his youngest daughter on the head and looked into her blue saucer eyes. "I'll see what I can do," he mumbled and went back to his paper. Ginny scrunched the paper as she threw her arms around his neck. "Daddy, Daddy," she cried excitedly, "I *love* you!"

The following Monday, Joan Johansen followed her husband's instructions and, after sneaking a little morning dose of the moonshine for herself, went up to the Goldblatt's store and got the dress for her youngest daughter. The other two girls had already agreed to wear their cousin's hand-me-downs for this Christmas.

Ginny spent the next several years still in hot pursuit of her father's attention. Being the youngest of the three girls, she needed to assert herself over them and the screaming tirades of her alcoholic mother. Although her daddy was often gone—after all, he had a very important job in the city and frequently had to take pretty ladies to dinner and couldn't come home 'til very, very late at night and sometimes not at all—she was nevertheless his favorite. She learned early that she could leverage "favored" status not only with her sisters, but also with her mother. By the time Ginny turned fourteen, she had decided that male attention was without a doubt her ticket to ride.

Meanwhile, back on the farm, young Tom spent his ensuing years trying to escape his mother's home and disavowing any knowledge of whoever in the world might have fathered Zona's baby. Tom thought he, too, had finally found his own personal ticket to ride when at the age of seventeen he chose to marry a perky local girl with a huge mane of shoulder-length dark curly hair and almost nonexistent ambition. Her name was Elizabeth. Only trouble is Tom's ticket didn't take him very far. He and Elizabeth moved in with her folks who lived just down the road from his. At the age of seventeen and a half, he and his bride became the parents of a daughter they named Molly.

Six years later, the character-challenged Tom and the under-achieving Elizabeth were hopelessly estranged. He desperately wanted his freedom—freedom from the farm, his emotionally mute father, his strident mother-in-law who turned out to be a long-jowled incarnation of his very own mother, and the all-too-bumpkinish Elizabeth. His pockets may have been barren of coin, but his mind overflowed with plotting. He discovered that his stepsister, Allie—large-boned, broad-hipped, and twelve years his senior—who lived in Chicago with her round-shouldered, concave-chested, but strangely successful husband, could be his get-out-of-jail-free card. Allie was deep in the throes of grief, for she had recently lost twin girls at birth. Tom wrote to her about leaving the farm as well as his broken marriage, and Allie, wanting to believe his stories about what a mess Elizabeth was, had encouraged him to bring Molly up to her where she would raise the child for him. Anything to relieve the burning ache of her empty arms. In return, she would give Tom a house to live in and enough money to get him started in the big city.

So with Molly in tow, Tom boarded a train bound for Chicago under the pretext of a two-week visit that would allow his daughter to meet her Aunt Allie and Uncle Hank. Little six-year-old Molly scrunched up her pretty face with wailing tears as she sobbed goodbye to her mother at the station. Perhaps some deep, hidden part of her knew that it would be decades before she saw her mother again. Of one thing Molly was certain as she stepped unwillingly into the coach car: She did not want to leave her mommy, not even for a brief trip to the Great Unknown North.

Tom, wearing his innocent face, nudged Molly deeper into the car, telling her they'd return soon. But he knew he wasn't coming back. He was, in effect, stealing his daughter. Had his actions taken place in today's world, Molly's face would have appeared front and center on the back of a milk carton. But this was 1938, and the best one could do for milk containers was either the bucket that held the liquid fresh from the cow's teats or, in more urban areas, heavy gallon-size jugs delivered to the back steps of houses.

Either way, the bottom line remained unchanged. Nary a carton in sight.

Tom leaned his head back and let the chug-chug of the train's engine lull him into a restless sleep while Molly tried to suppress hiccupping sobs, unaware that her daddy had walked away from the slim remains of his conscience and any potential within him of grace, sealing the deal instead with his own weakness.

Elusive whispers of freedom toyed with Tom in his troubled sleep, dallying with bon vivant fantasies, then distorting and warping off into the ether as he wended his way north to the town that, according to crooner Frank Sinatra, Billy Sunday could not shut down.

Chicago.

And that's how the two people who would eventually become my parents managed to get themselves into the same state and the same town at the same time.

2

HELL HATH NO FURY

When Tom first sojourned from that poor dirt farm in Tennessee to the bustle of a big city where, while making chocolate in a local sweet shop he ran headlong into the seventeen-year-old Ginny, he had no idea he was cementing the direction of his life. His attraction to her certainly didn't appear to be foreordained or even a matter of personal choice. Maybe it was just dumb luck.

But I don't think so. I don't even think it was merely happenstance that I ended up being their kid. That would make life simply random, although perhaps what might be interpreted as randomness is more accurately described as life in its multitude of possibilities. And in those possibilities we have what Victor Frankl had. We have what is at the very core of our being. In those potentials we have choice.

That's where the road to all inner healing and self-awareness begins. Although my mother and father came from relatively common, albeit dysfunctional backgrounds, together they succeeded in creating something greater than the sum total of their parts. Only they opted for the dark instead of the light. They made decisions—initially small and then quite large—that plopped them right into the pitch-black side of their weak characters. Together they managed to mutilate opportunities and unleash Darth Vader-esque life choices that were so much darker than their individual histories would appear to have indicated. I've been a therapist for thirty years. Trust me, on paper who would have thought their backgrounds were harsh enough or stupefying enough to have laid the groundwork for the aberrant tag team they ultimately became?

I am alone in the house with my mother. Her name is Ginny. My name is Sandy. Everybody else has already left. It is the first day of school, but I'm not old enough to go. I have to wait three more years. It's hot. I plop down on the floor in the kitchen with my paper and crayons. It's cooler here. I pick the red crayon to draw a circle. My mom is standing at the kitchen sink washing dishes and wiping sweat off her forehead with the front of her arm. Pieces of her hair poke out at all angles, escaping the tight round thing she had pulled her hair back into earlier this morning.

Oh-oh. She's starting to talk under her breath. She's mad. The veins on her neck are popping out like pieces of my pick-up-sticks game, tied together and sewn in under her skin. My belly is doing somersaults, turning over and over. I'm scared, and I want to look away. But I keep looking back at her like I'm one of those nasty old moths that can't stay away from the light bulbs. I hate those things.

Her voice is getting louder. She seems to be looking at something I can't see. Maybe that's a good thing. If she looks at me, she'll bug her eyes out, showing the whites all the way around them. Like two eggs with blue yolks and a black dot in the center of them. She does that a lot when she gets mad.

I had a doll with eyes like that once. I poked them out, but then the black holes scared me even more. So I hid the doll, and now I can't find her.

Ouch! Her voice has climbed to that real loud, high place. It hurts my ears. I must not breathe or even blink my eyes. I am sitting perfectly still, trying with all my might not even to move a muscle, trying not to draw any attention to myself. If she notices me, something very, very bad will happen. I know it will.

Don't breathe.

"If that goddamn kid hadn't been born," my mother yells, "I would have been home where I belonged."

I am the "goddamn kid" my mother is referring to.

Oh, no. I see it, but I am too late. I'm only a few feet away from her. That's too close! She can reach me with her arm. She can reach me with her foot. I feel my whole body jerk as if I have just been poked hard with a fork. One of those long, sharp ones that farmers use for hay.

And then it happens. She looks down at me with her egg yolk eyes. I can't move. Something has me glued to the spot. I barely see the flash of movement as her foot rises a second before it kicks into my ribs.

And then she picks me up and flings me into the air—although, in truth, I don't fully understand what has happened until after I have crashed into the wall and bounced hard onto the floor.

I lay there limp and dazed, staring into the black square of the checkerboard linoleum upon which I landed. My head has such a sharp pain, like a knitting needle has been shoved into it. But I am too scared even to cry.

I am two years and four months old.

My mother stepped over her fallen daughter—that would be me—and stormed into her bedroom that was adjacent to the kitchen. She slammed the door loudly behind her and sat in front of her large vanity mirror, automatically reaching for her brush. She was livid beyond livid. If she could have gotten hold of her bastard husband, Tom, she would have gladly ripped him apart rotten piece by rotten piece.

Ginny sighed angrily. She had set her sights on Tom from the minute she first saw him almost eight years ago when she was seventeen and he was a suave older man of almost twenty-four. She saw him as a hand-some fellow, a true gentleman made even more attractive to her with his southern drawl and "yes ma'ams" heavily peppered throughout his speech. And he liked the look of her, too. As a teenager, she had mooned over his story about how he, the youngest of the family, had migrated from the armpit of rural Tennessee to the bright lights of Chicago to escape the clutches of his God-fearin', Bible-thumpin' mom. Evangeline—all 4'11" of her—apparently went around in the midst of summer's one-hundred-degree heat garbed daily in a black floor-length, high-necked, long-sleeved dress, under which she wore full petticoats and ankle-length bloomers. There was no doubt in Ginny's mind that Evangeline, already well into her seventies, ruled her brood with an iron fist or, more specifically, an iron cane, with which she seemed to have amazing dexterity.

Tom had more stories, too, especially about his first wife, the infa-mous Elizabeth. Ginny was convinced that the guy with whom she was so enamored had been abandoned by evil Elizabeth and left to raise his daughter all by his little ol' self. Tom had somehow failed to mention his deal with Allie. Besides, it was part of Ginny's theatrical flair to play the magnanimous damsel who had taken in another woman's child. She got a lot of mileage out of that initially, but Molly had always been a prickly thorn in Ginny's side. She was way too much competition. The child had matured early, and with her dark hair, deep blue eyes, and hourglass figure, she now looked more like something out of the movies, for chrissakes, than the no-account hillbilly she really was.

And then this morning Molly had come to her with some horrific tale about Tom stalking her, kissing her, and touching her in all the wrong places. Ginny, of course, slapped Molly across the face for telling such outrageous lies and then proceeded to probe and prod until Molly finally blurted out that it had all begun on the night Ginny had had her own near-death experience giving birth to that total nuisance of a child, Sandy.

Ginny glared into the vanity mirror as she continued to readjust her hair absently. Of course, Molly was lying. Of course, she was. Goddamn bitch!

I am still lying on the floor. I know that my body hurts, but it's odd. It's here, but it also seems far away from me. I can't really feel anything except that I feel too frozen to move.

My mother returns to the kitchen. My eyes move with her, but no other part of me does. She pushes me aside with her foot and reaches into the refrigerator for a beer. She opens the cap, takes a long swallow, and continues to glare at me like she's throwing darts from her eyes. She gulps down the rest of the beer and reaches for another. Under the pressure of her stare, I finally look down, but all I see is the same deep, black hole of the square of floor that has become the hard pillow upon which my head still rests.

I stay curled up and try to pretend I am not here.

According to my actual memory, the scene in the kitchen is a composite although it may have happened exactly as I've described it. But my memory of this time is not as cohesively consecutive as I've just told it. I clearly remember my mother's voice, the abrupt change in my world, the sense of always being under siege. I remember the hitting and kicking and that split-second sensation, frozen in time, of flying through the air on the way to hit a wall. And I recall being too scared to remember any of it with feeling. Had I let the pain come in, I would have died. That's how much bigger than me it seemed, and that's how, even at such a tender age, I instinctively protected myself by separating into two. The ability, unconscious as it was, to buffer myself from the physical pain was a gift that would become a life-saving grace in years to come.

Historically, I do know that my stepsister confronted my mother shortly after my second birthday, and it brought my mother to a cross-roads. She was going to have to make a choice. And she did. Rational, linear thinking, which Ginny had trouble holding onto on a good day, rapidly gave way to what had always been a predilection to self-centeredness. Like her mother and her mother's mother, Ginny's world, when not directly revolving around her, revolved around her image. "What will the neighbor's think?" was a credo more dear to her than any Bible she had ever, albeit briefly, opened.

Lost in her own ego, Ginny flushed away her remaining values and potentials—the batteries that might have been a life-line to the spark of light within her—and plunged headfirst into the dark. Her indifference toward me turned to hate, for my mother had finally found a target for her embarrassment at being married to a jerk like Tom.

It was my fault.

It was the beginning of the end of anything normal for me. It was the beginning of the end of anything redeemable for Ginny....

3

DANCING TOWARD THE LIGHT

The secret of The Secret is that all things and all people are, at their essence, transmitting a frequency, a field of energy, which is the creative source of all that we are and all that connects us. This frequency can be perceived as a light. It is this light of our own intentions and dreams that moves toward us as we move toward it. Initially, it can seem to be a very distant light or even a non-existent one. But there is no darkness without light at its core. To know and experience this, we have to lift ourselves out of the limited and limiting world of pain and suffering as an ultimate reality. That, too, is a frequency that makes us feel like we're walking barefoot across broken shards of glass and the light, if it exists at all, is in a galaxy far, far away.

Years ago, I had a thirty-something client named Suzie. She had fabulous, penetrating hazel eyes and a perpetually turned-down mouth. An accident had ended her very promising athletic career in her twenties, and, in spite of her many other successes, from Suzie's angle her life had been nothing but a mudslide ever since. For months I'd been trying to get her to consider a point of view that transcended her moroseness. But she was locked into the cavernous vault of her own mind—locked into her history, her genetics, her habits of thought. One morning, as she sat across from me in my office dabbing a Kleenex at those now tearing, beautiful orbs of hers, she pleaded, "Will I *evvvvvvvvveeeeerrrrr*" (dragging the word "ever" into sentence-long proportions) "be happy?"

I watched her closely and with tongue-in-cheek answered somberly, "No dear."

Startled, her head shot up. Suzie looked into my eyes and saw the humor sitting there. I observed her hang in the quagmire of indecision for a nanosecond. And then she did something that was out of character for her at the time. She burst out laughing.

Light comes in many forms. When Suzie embraced the lightness of laughter, she also initiated a profound change in herself.

Like Suzie, I get to choose. That's easy for me to say now—I've been around a long time. It's supposed to be easier by now. But it wasn't always so. There was a time when a light heart and ironic humor were separated from me by a world of hurt. This is funny? Cosmic joke? Look for the light?

Get out of my face!

But with time and a lot of practice, I eventually came to understand the value of humor, ironic and otherwise. I found that the lighter my heart got, the more connected I felt with an energy or force (a frequency) within me that wasn't bogged down by my painful past. I found there was an interaction—a dance of sorts—I could do with this part of me that in my mind is the heart and soul of my being. And as I reached for this lightness, an amazing thing happened. I felt that this force had been hanging around for some time, waiting for me to show up. Because it wasn't just that I wanted to dance with it. It wanted to dance with me, too!

It's a power dance involving this force—this ever-ready battery of choice—that moves us into the light and away from toxicity, darkness, and suppression. It's the movement of lifting oneself out of the abyss of knee-jerk reactions into conscious, self-directed choice. It's like being stuck in a pitch-black space and slapping a waning flashlight against the palm of one's hand, trying to eke that last flicker of light out of it—then holding your breath, hoping like hell that, dim as the shadowy light might be, it'll stay on for as long as it's needed. Until, at last, the electricity comes back on.

Or not.

It's up to each of us as individuals.

Inherent in experiencing the power of choice is the awareness of the power of the mind. It's rooted in the principle that I'm only a victim if I give someone else my mind.

So, in the early days, the discipline was to teach myself to stay in charge of the focus of my thoughts. That became my definition of discipline—the ability to be in charge of the focus of the mind.

No small task, especially when there were so many times that it felt like a clanging cacophony of some deranged mechanical beast had been turned loose in my head with screeching under-used brakes, popping massive springs, and blowing pistons. Belching black smoke while it endeavored to control my mind and body. There were weeks—or was it months?—when my only prayer was, "Show me another point of view." I would barely get the words out of my mouth when my head would once again become encased in the god-awful sputtering and spewing of some story of how wronged I had been or how hurt I was or how unjust something was or yadda, yadda, yadda....

Through trial and error, I met the challenge of lifting myself out of the density of a wounded emotion into the possibility of a new thought. A new emotion. A warrior's dance of self-determination, intended to quiet the jangling noise in my head of needing to be right and to silence the voices of the past that scream about my lack of value and insist that pain and suffering are the only options in life. Beating the drums of the fearful, angry rapper's litany bombarding my head, screeching that life sucks and never, ever does it get better.

But with years of effort, braided together with a passion for discovering within me something greater than my pain, I began to hear—underneath all that internal noise—a different sound, a new drummer, and to feel an expanded movement from a resonance deep within me. I call it the dance of a potentially dying light.

Potentially dying, because if I had remained unconscious of the power of choice, well, this little light of mine, it would never have shined. The pressure-cooker environment that seemed to thrive inside of me wasn't simply the trauma of my past, although that was a large part of it. When I asked for change, in fact, fervently searched for change, another part of me, greater than the pain, also responded. The light of consciousness knocked at my door, responding to the subtlest of invitations, as it prompted, pressed, cajoled, and, on occasion, shoved me into expanded awareness, challenging the status quo, challenging the density of conflict and pain.

So, here's the dance. It's a four-step. Begin by picking up that wavering flashlight—that tiniest glimmer of potential or hope, no matter how vague it appears. Picking up the flashlight is picking up the potential. It's the choice that says, "Yes, I can." It's choosing that, all emotional evidence to the contrary, today can be greater than yesterday. Today, I can reach for a point of view that is not rooted in my chronological history.

Today, I can use my mind to begin to create the part of my life I have not yet experienced. I am not limited to my genetics or my past. I am a pioneer. Today, I can choose with love, because today I am not only enough, I am more than enough.

Now here comes the light....

Put on your favorite music—I'd go for Elton John or Jimmy Buffet. Grab that flashlight and move to the count of four. Slap-slap (across your palm—the light's there), flicker-flicker (let go of doubt—choose the tiny spark of light), cross your fingers (don't give up), try to breathe (it always helps to breathe). Twirl twice. Now once again: slap-slap—if you can't see the light at least think the thought of the light being here; flicker-flicker—don't focus on the doubt; cross your fingers; try to breathe. Twirl, twirl. Keep it up. Don't pay attention to the head noise. Do the dance. With practice, the cacophony will dwindle to a simper and then morph into a harmonic—a gentle, restorative hum of possibilities.

With practice—lots of it—I learned that I could skip the crossing my fingers part. I don't have to hope the light is here. It's always here, even when I can't see it.

By the way, I lied about the twirling. There is no twirling in this dance, but it sounded like fun. So, if you want to twirl, go for it.

I will be five years old in one week. I am so excited. I asked my mom if I could invite some friends over for a party. She said no. But she is having my aunts and uncles and cousins over in the evening. The adults will drink and fight as always. But I'll have some cake, and I'll get some presents. I'm crossing my fingers and hoping some of them won't be clothes! Clothes are sooooooooooooo boring.

My friend Harriet is calling to me from the sidewalk outside my house. She's not five yet either. She has a scar on her top lip from where they had to sew her up when she was a baby. She's shy, but I like her. I run out the back door and hop on the hand-me-down red tricycle that is now mine. Harriet climbs on the back step and holds onto my shoulders as I pedal around the corner and up the block. It's a sunny and warm day. I'm very happy to be outside.

We round the next corner, and there is Mrs. Palmer leaving her grocery store. It used to be a double car garage just like the one at my house. But now it's a store. Mrs. Palmer holds up a brown bag she's carrying and says, "I'm on my way to the shoe repair shop. If you girls want something, I'll be back in a few minutes." She gets in her car parked next to the curb and drives away.

"Got any money?" Harriet asks me.

I shake my head.

"Me neither."

We remain perched on my trike while we think.

"Want to go in?" I ask.

"Sure."

I park off the center of the sidewalk and together we open the unlocked door—nobody ever locks their doors here. My mother has sent me to the store lots and lots of times, but this is the first time I've been in a place like this without an adult around somewhere. Ever!

Wow!

I walk up and down the aisles in wonder. All the shapes and sizes and colors and no one there hurrying me along. It's magic. I feel like I'm under a spell like the stories that I've read in the fairy tale book.

Then I come across the cash register. I play with the buttons just for the fun of it. The cash drawer suddenly pops open and scares me so much I jump backwards. I look down at the money in the drawer. Then everything gets weird and speeds up in my head. Without thinking, I fill the pockets of my shorts with coins. It all happens so quickly. The next thing I know, Harriet has grabbed a handful, too, and we're both racing out the door, leaving an open cash drawer and a trail of dropped coins behind us.

Now here I am, sitting under a huge lilac bush. Its branches are bending over with dark purple blossoms. I breathe in the sweet smell of the flowers I love and count my loot. My eyes open wide, but not egg yolk wide. I have $2.32 in my lap.

I am rich!

A light bulb clicks on in my head, and I get an idea that makes me feel warm inside. I gather up the coins and rush off determined to round up every kid in the neighborhood. I soon learn not every kid is available, but a lot of them are. I'm like the Pied Piper leading them all to another corner store a few blocks away. When we get there, I treat each and every one of them to an ice cream and throw in some candy for good measure. I count the remaining coins. Seventeen cents. But I am strangely content.

I munch on a vanilla cone and bask in the accolades of my buddies—some of them quite new-found. The afternoon sun passes over me, and the other kids have drifted away. I am not happy the way I was an hour ago.

The light dims. Shadows sorrowfully deepen. It is time for me to go home.

I climb up the steps and enter my house through the back door into the kitchen. My mother is waiting for me. Her face is red, and she is glaring at me. Dread drops the bottom of my stomach about a foot. She knows. A highball is in her right hand. She raises it, and I think she is going to throw it at me. I am braced to be hit in the head by the glass, but my grandmother and two aunts are there, too, which actually keeps my mother in better control.

"You goddamn slut!" she screams. I do not know what a slut is, but now is not the time to worry about that. Whatever it is, I'm sure it can't be good.

"How dare you embarrass me like this!" my mother roars on. She keeps yelling and bats me around my head with her hands. I force myself not to protect my head with my arms. It will only make her madder. Finally, she sends me to my room. "You bitch!" she hollers after me. "You just wait until your father gets home!"

I go inside my room and close the door behind me. My twin-size bed is against the far wall opposite the door. I sit on the foot of my bed. I am numb. Time passes, and I am still numb. Then I see the doorknob turn, and my heart jumps in my chest. It is my father. He closes the door pointedly behind him. He is still in his dark green work uniform. He doesn't say a word. His dark eyes narrow. The left side of his top lip curls up in a sneer.

I am suddenly terrified.

Slowly he begins to pull his black belt out of the loops that had secured it around his broad belly.

I pull my legs up to my chest and scoot back rapidly to the top of the bed. He laughs. I crouch tightly and cover my head with my hands. He whips his belt full force across my body. I shriek. He slams his belt across me one more time and the pain pierces every sense I have. I howl and try to press into the wall to get away.

But there is nowhere to go.

He strikes again and again and again.

And then I am gone.

The sound of my own crying wakes me. It's pitch-black night, and I am still on my bed. My father is not in the room anymore. I put my hand on the stinging pain coming from above my right hip. It is wet and sticky. I wipe my fingers across my cheek in the dark.

Wet tears streak through the blood I have just smeared onto my face. My knees ache; my whole body throbs. At last I fall back into a painful sleep.

"It's chasing me," I cry, looking over my shoulder at the huge, dangerous locomotive bearing down on me. It is the dead of night, and I am standing in the street in front of my house. I turn to my right and race up the road. My heart

is pounding. The steam engine roars after me, belching out thick, black smoke. I can't see who is driving the train, but somebody—somebody—just rang the bell, shattering my ears and shocking my teeth into chattering uncontrollably. I turn left at the corner and run past Mrs. Palmer's Store. The train pursues me. I charge across the street and rush up the next block. It follows, closing the gap between us. I am panting for breath. My heart feels like it's going to rip apart in my chest. I try to hide under the shrubbery in front of the house on the far side of the road. The bright beam on the front of the engine rips through my hide-away, leaving me defenseless. I scramble to the end of the block. The train races right behind me. I turn right and then right again as I dart down the alley. The locomotive thunders behind me, matching my every move. I tear ahead, my lungs aching for air. I look around quickly. I am in the alley immediately behind my house. My eyes burn from the terrible smoke. The demon train is almost on me.

I wake up with a start and sit up abruptly. I am drenched in sweat, but I am so relieved. That horrible, horrible train! It had only been a dream.

I lean back against the wall and almost shriek out loud with the pain of it. The train had been a dream, but what happened before I had fallen asleep was real. My father's beating, Mrs. Palmer's Store—those parts hadn't been a dream after all. Oh, how I wish they were.

It is the day after my fifth birthday. The living room is filled with neighborhood children who, unlike my relatives, have actually brought me toys for presents. One of them is a toy clothesline and clothespins. And some doll clothes to put on the line. I get some paper dolls with pretty clothes that have tabs that fold over the shoulders to hold them on. Then I open a board game, "Go to the Head of the Class."

But I am not happy. I feel like I'm in a bubble, going through the motions of my first children's party. But I'm strangely not really here. My mother changed her mind about this party the day after my great shame at Mrs. Palmer's store. It is very important to my mother that the other neighborhood mothers understand that although I may be a very, very bad child, she is a very, very good mother.

Some kids who endure the level of pain that my father inflicted on me that day of the infamous Palmer Store heist are able to escape into an alternate reality or fantasy. Through the savvy of the mind desperately trying to protect them, they scoot into their personal version of a tropical paradise or the Land of Milk and Honey.

That wasn't where my mind took me on that painful day when my father's abuse escalated in such a frightening manner that I seemed to disappear from the moment. I didn't actually pass out, but I did cease to be connected—to my surroundings, my body, and my pain. Sort of like a twilight sleep without the fairy tale ending of a handsome prince. From that point on whenever I was able to separate fully—which in itself was an extraordinary life raft in the midst of a very inky, roiling sea—I was simply able to detach from all feelings. It was as though my nervous system, my capacity to feel physically or emotionally, had been severed from my body and brain.

It was a godsend.

My terrifying train was not a one-time visitor. The train dream became for many years my signature dream. A recurring nightmare triggered by the belt I could not flee from when Ginny turned Tom loose on me the night of my transgression—the night from her point of view that I brought such great shame upon her oh-so-sweet henna-dyed head.

What *would* the neighbors think?

Through the years of my childhood the train morphed into a metaphor for both the belt and the life of abuse I could not escape.

One night when I was around twelve, I had the dream for the last time. It all began the same way—running up the street on which I lived, turning left at the corner, past Mrs. Palmer's store, and on and on. But this time something had changed in me. The giant train closed the gap between us and was breathing down on me, its fiercely exhaled dragon-like acrid smoke catching in my eyes. I could feel its heat as the hairs stood up on the back of my neck. I blinked rapidly, trying to ease the stinging in my eyes. I was almost there. But this time, when I reached the alley at the back of my house, instead of waking up, I turned around and faced the steel beast.

It was gigantic. But some part of me had had it. I looked up at my terrifying monster and said, "I'm not running anymore. If you're going to get me, get me now." I planted my feet firmly and drew in what I knew—*absolutely knew*—was my last breath on earth.

And then a most amazing thing happened. At the moment of impact, that heavy, solid, dense locomotive became diaphanous—like a cloud passing through me—and I remained of substance.

4

MEANDERINGS THROUGH A NARROW PATH

In my twenties, pain and suffering were ingrained in me as though they had been tattooed on the inside of my veins. I lived on an inner planet of pain. It flowed through my blood, not as a perceived choice or a point of view but as an unimpeachable reality. Every day of my life I hurt. Had people mentioned to me at the time that pain and suffering were a point of view, I'd have thought—and probably said—they were insane. And I'd have been pretty pissed about it, too. How dare they? Don't they get it— don't they understand what I've been through!

Yep, big tattoos. Without a beacon of light in sight.

When I was a kid, I didn't know about flashlights and moonbeams, and I sure as hell didn't know about metaphors. I had no idea how to seek the light within me or that it might be a good idea to do so. By the time I was four, I was already rapidly losing the ability even to seek for hope. And then, in the midst of the worst of times, along came my train. It was my first lesson, initially unconscious to be sure, that there was something deeper and greater in me than the circumstances of my life— something stronger than my mother, bigger than my father, greater than my fear. Something that could be aroused and come forth to my rescue. A glimmer of light that birthed itself out of a most treacherous path and abysmal darkness—a little yellow bulb, initially no bigger than a Christmas bulb, that gave me the courage to face and ultimately deal with the increasingly dire circumstances of my young life.

Looking back, I can see what was initially obscured but is now clear. If the dark is totally, unremittingly black, it can drive one so deeply inward that the light reveals itself. That is what I believe happened for me.

If we're young or innocent enough, beaten down enough, or simply strong enough to get out of our own way, that little frequency of light from deep within us will make its presence known. And if we have sufficient courage or desperation to pursue it, it will guide us out of the darkness and into the direction that can make tomorrow so much more promising than yesterday. The good news is if we're not spending all of our time projecting our point of view about the past into the future, today can be pretty good.

But, as a little kid at home, life was more like living in a windowless dark room than a sunny meadow. I was way too young to grasp that I was not to blame for my mother's cruel anger at me. Fortunately, I was also way too stubborn, way too much of a fighter, to surrender completely to the ugly scripts my mom kept trying to layer over me.

Which doesn't mean a lot of it didn't get on me.

It did.

I am five years old. My cousin, Peggy, lives across the street from me. We will be entering kindergarten together in a few weeks. She's the teeny-tiny, pretty, pale blonde one. Or so I've been told. Oh, and she's also the smart one. I'm the chubby one, and they call my hair color dirty blonde.

My mom keeps telling me I'm stupid. Then she calls someone and makes fun of me over the phone. That doesn't make me feel very good. If I just quit doing so many things wrong—I forgot to brush my teeth last night, I can't figure out buttons, I have hay fever and sneeze too much…. If I could just do things better, maybe she would like me.

I don't know why I make so many mistakes.

Today is a warm August afternoon. My mother has ordered me to sit on the high, white painted, three-legged stool in the kitchen. I climb up with bad butterflies in my stomach. This is where she makes me sit whenever she wants to ask me a lot of questions or to tell me something and see how I react. Every time I go visit my Aunt Allie, my father's half-sister, I end up on the stool as soon as I get home. The other day I was sitting by myself at the soda fountain at the Five and Dime, and I heard someone use the word "interrogate." They were talking about a man who had been caught robbing the drugstore and the way the police were questioning him. I'm not sure, but I think that's what my mom is doing when I end up on the stool.

"Look at you," my mother says once again, sharply pointing her finger into my chest. "You are such a mess." She takes a swipe at my ugly-colored hair, which seems to be growing a shade darker every year. "What is this?" she demands angrily, yanking a clump of my hair so hard my head jerks around. "For Christ sake, can't you even keep your hair washed!" She slaps my face, and I cry out before I can stop myself.

She squeezes the two sides of my mouth together hard. "I hate you! I hate you!" she yells. She's getting pretty wild, and I am getting pretty scared. I try not to move or upset her more, but I'm not sure what to do next. I know if I try to get off the stool, she'll go crazy.

"Aunt Clara," my mother continues to yell, referring to one of her sisters, "agrees with me. Aunt Clara says you're stupid and Peggy is so smart and pretty. Jesus, Mary, and Joseph, Sandy, you're an embarrassment to all of us. Goddamn you, you'll probably fail kindergarten. I wish you had never been born!"

My mother turns around, then abruptly looks back at me and shouts, "Aunt Beth agrees, too. Even your grandmother says you're a slob and a goddamn disaster. You bitch! Nobody likes you. They all hate you."

She storms out of the room with one final "Goddamn you!"

I sit in silence, watching the back of my mother's red-and-blue flowered, cap-sleeved house-dress as she marches down the hall. I think, okay, so Peggy is bright and pretty, and I'm dumb and ugly, and nobody will like me. I feel a tear start to sting in the back of my eye, and I force it away. "You will not cry," I say to myself. "You will not cry."

If I cry, she just makes more fun of me.

As an adult, I look back on these types of incidents with my mother, which sometimes included her gaggle of female relatives and their scenarios in which I was predestined to failure and little Peggy to be a future Miss America. In the end it was a good thing these economically strapped, underdeveloped women with way too much time on their hands didn't have the means to go to Las Vegas. They'd have lost the Sears and Roebuck shirts right off their backs.

My mother didn't succeed in breaking me, but she did manage to create a competition between Peggy and me—or more accurately, between me and Peggy—from which we never recovered. Of course, Peggy had problems of her own. She, too, had a secret. Hers was a deep, dark, damp secret. She was a bed wetter. One day shortly before our great kindergarten debut, Peggy's mom, Aunt Gwen—who, taken in the context of my extremely screwed-up family, wasn't actually that bad—used incredibly bad judgment and decided to make her daughter's private life public. She put diapers on her little girl, covered them with a short skirt, and invited all the neighborhood kids to play in their fenced backyard. When everyone was gathered, Gwen announced that Peggy was wearing diapers because she wet her bed. So all us little munchkins, being just as ignorant as the adults around us, chased poor Peggy around the yard for who knows how long, pulling at her skirt and taunting her.

Aunt Gwen's version of tough love worked. Peggy never wet her pants again. Neither did she ever become popular in school or get above a "C" average.

Like most kids, Peggy and I, each in our own way, stumbled through the challenging morass of early childhood, making choices—some of them conscious, some of them not. My cousin instinctively chose to stay safe by staying inconspicuous while the Mad Hatter mentality of my entire family pressed me into the opposite direction.

But heads or tails a quarter is still a quarter, the quarter here being a metaphor for insecurity. Neither is better or worse. They're just opposite ways of expressing the same fear. Peggy became withdrawn, less verbal, and introverted. I became forceful, aggressive, and driven to achieve.

Heads or tails.

In spite of my mother's wooden stool inquisitions and Peggy's backyard shame, we finally made it to kindergarten, where we promptly went our separate ways. Peggy quietly melted into the background, and I became mesmerized by a popular classmate named Marsha.

Moon-doggishly, I would follow Marsha all around the classroom. She was the prettiest, the smartest, the best of everything. Marsha is who I wanted to be. Not sure of how to pull that one off, I came up with a Plan B. I would be her shadow. She would walk up to the chalkboard, and I would be there with the eraser. She went to the bulletin board to hang a picture of her hand that she had just outlined, and I stood next to her with the thumbtack. Miss Barton, our kindergarten teacher, would tell us it was time for our naps, and I would race to lie down on the mat next to Marsha's. It's amazing that I hadn't already irritated the hell out of little Marsha, but instead she would smile at me as we closed our eyes for our ritual nap and pretended to be asleep. I sighed happily. Marsha liked me. In a few minutes, Miss Barton would bring out the gingerbread cookies and milk.

Kindergarten was good.

And then one day I didn't just pretend to fall asleep as Marsha winked at me. I actually did. At first the sun was shining so brightly it made me want to laugh. Then I saw a black disc begin to eclipse the light. It really scared me. I didn't know where the sun was going. I thought maybe it was disappearing from the sky. Forever. A cold shiver of terror twitched through my body. I opened my eyes in alarm. I was so frightened. What was happening? Even in the dim light I could see that Marsha's face had turned impossibly ugly! She was pointing at me and laughing at me in a nasty way. I looked down and saw that my sweater was once again buttoned wrong, leaving the top and bottom edges foolishly uneven. I pulled at it hastily, so angry with myself. Why can't I get those silly buttons right? Am I stupid or what?

I looked at Marsha again. But she had disappeared and been replaced by the image of my mother sitting on the stoop of our house that morning as I waited across the street for the school bus. My mother was pointing at my coat, which of course was buttoned wrong. Her finger shot out at me, poking fun at me, like a sword wounding my chest. The yellow bus with the black writing on it pulled up in front of me and blocked my view of her, but not before her words had found their mark.

"Sandy, you are so stupid!"

A noise pierced the fog of my dream. And then I realized the cry had come from my own lips. I opened my eyes. Everything was back to normal in my kindergarten classroom—except for Marsha, who was looking at me oddly, and the two little girls behind her, who were starring at me with their hands cupped across their mouths, trying to hold back their snickers.

Marsha and I remained friends all through the year, but in the summer her family moved to Cleveland, and I was left to fend for myself. I learned a lot from her. She'd been a great model for me of acceptance, popularity, and youthful intelligence. It made "fending" over the next few years a whole lot easier.

It is a sunny Friday afternoon in late April. Since the beginning of the second grade my teacher, Miss Drew, has appointed me to lead the class every single day in our prayer before lunch. It's a very important job, and I'm quite good at it. At Miss Drew's signal, I stand up in front of the class. Then I ask everyone to be quiet. As soon as they are, I start the prayer; then, we can all eat. No one else in my class has ever been invited to do this. I think maybe I'm special in Miss Drew's eyes. I think she likes me. I think some of my classmates do, too.

"Amen," I say with the other kids, concluding today's prayer. I start to return to my seat when Miss Drew calls me up to her desk. She's pretty with dark hair and eyes—and she's getting married a week from Sunday. All of us in her class are going to the wedding. Actually, we're going to be in the wedding, standing along both sides of the pews with ribbons and bows as she walks down the aisle. It's all so exciting.

Feeling happy and at ease, I walk over to where Miss Drew is seated at her desk.

"Sandy," Miss Drew begins in her soft voice, "you've done a very, very good job at being the prayer leader all this time...."

She seems to be studying my face. I am suddenly filled with tension. Something is very wrong here. Something bad is about to happen. I'm sure of it. My whole body goes cold inside.

"But," she continues, "it's occurred to me that I haven't been very fair to the other children. None of them have had a chance to practice being a leader."

I hold my breath. My stomach is wadded into a big knot. I can't lose this. I can't lose what makes me feel okay. I can't lose what makes me feel special. I stare without blinking past my teacher's head where a bunch of penmanship papers are taped to the wall. My head goes blank.

"As of Monday, I'll choose others to lead the class."

I close my eyes. The gauntlet fell.

"I'll rotate a new student every week. Sandy?" she queries. My eyes open, and I see her searching my face. "Are you okay?"

I nod. "Can I be excused to go to the bathroom?"

"Sure."

I walk past my desk, past the murmur of my classmates eating their lunches. I walk past the bathrooms, past the principal's office, past the nurse's office, and right out the side door of my school. I don't know who or what is in charge of me. But I am not. I walk calmly and directly down the block and across the street, like a homing pigeon—only I'm without a home.

I arrive at a narrow pathway that cuts through to a beautiful but forbidden sprawling Catholic monastery. I look around at the manicured lawns, flowering lilacs, and towering trees and am drawn to them. Ever since I can remember, I've always loved the tall, green trees and the lilacs. I plop on the grass underneath a large maple and rest my back on its broad trunk. My head is empty. I have no other thoughts.

Two brown-robed monks walk by. Their hands are clasped in front of their waists, which makes the long sleeves of their garments almost touch each other. They smile at me and appear friendly, but they don't say anything. I watch them as they walk down the path away from me. They don't speak to each other either.

"I wonder if they're doing that silence thing I heard about last year?" I think to myself.

I remember when I first learned of it. I don't really understand how silence could be a good thing. I tried it a couple of times, and nothing happened. So then I decided to try it out on my family—of course, I didn't tell them about it. They would have laughed at me for weeks and weeks. Last Christmas Eve everyone came over, and I watched to see who was talking and who was silent. Well, everyone started yammering right away. My mom and her sister, Aunt Clara, were as usual the loudest. But then I noticed Aunt Clara's husband, Uncle Joe, hadn't said a word after he had said hello to everyone. Tall, thin, and stoop-shouldered, he quietly stood around toward the back of the room with a pleasant look on his face. Maybe not talking was working for him. But then my mom and Aunt Clara got so loud that everyone else in the room quit talking. It was hard to tell for sure, but I think the problem was that Aunt Clara had baked a pumpkin pie in a pie tin that my mother claimed was hers. Aunt Clara took another gulp of her highball and hollered, "Are you calling me a liar?" My mom shot back, "You're goddamn right I am." Then she picked up the pie in question and threw it at Aunt Clara, who ducked just in time to have the pie nail Uncle Joe, who looked perplexed. Pumpkin exploded all over his face and hair and shirt and tie. Then it splattered onto the wall and carpet.

I saw Uncle Joe later that night. He had cleaned up pretty well. But as he bent over to say something to my cousin, Joe, Jr., I couldn't help but notice a big glob of pumpkin sticking out of his ear. That was worse than any booger I've ever seen in my whole life.

I haven't eaten pumpkin pie since.

I am pulled out of my memories by the presence of another monk walking past me. He's not quite as friendly as the other two, but he's not unfriendly either. He nods without speaking and continues on his way.

I stretch out on the grass and think. I've been in parochial school since kindergarten, so I've had almost three years of religion classes now. Missouri Synod Lutheran. I guess there are other Lutherans, too, but I don't know much about them. Actually, I don't know anything about them except that they exist. Other than that nobody mentions them. Catholics I've heard about. I think our religions are pretty similar except for the prayer beads, the Pope, and that genuflecting part. Oh yeah, and the Blessed Virgin. Nonetheless, I'm supposed to convert them. But I have a secret fear that they'll convert me, so I stay pretty close-mouthed on the subject of religion around the few Catholics I know. There is a Jewish Temple not far from here, but my parents don't like Jews. They don't like Negroes or Polish people either. My religion class hasn't told me yet what I'm supposed to do about the Jews, which is just as well. I don't know any.

I close my eyes and relax into the soft green grass and the sweet smell of spring. I fall asleep listening to the sound of the birds. I awake with a start and have to remember where I am. The sun is going down in the sky, and I realize I'd better get home before dark. I know it's a long walk, probably three or four miles, and I have to cross a very busy street, but I've done it before, so I know I can do it now. I am standing in front of my house before I realize what I did today. And suddenly I am upset and frightened. I left school without permission. It is against the rules. Never, ever, ever do I break the rules at school.

I entered my home from the back door into the kitchen. My mother, highball in hand, immediately launched into a tirade, my father by her side in mute support. But, amazingly, it was fifteen or so minutes of yelling, to bed without dinner—and that was my punishment.

It could have been so much worse....

It's springtime again but a year later. I will soon finish the third grade. Oddly enough, nothing bad happened to me after I bolted from school last year following my dethroning by Miss Drew. It seemed to me that all the adults wanted to forget about it, so I pretended to do the same. But it really threw me, and, for a while, I didn't know how to be. Some of the kids teased me about not being in charge anymore. I acted like I didn't care. But I did.

There is a teacher's college that adjoins my school's campus. Every spring the college holds an annual talent festival for elementary school kids. Last year I decided to try it. It was only a couple of weeks after my life at school had changed so abruptly, and I don't believe I was thinking very clearly. I went to the contest completely unprepared. What was I thinking? That was so stupid, and I made a fool of myself, standing in front of all those people blathering on aimlessly for five minutes. I'm still embarrassed when I think of it.

This year I am determined to do better. This time I have read the suggested formats very carefully, and I have reviewed the categories from which I can pick. There are a lot of possibilities—Bible Story Telling, Book Reports, Singing, Short Pageants. You name it, they've got it. The icing on the cake is that the judges will pick the best of the best from the primary categories to repeat their performances in the evening presentation on stage in the college auditorium. Wow!

My classroom has two student teachers from the college in it. I have asked the male one, Mr. Johnson, to help me prepare, and he has agreed. So now I am spending every recess sitting under a tree with him, going over the presentations I have written. I was surprised—and a little mortified—when he told me he had heard about my belly flop last year at the festival. And he was surprised at how determined I was to get it right this time.

My birthday was this week. I have just turned eight, and the day of my big chance—well, really, second chance—has finally arrived. It is a Sunday afternoon. My dad drops me off at the college an hour before the contests start. I scurry around and finally find my way to the two different rooms I'm supposed to go to for my categories. I look at the posted schedule again to double-check the times. Yep, Bible Story is first; then, one hour later, I am to go and do my Book Report. I enter the room assigned for my first presentation. I'm excited more than scared. I've been rehearsing in my head all morning. The room is overflowing, mostly with other participants and their parents and grandparents. There's also a three-judge panel at a table to the side. This time, instead of murmuring quietly while I'm presenting, people are actually looking at me with interest. They have smiles on their faces. I'm sure I'm doing better than I did last year.

After my presentations, there is a nice round of applause, and I make a little bow. I spend the afternoon walking around the campus then taking the connecting road that leads to my school. No one else is on the road. I sit on one of the swings and do what I do when I am feeling nervous or scared. I try not to think about anything. It helps me not to feel anything.

Before I know it, the time has passed, and I race back to the college. Now I feel the excitement. I'm caught up in the clamor of many kids who have been hanging out with their families waiting eagerly for the judges' results.

And then the postings!

Now I'm more than excited. I'm really nervous. I hold my breath as I poke my way toward the front of the group, edging close enough to see. I search anxiously for the two categories I competed in. Oh, my! I am awarded a Blue Ribbon in each of them.

One more wait. I pace, more anxious than ever. I just heard someone say that this is the crème de la crème *moment.*

The results are finally posted.

Yes! I am chosen to present my Bible Story tonight on stage.

I am so happy that I feel my eyes brimming. How odd. I have never before cried tears of joy.

I close my eyes, and a deep sigh of relief escapes me. Then I find a pay phone and call home. My father answers. I know better than to express my feelings to either of my parents, so I simply tell him I won and ask to be picked up at 8:30 tonight instead of five in the afternoon.

It never occurred to me to ask my mother or father to come to the show. It never occurred to them to come either.

Succeeding at the talent festival was part of a childhood rite of passage for me. School-wise, the third grade was a very good year. It offered a plethora of positive events that helped me establish confidence in my choice, confidence in my determination to be somebody, and confidence in my ability to establish a façade of normalcy that was in such stark contrast to the reality of my home. School was the one salvation I could find, the one environment I felt I could control through my own efforts. It was the one place I could strive for success and pretend that I was okay.

Formal class elections were held for the first time in the third grade when I was eight. Term of office lasted ten weeks, and then new elections would be held. I was elected president first time out. Thank God! It resurrected my belief in myself at school, which I sorely needed. From that point on, I was elected president of my class every year through the eighth grade—except for the seventh grade, when I was impeached for not setting a good example by passing notes during an interminable religion class taught by a just-returned-from-Korea-and-slightly-rabid young minister who was determined to make us kids feel bad for being so privileged. I tried to talk my teacher, Mr. Boman, into relenting, outlining for him all the reasons his punishment was too harsh. But he stood there, hiked up his brown-belted gray pants to the center of his waist, sniffed through his patrician nose, and pointed to the confiscated note. My request for leniency was denied, and I was banished from that term of office. But in my child's mind I had been elected, so technically my string remained unimpeached.

My true crowning glory in school, however, came during the sixth grade. Television was still in its infancy, but growing exponentially in popularity. *Angel Casey's Sun-Times Quiz Down*, a quiz show for Chicago's finest youngsters, was the local hot ticket. As a twelve-year-old kid, I was impressed. Then one day the producers came knocking on the door of my school. The faculty would select three outstanding students: two regulars and one alternative—just in case one of the regulars pooped out.

The buzz among the students was incredible. We were giddy at the prospect of celebrity. My head bobbed with such excitement every day that my shoulder-length light brown ponytail began to look like it really was flicking off flies. The quizzing and testing began. The field was narrowed to ten. I had made the cut. Then came another round of drilling and quizzes, which seemed to last forever, but in actuality was probably only a week. The final day arrived at last. Peter and I sat in front of my classroom while teachers from all the upper grades fired questions at us. We passed and were named the regulars. Freddie was the alternate.

On the day of the live telecast, I arranged for a ride to the studio with one of my classmates. About an hour before I had to leave, my mother sent me to the store—the same one where years earlier I had treated my little friends to ice cream from my ill-gotten gains. As I was paying for the roast and potatoes my mother wanted, I told the cashier that I was going to be on television that afternoon. She stopped everything, called the owners out of the back room, and they all applauded me for what a great day this was for me. I was overwhelmed with emotion. It became the second time in my life that I shed tears of joy.

It was also the only acknowledgment for my television debut outside of school that I can remember. But it was sweet.

I went home, changed into my best outfit—a matching yellow sweater set and swirling gray skirt—pulled my hair back into my finest ponytail, straightened my bangs, and rushed outside. My ride showed up in a matter of minutes. I climbed into the back seat with my friend, and we were off. As my house disappeared from view, so did any thought of it. I turned to my friend, and suddenly the hyper-excitement I was really feeling bubbled out of me. I laughed, giggled, and talked spitfire rapidly all the way to the television studio.

I did okay on the show that day, although I didn't win. But I had found a place to shine, and I had gotten there. In that moment, that was good enough for me.

My mother, bless her pickled little—and we are talking small—heart, made a choice when I was only two years old that altered my life. She decided that I was the enemy and from that point on campaigned hard for my failure. As a personality, she was truly awful and suffered no conscience about sacrificing anyone weaker than she who got in her way.

For a long time, who she was and how she was got in *my* way. Then, as I grew older and mercifully wiser, I began to consider the possibility of inner healing, even for me. I started to contemplate choice. What if it wasn't just dumb luck—or lack of luck—that landed me in Ginny's womb? What if some part of my being or soul had also chosen her?

What were the odds? Ginny *and* a stupid soul.

Well, assuming I did choose my mother, it obviously wasn't for the life of luxury and tenderness that she so clearly could not provide. Could there be a long-term upside for the intensity and consistency of rejection that she offered with such pristine consistency?

Her capacity during my youth to become more and more vile in the ways she threw me to the wolves actually limited my choices and made them pretty clear. There was no middle ground—no gray area to burrow down into. I was either going to drown in the pain and self-hatred of primal rejection or I was going to grab that flashlight and hang on to it for dear life. Those were my choices. Descend into the abyss of a man-made hell or hang on until I grew strong enough to realize the source of the light was not external but came from a universal presence that many of us call God and that dwelled deep within my own being.

To me, my mother's behavior is no longer about right or wrong. It's just the way it was—a reality I experienced. I don't hate who she was; I don't love who she was; and I don't need her to be any different than how she was. Eventually, I came to understand that, like the scary train of my recurring nightmare, she was one of my greatest teachers.

But as a child all I knew was that her rejection initially made me want her affection more and fueled my drive for approval. It made me fight harder to prove that I might be of value. Ginny was, for all practical purposes, like a mama guppy that eats her young alive at birth. And I was a baby guppy trying really hard not to get eaten.

5

THE FALLING LEAVES

My parents: Ginny and Tom, Tom and Ginny. Fred and Ethel gone bad. Really bad.

It is a Friday night in October. I am ten years old. I am sitting at the dinner table with my family. If I could have my way, I would never, ever have a family sit-down dinner again. It's dreadful and totally impossible to know or prepare for what might explode on any given evening. My mother is the dynamite. Any one of us could unknowingly be the match. But mostly it feels like it's me. I poke with my fork at the green peas on my plate.

I look at my father. He is eating his pork chop with his hands. A small stream of grease runs down to his wrist, dripping onto the cuff of his thick, dark green work shirt. At our table any meat that has a bone in it is automatically eaten whole with our hands. We do not put napkins by the plates. That is reserved for company and the occasional restaurant we go to.

Unfortunately for me, attendance at dinner is not optional. Tonight my mother has once again zeroed in on me. I have made her mad again, but I haven't a clue as to what I did this time. My mother is in the middle of a rant at me. She doesn't really need a reason why. From experience I have learned that although her reasoning frequently doesn't make any sense to me, it's all strangely logical to her. I do not say a word. If I do, it will only make things worse. She glares at me angrily and continues to yell. "Just for that, missy"—I have no idea what the "that" she's referring to is—"you will go with your father tonight. Get your goddamn ass out of my house and out of my sight!"

I stifle a sigh. Siberia. We've been studying that bad Soviet Union in geography the last few weeks. My Siberia tonight is in reality my father's business, a soft drink bottling plant. It's about a forty-five-minute drive from here. I hate it there, but then again I don't much like my father either. I don't trust him. He always makes me feel creepy.

I look at my mother and know that there is no room for negotiation. Then I notice my dad is looking at me. There is the dreaded sneer on his face, but there is something else in his eyes, too. My skin crawls. It's like a scary, scary wave is washing over me. I don't understand it, but it makes me want to throw up. I swallow with difficulty and try to control myself. My mom is the queen of puking and fainting, so I try very hard never to do either.

My father and I arrive at his business, and I sit in his office as instructed while he goes into the plant to tinker with the bottle capper that is giving him trouble. I look around for something to read. I read all the time, but there is nothing here. I twirl in the desk chair several times and then stare out the window. It is dark outside. After a while, I get up and go to the bathroom, more from boredom than anything else.

The bathroom is small and narrow. The toilet is located opposite the door. I am just starting to pull up my underpants when I hear the doorknob rattle. Without even thinking, I instinctively ram my body against the door, trying to hold it shut and struggle with my panties at the same time. I have no idea who or what is on the other side. I fumble with the chain midway up the door, trying to latch it. I didn't think to do that when I came in. The bathroom in our house doesn't have a lock on it.

I push harder against the door. And then I hear his voice. "Let me in, honey."

It is my father.

My heart is pounding in my chest. Something is very wrong. I grunt out loud and try with all my might to hold the door closed. But he is huge, and I am ten. He pushes through the door, his arms outstretched toward me. Everything is happening so fast. "Come here, baby," he coos weirdly. I manage to twist out of his clutch, and I race from the bathroom into the darkened hollows of the bottling plant. He follows me. His eerie chuckling terrifies me. I dart through an open door and wind up in a small, square room. He enters right behind me. I am trapped. I start to shriek and to plead. For what I am not sure.

He catches me and pushes me down hard. My head hits the concrete floor. I try to squirm away. He rolls me over and puts the full force of his 250 pounds on my body.

I can't breathe.

I CAN'T BREATHE!

Then there is a piercing pain between my legs. And then I am not there. I am in a somewhat familiar place that sees but does not feel.

The survival gift of being able to separate from one's immediate experience is akin to the gift of a post-surgical epidural to block the intensity of the pain. It gives you room to heal—just a little bit—and it gives your brain and body room to adjust to the intensity of the extreme shock it has just endured. As a child, I was given the gift of mental "separation" many times. As a woman, I am grateful for that merciful gift so desperately needed by the child I once was.

It is a short time after my dad hurt me. He is locking the outside door to the bottling plant. He motions toward the car and tells me to get in. I open the door to the back seat on the passenger side. It's as far away from him as I can get. He snickers. It hurts to lift my leg to climb in. It hurts to walk. There is a sharp, throbbing pain in the back of my head. My whole body aches like something just ran over me. My ribs hurt. I am still having trouble breathing. My stomach cramps painfully, and I want to throw up. But I can't. My mom would. But I refuse.

I huddle in the back seat until we get to an area that I recognize. My father comes to a stop at a traffic light. Just as the light turns green again, I open the back door and jump out. He yells, but I have already slammed the door shut, so I don't hear what he says. The car behind him honks. I open the gate to the backyard of the second house on my right. Just like at my house, there is another gate on the opposite side of the yard that leads to an alley. I go through it and find a way to get lost in the darkness. I crouch in a wedge of a nearby garage, pull my skirt down over my legs, and think no thoughts. I have no idea what just happened to me, but mercifully I cannot feel my body right now—at least not as much as I could when I first got into the car. All that I'm aware of is that my heart is still pounding in my chest….

I awake with a start and the shock of the pain in my body. I touch the back of my head where it hurts so bad. Blood has crusted over. There is a sticky mess between my legs. I have no underpants. I don't know what happened to them.

I am so ashamed. I don't know why.
Where can I go? Who can I talk to?
I have no place to go.

I do the only thing I know to do. Slowly, I limp home. My head is once again blank. By the time I walk through the back door of my house into the kitchen, it is close to midnight. My mother takes one look at me and starts screaming. She is furious. Even madder than she had been a few months ago when the parents of Diane, the twelve-year-old girl who lived across the street, came over and told my parents off. Their daughter had accused my father of trying to fondle her breasts. More than once.

Tonight, my mother is actually out-screeching herself. My father is nowhere to be seen. I do not have the energy to stand. I pull out a chair and sit painfully, propping my elbows on the table and holding my head in my hands.

I think—but only briefly—about cleaning myself up. Maybe a bath. But there's no way I can get naked in a house with so many doors and no locks.

I can't take it anymore. I get up and slowly walk down the hall to my room with my mother's tantrum still ringing in my ears.

All of my life I have loved the falling leaves of autumn. The morning after being raped I rose early, struggled with my hurting body to bundle up, and went outside. I used the rake to gather some of the leaves that had fallen off the giant elm trees surrounding my house into a huge pile next to the curb. I tucked two potatoes into the center of my stash and lit the leaves with a match. I spent the morning tending my fire and cooking my potatoes. It's something that I had done often, although it took forever to cook the potatoes. But I loved the leaves and the smell of the potatoes cooking within them.

In the early fifties there was no sex education. We were gentrified. Mamie Eisenhower, Doris Day. White gloves and pillbox hats. Happy Days without the Fonz. S-e-x was a four-letter word and perverts, if they existed at all, certainly did not live in the suburbs. As a ten-year-old, I had no idea where babies came from, and although I regularly won spelling bees, I would not have been able to define the word rape.

On the morning after my father first raped me, I was having an almost out-of-body experience—although I wouldn't have known that term, either. Metaphysics was not exactly my neighborhood's genre. Nevertheless, as I prodded and poked the fire for my precious potatoes, instead of being involved in the normal experience of the cooking and the tending, I was only aware of me watching me cook and tend. The shock and horror of the previous night was sending me into the next level of me separating from myself.

Like Alice through the looking glass, I was slipping more deeply into two caves with fading lamps and very different realities.

6

THE ABYSS

It is the night before Thanksgiving, barely a month after the first time my father attacked me. I am sitting on the edge of my bed alone in the dark room sobbing.

"Sandy, Sandy…." I can still hear my father's voice from earlier this evening, whispering into my ear right before my mother left the house. He squeezed my arm painfully and looked me in the eye. It made my skin crawl in a way that made me feel naked and ashamed. Then he chuckled softly. "It's payback time, kiddo."

His words scared me as much as anything had in my ten years.

And now the payback has happened.

I try so hard never to break down.

But I am crying and broken tonight. I can't help myself. I know I am only ten, but I feel old and beaten. I must be a hundred. Maybe a thousand.

I don't know how I will get through this. I have no hope. I want to die. But I don't know how to. What am I going to do? How am I going to do it? How am I going to make it through this night?

I don't want to.

Oh, my God, it hurts so bad inside. I swear to God, I will kill anybody who touches me again. I cannot bear for anyone to touch my body again. Not ever, ever again. I will kill him. I will. I will just goddamn kill him.

I don't care if my mother would try to rip my tongue out for even thinking those words. Well, goddamn her, too.

Stupid me. WHAT AM I THINKING?

I know I can't win. I can't….

My father's not here, but it feels like his hands and slobbering mouth are still on me. Oh God, get his hands off me. Get him away from me. Please, please, please. No more. No more.

I can't find a hanky. I wipe the running snot off my face with my sleeve. I don't even care. I sink deeper into the sobs that I cannot control.

"Leave me alone," I cry out loud. "DON'T TOUCH ME!"

I hear my shouts echoing in the empty room. The tears keep coming. I can't stop them.

Ever since that first night at the bottling plant, my father has kept doing it to me. Time after time. A few minutes ago was the last time. Until the next time. I know it will not end.

When he first started attacking me at home, I screamed and yelled and fought. But nobody helped me. I know my mother heard me. Her bedroom is very close, and she hears everything.

A few weeks ago I made a terrible decision. I decided that my only choice was to fight harder. So I stole a small, sharp kitchen knife and held it firm under the covers. I stared into the blackness of the room, knowing that my father would come. It wasn't long before I heard the floorboards squeak, and I knew that he had entered my room. I was ready for him. He pulled the covers back and climbed into my bed with me. I waited until he started to pull down my pajama bottoms. Then I screamed and plunged my dagger into him. I wanted to hit his neck or his chest or his eyeball, but all I got was his shoulder. He howled loudly and wrestled the knife away from me. "I'll get you for this," he whispered into my ear before he left my room, dripping blood everywhere.

Two weeks have passed. Yesterday the bandages came off his shoulder. Tonight was his revenge. He told me so. Earlier this evening my mom, who no longer makes any effort to conceal how much she hates me, slapped me in the face again for who knows what and screeched out her punishment. Tonight I would not be allowed to go over to my grandmother's house with all the girls and women in my family to help prepare the big family feast for tomorrow. Mom said there was no one who even wanted to be around me anyway. She called me a goddamn whore and stormed out of the house.

I am condemned to stay at home with my father. Shortly after my mother left, my father came into my room. I glanced over at him. His face broke into a snarling grin. A tremor rumbled through my body.

He grabbed my arm and pulled me through the house and down the stairs into the basement where I saw that he had laid out a rope, a large black spider in a jar, and a raw onion. I hate raw onions and am more than a little terrified of spiders. He ordered me to take off my clothes. I resisted. He twisted my arm until I cried out and complied. I stood there naked and so humiliated. He took the rope and wrapped it around my bare legs and unclothed torso, pinning my arms to the sides of my body. Then he knocked me down onto the gray concrete floor.

"You stupid girl," he growled, "I will teach you not to ever try a stunt like that knife again."

He picked up the onion and forced it into my mouth. I twisted my head, gagging and choking. He pulled the top of my hair hard to get me to hold my head still. Tears streamed down the sides of my face. He pressed more of the onion into my mouth. I tried to spit it out. He pressed it in harder.

"Chew it or you'll choke," he sniggered. I caught a glimpse of him. His eyes were wild, but excited. And I knew he was enjoying this.

Finally, he was satisfied that he had choked enough of the onion down my throat. Then he picked up the jar with the spider. He held it up in front of my terrified eyes. "It's a black widow," he said with that same weird delight. He opened the jar slowly and placed the spider on my naked belly. I screamed. "If you move," my father sneered, "it'll bite you." He picked up a small stick and began to inch the horrible, horrible insect up my body.

Then he chuckled—that same evil chuckle that had terrified me in the bottling plant—and said, "When it gets to your face it's going to bite you. And then you'll die."

The spider did not bite me when it got to my face and crossed over my eyelid. So, I guess I will live. I don't even know for sure that it was a black widow. My father ended my torture by untying my legs and raping me, but by that time I was so completely terrorized it was almost unimportant.

I continue to sob alone sitting on the edge of my bed. I have never cried this hard in my whole life. I try rocking my body back and forth. It does not help.

How will I get through this night? How will I live? Can I live?

Do I want to live?

I do not know. I don't think so.

Maybe ten years is long enough....

7

SEEDLINGS

Okay, so this would probably be a good place to pull up that four-step dance of light, include the twirls, and throw in a little of Jimmy Buffet's "Cheeseburger in Paradise." Hold the onions....

It's true, life can be unbearably hard. The miracle is that there *is* light in the midst of it. My miracle is that the light is a healing light, 'cause it truly doesn't hurt anymore.

Obviously, it did as a kid, though, where too much of my life at home was like living within a shroud of painful darkness way before such things as symbolic batteries and flashlights were part of my reality. As a result, I spent my first thirty years under the mental guise of a confirmed victim, although it had never been my goal to be a victim.

Is it ever anybody's?

But a victim I was. For most of those thirty years I covered my seeping wounds with a façade of "Let's pretend I'm okay." But I wasn't. It's not that I was trying to feel sorry for myself or consciously wanting to stay in grief, pain, and anger. I just had no idea there was another way.

It sounds so simple to say, "Just make a choice." It is simple, as in not intellectually complicated, but emotionally, it's often not even a little bit easy. And sometimes it feels damn near impossible. For decades I suffered from maintaining the perspective that I was what happened to me or, as a minimum, I was the result of what happened to me. That was my reality because that was my point of view—namely, that of a victim. But the truth is my problem wasn't what I experienced as a kid. I managed to survive it as it was occurring, so technically it was already behind me. My problem was the conclusion I drew about myself as a result of what happened to me.

Years ago, I remember watching mallards on our creek attacking an older female duck. At least in my mind she was older. They went after her mercilessly with their squawking beaks and flapping wings. She fought them off and got away, but they returned and returned. One morning, I found her dead body washed up on the shore. Makes Huey, Dewey, and Louie look less inviting.

Trauma is that kind of a critter, a difficult duck with a very annoying quack. It gouges out a jagged-edged journey, instantly clouding one's vision and returning time after time. For trauma can paralyze an individual in a compelling, repetitive loop, temporarily freezing the seed of one's soul like a barren winter preparing itself for the long, dark night.

In other words, educational and enlightening as trauma has the potential to become, initially it sucks.

With maturity, however, comes the decision to do more than merely survive, to do more than just make it through the challenges of a personal "night." It takes courage to let the spring thaw happen in one's heart. It is a conscious choice that, like a fragile seed, must be gently planted, caressed, and nurtured.

Here's the thing: the light *will* reveal itself. Really. With participation, it will. It'll require stubbornness, tenacity, will, lots of practice, and maybe just a little watering can from whatever one perceives the "other side"—the spiritual side—of life to be, but the desire for change can, one fine day, blossom spectacularly into anyone's personal life.

I was in my thirties before I could reach beyond the trauma for what was then a completely foreign point of view for me: I am only a victim if I give someone else my mind. I am only a victim if I give some person, situation, place, or memory the power to control what I think of me. It's not like I got that thought and went, "Wow, what a great idea!" So ensconced was I in being a victim—after all, my parents really did the things they did—that I had to chew on the concept for several years. I thought about it. I am not a victim of the world around me or within me. I am only a victim if I give someone or something else my mind—if I give someone or something else the power to choose my mental or emotional point of view. If I give someone else the power to validate or invalidate me.

I thought about it again and again. And then I thought about it some more.

Choices. Would I ever be able to choose not to be a victim? My history so supported the idea that I really was one that I feared I was stuck there for all eternity.

Slowly the seed of a new possibility I had been so carefully tending began to sprout. My life always appeared to me to be about a victimized, abused child. But then I began to think, "Maybe it's not. Maybe it's more than that." I pondered the early years. "Perhaps," I actually muttered out loud to an empty room, "mine was a story about flying—not to be confused with Erica Jong's *Fear of Flying* treatise."

I shook my head, chuckling. No, my tale was hardly about sexual liberation, although, thankfully, I did achieve that, too. My story was more about short flights—like when Ginny took to tossing me through the air when I was a very little girl. Sort of like the Wright brothers, with some equally bad landings.

"Or could it be," I continued my conversation with the air, "that my story has been about what is without a doubt one of the unkindest cuts of all? The absolute rejection of a mother to her child, which can only lead to the absolute rejection of the child to herself?"

Amid the broken shards of glass strewn about in my thirty-something brain, a light bulb popped on. For the first time I understood what my brief adult forays into beating on my own face had been about. I was mirroring my mother. Standing in for her. Replaying her rejection of me by rejecting myself. Awareness opened the door for a new decision, and I promptly knocked off self-pummeling as an option for acting out unworthiness.

Good choice.

Of course, vanity helped a little.

So, face intact, I continued to ruminate. Not for every moment of every day but for a long time, nonetheless. Pondering—not the replay of the story but the curiosity and passion to find some kernel or pearl of wisdom within the story—became an almost sacred quest for me. Especially in my thirties and forties.

Although my story is factually accurate, the facts are not what will make it real in my life today. How will it actually impact my life? It all depends on how I identify myself as a result of the things I've experienced. What will make it real is the emotion I hold around what happened and how I use that emotion to identify myself. I have had the experience of a victim—many times over. But I am not a victim.

Why?

Because I said so. Because I choose so.

Because choice is my reality.

Because I am in pursuit of light.

And just like that we're back to the premise that what happened or is currently happening, difficult as it might be, is not the problem. The conclusion we draw about ourselves as a result of our experiences—good or bad—that's the juggernaut. The way we have identified ourselves will determine how we personally interpret the past, whether we fear or embrace the future, and how we experience our now.

So, is this a little girl's tragic story? Or is it the story of a soul in a young body ultimately wanting to discover something in herself and others greater than the dark? Is she a victim or a pursuer of other potentials? What *is* her reality? Who gets to choose?

I do.

Excuse me while I go in search of that flashlight.

8

BREAD PUDDING

Every moment is a choice, and every choice reverberates. It's a frequency that echoes not only within the walls of our own personhood, but it pulses like an ever-expanding eddy into our environment, touching and potentially influencing everyone who comes in contact with it. Every moment presents an opportunity to "pay it forward." Ann Poplis taught me that. She was someone I knew in my childhood, a middle-aged, angular-faced German woman with a ready smile who made a simple choice—a simple act of kindness that impacted me deeply, not because of the magnanimity of the act but because it gave me a feeling I had not known. It gave me the feeling of what it was like to have someone be truly considerate of me and put me first. It made a tiny air pocket in my inner cave of unworthiness.

The memory of Ann had been tucked back in the craggy, cavernous recesses of my mind for several years until one day when I was in my mid-forties. I was on the podium in front of the student body of Pepperdine University as the guest speaker for the assembly.

Now, I know that Pepperdine was probably not the most congruent alignment for me. It's a great school, but it's also a fairly strait-laced, conservative institution. Me? Not so much. So, there I stood—a liberal, somewhat non-traditional thinking, unorthodox woman. A maverick in mid-life clothing.

I was in trouble.

I looked out at my audience. Papers rattled, students murmured among themselves, textbooks and notebooks were pulled out of backpacks. Others slouched in their chairs with their arms folded across their chests and heads bowed forward as though they were settling in for a long winter's nap. Study Hall 101. And that's when it dawned on me that attendance for these weekly conclaves was not optional.

Nothing like a captured—not captive—audience to put icy fear in the heart of a motivational speaker.

Did I mention I was in trouble?

And to make matters worse, the last guest speaker for this assembly had been Ronald Reagan. As in former President Ronald Reagan.

Big trouble.

I stepped up to the podium and began to speak. Maybe one out of every ten or twelve kids glanced up. I was screwed. I didn't have to be psychic to know that this was not going to be one of my better speeches.

Was it too late to take up house painting?

How the hell was I going to get their attention?

Wow! This is an exciting but very scary day. Now that I am age eight, with school out, I have decided that it is time—absolutely time!—to learn how to swim. I tried last year when I was only seven, but just like my first time at the Talent Festival, my attempts at learning how to swim were a bust. Somehow, I just kept sinking to the bottom and swallowing a ton of disgusting water.

This morning I wrap my bathing suit and swimming cap—they make you wear one of those in the city pool—in a faded green towel, talk my mom out of seventy-five cents (it's not too hard when she really wants to get rid of me), and accidentally let the screen door slam as I run out of the house. Today is the day! Today I will conquer the water with the mastery of the best swimmer ever.

Move over Esther Williams!

I almost run the whole seven blocks to the bus terminal, counting my money in my head. It is a two-bus journey each way. Twenty cents for the round-trip bus fare and transfers to the second bus, twenty-five cents for the ticket to get into the pool for the one o'clock double session swim, five cents to rent a locker for my clothes while I swim, and twenty cents for a root beer soda and the world's best hotdog from the street vendor outside the pool. Ketchup, mustard, pickle relish, tomatoes…I can almost taste it already.

I get to the pool, pay the fee, change clothes, take the required shower, let an attendant check my feet, and am finally cleared to enter the already crowded swimming area. Kids are playing and hollering in the water. Perched atop towering chairs on either side of the pool sit two bronzed-skinned lifeguards who occasionally yell at one of the kids in the water but mostly are involved with the pony-tailed high-school girls right below them. I take a deep breath and quickly walk past the three-foot end of the pool, which I would normally slide into. I march down to the far end, look for one brief moment into the bowels of the nine feet of water below me, and throw my towel off to the side. I back up all the way to the chain-link fence and, as if my life depends on it, run to the edge of the pool, and hurl myself into it.

The cool water engulfs me completely. I descend to the bottom. My feet touch the cement floor, and I push hard against it to propel myself to the surface. My head bobs into the air, and I am immediately inundated with the noise of all the kids around me who are playing, swimming, and diving into the water. Me? I sputter, cough, and sink again.

I surface one more time but only briefly, and then I am once again under the water.

"Oh, my God," my mind races, "I am going to drown here in front of all these people."

Why I think dying in front of an audience would be worse than dying quietly alone, I have no idea. But that's what I think.

It seems to me that death could not be more than seconds away, when my head suddenly breaches the water, and I am greeted by blue sky, sun, and—above all—air. This time, I start kicking my legs and moving my hands in tiny little claw-like motions in front of me.

I am holding my own but going nowhere and starting to get tired. So, I begin to stretch my arms out farther in alternating motions and kicking my legs harder, and just like that my body planes out. Before I know it, I am at the side of the pool. I get out, rest by the side of the pool for a few moments of deep relief, and then decide to try again. I do this better and better until the end of the swimming day. Now I can call myself a swimmer. And that hotdog? It is the best I have ever eaten.

So far, it is a really great day.

I'm aware that I am proud of myself and walking with an extra bounce in my step as the afternoon grows late and I head toward home. I round the corner leading to my house and am shocked to see the dogcatcher's truck parked by the curb on the side of my house. Oh, no. Jiggs, my wonderful, tan, fifty-pound mutt—my dear, dear Jiggs—must have gotten into some kind of trouble in the neighborhood. My mom is on the grass, her behind resting on her heels in a full knee bend, her hand outstretched trying to coax Jiggs to come to her. The dogcatcher is just barely off the property on the street, trying equally hard to get Jiggs to come to him. Before I can call to him, my dog's curiosity gets the best of him, and the next thing I know my best friend has been snatched up by the stranger in the white coveralls and tossed into the back of the paddy wagon.

My heart sinks. I yell out at the truck as it pulls away from the curb, and I chase it down the street. "STOP! STOP! PLEASE STOP!" I fight back tears. I am so scared that I will never see Jiggs again.

Two days pass. I feel miserable but do not talk about it. My parents call me into the kitchen. Jiggs, they say, has been run over by a car and killed. I feel like a piece of me has been killed, too.

A few hours later my parents are having a party. I feel numb except for the ache in my chest because of Jiggs. I look at all these people in the living room and once again have that odd feeling like I'm here but not here. It is a little like being under water.

The night wears on. I watch my father go into his bragging mood. He likes to tell stories that make him special. I've seen him do it many times. Tonight, not realizing or perhaps not caring that I am in the room, he boastfully tells a story that stabs my heart. He tells how a car had not killed Jiggs at all. He had actually dug out from under a double steel fence. "He was a mess," my father says chuckling. "Bloody and limping, but I'll be damned if that sonuvabitch dog doesn't find his way all the way home." My father laughs as he tells how he grabbed my dog and returned him to the terrible, terrible people who broke my heart and killed my Jiggs.

It is only a few weeks since I lost Jiggs. All the neighbors and cousins and aunts and uncles are gathered in front of Ann Poplis's house for an impromptu picnic. Ann lives two doors down from me. She is a very nice elderly—she must be at least 50!—lady. It is Friday night. Ann is Catholic. She makes the sign of the cross over her hotdog and then pops it into her mouth. She says the sign of the cross makes the hotdog holy or meatless or something, so she can eat it on a Friday. She also says "no meat on Fridays" is a silly rule.

My dad starts to talk about how it is a perfect night to go fishing. The other men in the group agree, and all of us kids shout we want to go, too. The men say okay. All the kids cheer. I forget myself and cheer, too. I look around quickly. Too late. My mother has noticed.

My chest drops heavily inside of me.

My mother comes up to me and whispers in her meanest voice, "Forget it." Then she turns to Ann and others around her, puts on her fake smile, and says, "Sandy can't go. She was sick last week, and I don't want her to get sick again." I look around as all the other kids excitedly rush off to get their things together. "Please," I beg, "Please let me go. I haven't been sick all week. Please."

But my pleas fall on my mother's deaf ears. "You will be staying home tonight," she says. I feel emotion starting to overtake me. I pinch myself hard in an effort to hold back the tears, but I start to cry anyway. Ann, who has been in earshot during the whole conversation with my mother, comes up to me quickly and puts her arm around me. "You stay right here, honey," she says. "I have something just for you and you alone." And with that she disappears into her house.

Ann returns almost immediately with one—and only one—bowl of warm, freshly baked bread pudding topped with twin peaks of whipped cream.

Okay, so there I was more than halfway through the time allotted for my Pepperdine speech, and the rustling of newspapers was still thundering in my ears. Not that it was really that loud in the auditorium, but as a speaker I was having a terrible time getting past it. I was putting myself through hoops, fixated on trying to get their attention. And then out of the blue I remembered Ann Poplis.

When I finished the story of the fishing debacle and Ann's act of kindness, I told the Pepperdine students that I couldn't remember if I had even liked the bread pudding. But I had always remembered Ann and how her simple act of kindness had wiped away my lonely tears that fateful Friday night. I had always remembered how her caring had touched the heart of a little girl whose heart was rapidly closing. Ann, by her simple, spontaneous act, had made a difference to me. She had been a rare candle in a youth filled with too many dark nights.

I looked out at my audience. I had forgotten about the newspapers, books, and heads looking down. I had forgotten about my need to grab their attention. I had forgotten about my ego and gotten back to speaking from my heart.

"Choose kindness today," I concluded. "You never know when you might be somebody's bread pudding."

I stepped away from the microphone. The students actually applauded and with a fair amount of enthusiasm, although blessedly that was no longer my goal.

Thanks, Ann.

9

THE BOY FROM THE BAKERY

You know the song that laments, "Sometimes I feel like a motherless child..."? One would think that might have been a theme song from my early life. But it wasn't. Like children who grow up in poverty unaware that they are poor, my only experience was having a mother who hated me. I didn't know anything else. In my vocabulary, the word "mother" was not a synonym for love. I never longed for a mother who loved me because I had no understanding of that concept. And I never tried to ferret out a substitute mother. Although I don't adhere to this position now, as a teenager and young adult I believed that you get one chance at having a mother. If she's good, you don't need another one. If she's bad and you've already been burned, you won't want another one.

And Ginny? Well, it goes without saying she was not just bad, she was horrid....

I am ten years old. It is a cold, cold Saturday evening. A little over a week has passed since the worst Thanksgiving of my ten years, when my dad punished me in ways I can't bear to remember. Last night I prayed hard, and while I was praying, I started to cry again. And then I cried and cried. My body heaved up and down with the pain of it all. I have got to stop doing that. I told God I am sorry, so very, very sorry for how bad I have been. Why else would these horrible things be happening? I am so sorry that I have been so bad, and I know God is very disappointed in me.

Today is a little better, but I still don't think I can live. I'm not sure I'm good enough to live. But I have not yet found a way to die although I have continued to think about it. But not all the time. Sometimes I even forget about it.

Like this afternoon when I bundled up warm and went to the movies, which is something I really like to do. My favorite theater is the brand-new Mercury. It's big with clean red seats and large bathrooms. Well, at least the girls' is. I don't know what the boys' looks like. Two weeks ago I left my glasses with the pink pearl frames in that bathroom, and I never did find them. Boy was my mom mad. She said I can just blankety, blankety do without glasses from here on out. Which is fine with me, 'cause I don't like to wear them anyway.

The Mercury Theater is in the opposite direction of the ones I have usually gone to—the Montclair and the old Elm Theater. They're all about an equal walking distance. Both the Mercury and the Montclair charge a quarter to get in. The Elm is still fourteen cents. My mom didn't want to give me any money today, so I had to think of something. I had a dime left from last week, and I dug through the cushions in the couch and hit the jackpot when I came up with a nickel and four pennies. Sometimes it felt like maybe God didn't hate me so much after all.

The Elm Theater it was. Unfortunately, Randolph Scott was in one of the double features playing today. I like cowboy stories—I especially like the horses— but I do not like Randolph Scott.

I am home from the movie, plopped on the floor in the living room where I have been sitting cross-legged, trying to warm my toes while I think. My mother has just hollered at me from the kitchen to go to the basement and get a jar of what she calls her "famous" canned peaches. Actually, they're pretty good. She is going to serve them layered around a scoop of cottage cheese as part of tonight's dinner. "Hurry up," she yells. I don't even think she's mad at me right now, but her voice is like the men who talk during a movie. She just does not know how to whisper.

I get up from the floor. I am still wearing my green-and-yellow-striped dress from this afternoon, but I have taken off my shoes and socks. I always take off my shoes as soon as I can. Barefoot is the best.

At the top of the basement stairs, I reach for the light switch and notice a dim light already coming from the cellar. My pulse suddenly races. This is not a good thing.

I hesitate. I do not want to go down those stairs. But what choice do I have? None that I can think of. She'll kill me if I don't get those peaches. Maybe someone simply forgot to turn the light off. "Don't think," I tell myself, clenching my teeth, "just do. Do what you must do."

My heart starts to race again. Is it possible for a ten-year-old to have a heart attack? I don't think so, but it is exploding in my chest anyway. I descend reluctantly to the cellar, which runs the full length of the house. It is eerily lit by a couple of naked light bulbs.

Thump, thump, thump. It's so loud, it's like I can hear my heart making noise outside of my chest. I suddenly feel clammy and hot, even though the basement is cold and damp. It smells musty. I start to run, racing past my father's large workbench all the way to the back of the room and turn into the partitioned-off area directly underneath the kitchen that houses the hand-cranked washing machine, a big sink, and my mom's makeshift pantry. The light bulb is burnt out in this cubicle, but there is enough shadowy light coming through for me to reach for the peaches.

I'm almost outta' here.

Thump, thump, thump.

He steps out of the shadows and grabs me from behind. I jump right out of my skin and yelp loudly. I am so startled I almost drop the peaches. He presses me against the shelves and works his hand under my skirt and inside my pant-ies. My mom's screaming voice pierces through the rafters. "Sandra Lee! Goddamn you, what the hell is taking you so long? Get your ass up here. NOW!"

All I can feel is panic. It almost paralyzes me. "Relax, baby," my father says in that icky sweet tone of his that makes me want to puke. "Be Daddy's good girl now." And with that he plunges his fingers deeper into me.

My mother continues to scream down from upstairs. It is more than I can take. I push hard against the shelves and twist a half-turn. The peaches fall from my hand, crashing against the bare concrete floor. Glass and sticky peach juice everywhere. The surprise of it catches my father off guard, and he loosens his grip on me. I squirm away from him, dart the full length of the basement, and head up the stairs. Only this time, when I reach the landing, I do not reenter the main part of our house. I open the front door and, shoeless and coatless, shoot out into the icy cold winter night.

I do not have a plan. I do not think. I do not even feel the cold on my bare arms or feet. I am running and running.

I am almost to the end of the block, panting hard, when a uniformed cop whose house I have just passed catches up with me. He was pulling up in front of his house, returning home from his shift, when he saw me. I know who he is. I have seen him in the neighborhood before. The no-name cop matches me pace for pace. He is starting to pant, too.

"Hold on for a minute," he says.

I keep going.

"Slow down," he says. "You can't be outside in this weather without a coat or shoes." He puts his hand on my shoulder in an effort to slow me down. We are on the next block by now, and I am getting pretty winded, so I cooperate.

"What's wrong with you?"

"He's hurting me," I cry out.

"WHO is hurting you?"

"My dad."

"Your dad?" he asks incredulously.

I stop running and look at him. Even though it's dark, there is a street lamp close by, and I can see his face. And then I know it's no use.

"I'm sure it's some kind of misunderstanding," he says. The cop takes his jacket off and wraps it around my shoulders.

I look at the dark night and the dark sky. I look at the dark jacket wrapped around me. There is no place to run anymore. It is all just dark.

I am sitting on the hard-backed kitchen chair, shivering. I have wrapped a scratchy, wool army blanket around me. The heel of my left foot is starting to throb. I think there is some glass in it. The light from the overhead-ceiling fixture feels like it is piercing my eyes. I remain silent and stone-faced while my mother, father, and the cop discuss me as though I am not here.

That evening my world continued to fracture along its deepening and inevitable fault line of duality. This was not about conscious choice; this was about survival—that precious instinct of the mind/body connection that helps people get through situations they shouldn't have to get through. Light and dark, good and evil, pain and numbness. The oneness of me began to split into the twoness of me—like conjoined twins being surgically separated. But the split, by giving me a way to contain the pain, would also provide a potential pathway for me. Such is the essence of survival and life. There's a secret window inside of us someplace if we can just find that little spark of light. My personal salvation was the home and school split. Home was obviously the downside of that equation. But school! School was like the benediction at the end of a church service. It was that which blessed me.

On that night with the cop and my parents when I was ten, there were no blessings to be had. Only shame and hopelessness. I sat in the uncomfortable, hard-backed kitchen chair watching myself as though I were not there, even though another part of me knew that I was. Duality and separation from self at its finest.

Through the years, I have observed in awe the quintessential capacity for these human organisms of ours to persevere. The innate ability to separate, temporarily, or, alas, sometimes permanently, a part of oneself from the mainstream of one's own self-awareness in effect forms a separate unit that functions as if it belongs to another person. It is a life raft in the midst of one's personal perfect storm.

It is this brilliant survival mechanism of the brain that allowed me to endure and to become more adept in the two worlds in which the destiny of my youth lay.

A part of me listened to my mother, my father, and the cop discuss what needed to be done with such a disobedient and naughty, naughty girl who had, according to them, thrown a jar of peaches at her father and run out of the house when he was disciplining her. Another part of me was disinterested and, for all practical purposes, not even there.

Any remaining shred of innocence, as well as most shreds of hope, died within me that night. As my duality intensified, my antennae grew. I became like a silent snake that could slither around the corner and take in the whole room while no one noticed me lurking right there in the background.

It's how I survived and how I almost died.

It is less than one week before Christmas. I have not seen that cop since that horrible Saturday night, but I have gone way out of my way to avoid walking past his house. I don't know what I would do if I saw him again.

Something is going on in my house right now. I don't know what it is, but it's something. As I was walking from the kitchen back to my bedroom, I noticed my parents sitting at the large claw-footed formal dining table. Nobody ever sits in the dining room in my house unless there is company. It simply is not done. Plus, my mother was actually talking in a low tone. That just doesn't happen, either.

Something is up.

I leave the red apple I brought from the kitchen on my bed and sneak out into the hallway. I press tightly against the wall that separates the dining room from the hallway. Slowly, carefully, I inch closer to the edge of the archway. A piece of chipped paint flakes off the wall and drops onto my sweater. I flick it off irritably. This is not the time to have my concentration interrupted. I am on a mission.

I risk a rapid peek around the corner into the dining room. They are still there, huddled together. I duck back quickly. I do not move a muscle. I don't even breathe. But nobody yells at me. They didn't notice me. I start to breathe again. I am as close as I can get. I stay absolutely still. My mother's voice, restrained as it is, begins to carry toward me. Even through her hushed tones it is obvious that she is angry.

"You are such a goddamn loser, Tom. You are a goddamn piece of shit. Jesus Christ! I'm telling you that cop won't be the last time. She'll tell others. She'll destroy me."

My dad mumbles something that I can't hear.

"You're going to fix this, Tom. You goddamn got me into this. You are going to goddamn get me out of this."

For a minute all I hear is silence. Then my mother's voice.

"Get rid of her. I talked with Doc Stevenson today. I'm going to have my varicose veins taken care of right after New Year's. That's when you do it. You take care of her the first night. Do you hear me? The first night." Her voice rises in spite of herself. "And you better goddamn well do it right. Make it look like an accident. I swear to God, you blow this, and I'll turn your piece of shit ass in. I swear to God I'll get you for this."

I am stunned. I cannot take it in. Her words are bouncing off my brain like pebbles against a wall. I shake my head to clear it. Then I shake it again.

Was it real? Did I imagine this?

Silently, I move away from my listening post and tiptoe into my bedroom. It is still light outside. The yellowed paper shades that cover the two small windows in my room are at half-mast. The mirror over the beige paint-it-yourself dresser is still cracked the way it has been for months. My narrow pink-and-black stretchy headbands are tossed willy-nilly across the wide, furry white one and nesting on the right edge of my dresser. The thin blue chenille spread is still all crumpled, forming a blue puddle of fabric on the floor near the bottom of my bed. My black three-ring notebook and schoolbooks are still stacked on the floor near the head of my bed. My clear plastic pencil box lies next to them. My tan-and-white saddle shoes are still tossed lopsided on the floor.

Everything is just as I left it. Everything is still the same.

Only my life is changed.

I sit on the edge of my bed. I am hollow inside.

I twist a lock of my sandy brown hair between my thumb and forefinger. How many days? I count. Ten, maybe eleven.

I hope it goes quickly.

My arms are too heavy to lift. I am more tired than I have ever been in my life.

I am ready. I am done. It is okay with me.

It is the second day of the New Year. The holidays have passed. They are all a blur to me. Even the rapes. Earlier today my mom checked herself into the hospital.

No one is in the house but me. I sit on my bed with the bedroom door open, picking at a snag on the sleeve of my yellow sweater.

Waiting. Empty.

I am ten years, seven months, and two weeks old, and I am very tired. It has been a very, very long life…

There is a rattle at the back of the house, and I hear my father enter through the back door. I wish I had the energy to hate him, but I don't, even though I know he is such a horrible person. Still, there's a part of my thoughts that tries to pretend he's a good person, and all this other stuff is just some weird nightmare. Last night it was the nightmare again. This morning I didn't even wash away the sticky stuff between my legs. I haven't even taken a bath in at least a week. Why bother? What difference would it make?

I hear him continue to stir about in the kitchen, and I feel nothing but overwhelming fatigue. A cabinet door squeaks open and then is shut. A glass or dish clinks against the sink. The faucet splashes fresh water, then it becomes silent again. He goes into the bathroom but does not close the door. I think he is rummaging through the medicine cabinet that hangs above the sink. It sounds like one of my mom's many prescription bottles has clattered into the sink. My father curses, and then I hear him go back into the kitchen. A spoon or something is being clanked against a glass. Now everything is quiet. He seems to disappear for a minute or two.

I close my eyes. I am not afraid. I am numb. Ready.

When I look up, my father is standing in the doorway. My eyes are drawn to his right hand. A gun is in it and pointed at me. My head seems clear enough to me, yet everything is also strangely unreal.

It is all so unimportant.

"Get in the kitchen," my father snarls waving his weapon in my direction. I look into his face. Menacing. Some part of me knows that he is capable of pulling that trigger. It is difficult for me to get my legs to move. I shuffle with leaden legs out to the kitchen. "Sit there," he orders, pointing with the gun to a chair by the table. I sit. Some thick rope is curled up on the table near a tall glass of his precious Nesbitts orange soda.

And now I get it. The soda is poisoned with my mother's drugs.

So this is how it ends.

"Drink it!" he barks.

Why would I care? I have no reason to live.

I try to obey, but my body is not listening very well to me. What's wrong with me? Why was I such a terrible person that my mother hated me so much? Why couldn't I run faster the night the cop was chasing me down the street? Why wasn't I stronger the night I tried to stab my father? Why....

I hear him yelling at me again, and I try to reach for the glass, but time for me has stopped, and my body is slow to follow through. Why doesn't my body listen? Maybe that's the problem. My body lets itself get raped, lets itself get hurt. Maybe the only one I should be hating here is myself—or maybe my body.

Not that any of it will make any difference now.

My father's voice, like flour being ground out of a sifter, filters through the dense fog in my brain.

"Drink it," my father commands again. I am trying to lift the glass to my lips, but it is like I am trying to tap dance under water. I try again, but I am not going fast enough for him. I sense more than see a rapid movement of his arm. And then suddenly I am aware that he has placed the cold nozzle of the gun against my forehead. I am startled by the chilling hard steel pressing into my skin.

It is the first thing I have felt for hours.

And then in his impatience he cocks the pistol or releases the safety—or something. The only thing I know for sure is that the noise erupts in my brain, crashing through the barren emptiness I have been in.

A deep-woods animal yowl bellows out of my mouth. At the exact same time I grab the glass that a second ago I could barely lift and throw it violently into my father's face. It drenches him. Some of it falls back onto me. In my hair, on my clothes, on my face. But not in my mouth.

My father roars with rage. He pushes his knee into my gut to hold me in place and reaches for the rope. It has all happened in what feels like a split second. And then it is over. The fight in me has fled. I am numb again. He ties me to the chair, cursing and sputtering. I hear him searching through the house and know that he is looking for more drugs. I watch without feeling as he brings what he could find into the kitchen and dissolves it in more orange soda. He throws in some aspirin for good luck. This time he presses the glass to my lips himself. I submit and drink it.

A pounding, bass-filled voice showed up in the pre-dawn hours of the following morning. I know in retrospect that the voice was in my head. But when I first heard it, I thought it was outside of me in surround sound. Loud and demanding and compelling.

Stereo before we had stereo.

What caused it? I don't know. I'm sure there is some scientific explanation about brain cells dying or some hallucinogenic properties attributable to the drugs I had ingested. But I like to think it was my angels. That non-physical team that in my darkest hours I have frequently felt around me, urging me on, reminding me that I can do this. Reminding me that even when it looks and feels like I have absolutely no choice, I do.

A voice is coming at me from all directions.

"GET UP. GET OUT."

I try to open my eyes. My eyelids are so heavy….

"GET UP. GET OUT."

I work at it harder, and this time I am able to squint my eyes open. I am in my bedroom with its matching twin beds, one near the far wall where I sleep and the other one next to the door. It is dark in the room. The inside of my head is swarming with a gauzy fog. And it hurts. And then there is all this noise. Who is shouting at me? I can't see anyone. And then I realize I am in the wrong bed, the one closest to the door.

What am I doing in the wrong bed?

The voice rings out again. Deep and loud and blistering my head with its volume. But I still don't know who is talking. No one is here.

"GET UP. GET OUT."

The voice bounces off the walls from every angle. My head is mush, but the voice is so consuming I struggle to obey it. I pull myself to the edge of the bed and try to stand. My legs cramp and crumple underneath me. I fall to the floor, hitting my cheek on the rough edge of the narrow, knotted pink throw rug that separates my bed from this one. I try to lift myself up on my knees. I can't.

I look around again. My eyes have adjusted to the dark, and still no one is here. The voice grows louder anyway.

Thundering in my head.

"GET OUT, NOW!"

I try my arms again. I can push up with them. My shoulders feel okay. So I pull with my arms and shoulders. My useless legs drag behind me as I inch my way toward the bedroom door. Something inside tells me I must be very, very quiet. The voice propels me out of my bedroom. I creep around the corner, hunched up on my elbows, and pull myself through the small hallway into the dining room. There is no use heading for the back door. I would have to pass my father's room to do that. The front door is the only way out.

My legs are a little stronger now. I am able to use my knees to help crawl through the dining room into the living room. I am finally next to the front door. I want to rest here, but the voice is still raging all around me. I have to keep moving. The Christmas tree with the homemade Ivory soap snow on it is still up, standing tall, centered in the middle of the front windows. To make room for the tree, an overstuffed chair has been placed next to the door. My legs are still weak and unsteady but working enough now to help me prop myself up on the chair and rest on the cushioned arm. I lean my head against the door.

PLEASE, can I go back to sleep?

"GET OUT!"

The voice is everywhere!

I fiddle with the lock. It won't turn! I stay with it and am finally able to get the teeth at the end of the long, skinny metal key to line up right.

I'm almost there....

There? Where? Where am I going?

I slide to the floor. I think I am too tired to hoist myself up again, but then I do it anyway. It's way too dark to see anything, but I keep working with the key. Finally, I hear it. The bolt slips back, and I am at last able to crack the door open. I use the doorknob to help pull myself up. There is one more door to go. I need to be able to take only one step to get there. The voice pursues me. My wobbly body holds up, and I cling to the second doorknob. I wedge my way around the outside door and onto the front porch. I lose my balance and fall flat on my face onto the icy porch.

It is still too soon to stop.

"GET OUT."

I crawl to the edge of the stoop and tumble down the steps. From some place a very, very long way off, I feel a sharp pain running up and down my back, the scrapes and cuts on my palms, and the sting of the cold.

But I have to keep going. I am sprawled out on the sidewalk in front of my house. Now I keep pulling myself forward without any thought. Inch by inch, I draw myself out into the street, not even realizing I am out in the street.

I can go no farther. Exhausted, I turn my head to the right and lay my cheek on the hard, snow-packed road. I look straight ahead. Two sparkling stars are coming for me.

Like a bolt out of the blue, Fate steps in and sees you through. When you wish upon a star….

My own private "stars" on that difficult and perhaps fated day were the headlights on the car a teenage bakery worker was driving on his way to work in the pre-dawn hours of that morning. He lived less than two blocks up from my house, but it was a block I didn't spend any time on as a child. When he came across my semi-conscious body, he knew something was definitely wrong. He was even afraid he might have hit me. He fish-tailed his car to a stop and, not knowing which house was mine, went to the house next door to mine for help.

Camus wrote, "In the midst of winter I have found within me an invincible summer." To me that invincible summer is the recognition of a divine game plan, one that once we get beyond the experience of unutterable chaos and pain ultimately makes sense out of the incomprehensible. That somehow, some way, if we have the opportunity to hang in there—and if we grab onto it—the darkest night will reveal the purest dawn. That's my invincible summer.

I still remember the sense of hope and, strangely, peace I felt when I first saw the shimmering stars that turned out to be headlights. In a nanosecond of time they opened for me the possibility of another day.

Millions of children in our world are today looking for a thread of light that will give them their chance to hold on for one more day—their chance to live long enough to wish upon a star.

To this day, I've never met the boy from the bakery—or more accurately—the boy on his way to the bakery. I've never known his name. I've never seen his face up close. But on that winter morning, unknown to him, he became my angel of life.

And that's how I lived longer than ten years, seven months, and two weeks.

10

SHE WON'T DIE

I was eighteen when I made one momentous decision. It formed the raw beginnings of a course that would ultimately lead me into a future so beautifully different than my past. Not that I made my choice in hopes of any kind of nirvana. No, I actually had no hope. Just a decision.

There was no great drama that Saturday morning in late May. I was two weeks away from graduating from high school and being able to leave home legitimately. My plan was going to get a jump-start on college by picking up several quick credits in summer school on a campus almost six hundred blessed miles away from my parents' house. Fourteen days and counting. Uncharacteristically, I awoke early even though I didn't have to be at work until noon. I dressed quickly, slipping quietly out of the house and into the dirty tan 1953 Oldsmobile two-door coupe I had purchased with my work money a year ago. I rolled down the windows, breathing in the pleasantly cool, fresh early-morning air. I had a big dilemma to figure out. Was I going to plunk down some more money and upgrade to the sleek orange-and-white four-door 1956 Buick I was starting to fall in love with? Or would I stick with my klutzy albeit semi-dependable Olds?

Power thinking required the proper setting, so I drove the twenty-minutes to my favorite forest preserves. For the benefit of non-Midwest urban dwellers, forest preserves were strips of woods with towering trees set aside in the megalopolis of Chicago to help trick us into believing that we were not already living in concrete-infested jungles.

I parked and found that I had the walking trails pretty much to myself.

I started out at a fast pace. Not a power walk, of course. That terminology didn't exist yet. No power walks and no hikes—they were for mountain climbers. For the rest of us, it was just a plain-old walk. But on those wonderful walks, I never felt diminished by the huge, sprawling canopies of trees, only embraced by them. I was forty-five minutes into my walk and close to out-of-breath when I decided to rest for a few minutes by sitting on top of a nearby picnic table. My thoughts drifted from the car quagmire to my other life—my life at home. At eighteen I was still unable to connect with the compartmentalized part of me that held the momentous pain buried deep within me of my father's perversions and my mother's desire to have me dead. But I was aware of the blank, missing pieces of my life. I just didn't know what they were, and I had no one to turn to, no one to ask about it. Those strange, empty, dark circles in my memory banks were black holes that terrified me. Black holes that I was afraid to look into.

Of one thing, however, I was absolutely sure: Everything about the way I had been raised was wrong.

Immersed in this side of myself, the indecision of which car to go with became insignificant. Everything else did, too. Any hopes of going to school, and what that might do for me, faded into the background like an out of focus camera. My passionate teenage romances suddenly belonged to someone else, someone I couldn't, in that moment, relate to. I succumbed to that dark place inside of me. The aching pain of hopelessness. Sitting in the woods that Saturday morning, I did not—absolutely did not—believe that I had any future to look forward to. I did not believe that I would ever be happy or that I would ever have my own children. I did not believe that I would find true love or that I would be successful or prosper in any way. I actually thought I'd probably be dead by the time I was twenty-eight.

But with tears rolling down my cheeks, I swore that the one thing I would accomplish in my life—no matter how long or short I ended up living—was that I would *not* pass it on. The cycle of abuse would go to my grave with me.

I would *not* pass it on.

It was the only thing I believed to be absolutely true about me. I accepted it unconditionally. The cycle of abuse would end with me.

That was my first total albeit unwitting commitment to healing and change. Because without true, core-level change, the past *will* repeat itself in some form, in some way, whether an individual means to or not. So, on that late spring morning shortly after my eighteenth birthday, I set in motion—without any awareness of what I had actually done and without a road map of how to do it—a course change for my life that I never veered away from. I would not become my mother. I would not become my father. I wasn't sure I would ever truly become me, but I sure as hell wasn't going to become them.

Much later that day, I made another but significantly less monumental decision.

I got the Buick.

Obviously, twenty-eight was not my death knell, but it did turn out to be a very rough year. Through hard work and lots of practice, I grew in my life and prospered. As I did, my natural talents grew and blossomed, too. For many years, one of my favorite things to do in my work was to present workshops.

It was a December in the mid-1980s. A new snow crunched under my feet as I made my way to the Marriott Hotel in Denver, Colorado, where I was conducting a three-day workshop under the latitude-expanding banner commonly referred to as "Personal Growth," which, of course, leaves room for almost anything either the attendees or I appear to be in the mood for. Or to put it more concisely—it was a "let's just go with the flow" workshop. A group of fifty adults sat on chairs horse-shoed around me. I liked this size group. Not too big, so I could still get personal with participants. And not too small, so I could enjoy the fruits of my labor. It felt good not to be struggling about money anymore.

I was addressing Gloria, an attractive sixty-two-year-old woman with stylishly short silver-gray hair and a seemingly spunky attitude. Her unlined face and high cheekbones, *sans* "freshening" scars tucked behind her ears, were a testimony to some very good genes. Gloria was a divorced, well-to-do frequent world traveler. Her Sky Miles alone could easily fill a small bank. But in spite of her six-plus decades and world traveler status, she was still joined at the hip—or rather the navel—with her eighty-eight-year-old mother. A tear slid down Gloria's cheek as she spoke of her fate with her mother, who required her daughter—a grandmother in her own right—to phone home at 10:00 A.M. mountain time every day no matter where Gloria was in the world.

I looked into her misty blue eyes and went for the obvious. "Are you afraid your mother is going to die?" I asked.

Gloria looked at me with large, pleading eyes and bemoaned loudly, "She *won't* die!"

Soon we both had tears in our eyes, only mine were from laughter.

Although Gloria never quite caught on to the fact that it was okay to tell her aged mother to back off, her words "she won't die" lingered with me later that night. I thought of my own mother and her attempt to have me murdered so many years ago when I was only ten. I wondered how words like "she won't die" might have rankled Ginny when she learned that I had survived. Like all good predators, she was the victim. Lying in her post-surgical hospital bed in January of 1954, poor thing, her legs hurt like hell, I was still alive, and her roots were starting to show....

Perhaps from her twisted point of view she viewed the whole incident—the failure of her poisoning ploy and my father's ineptness as a child slayer—as bad luck for her and nothing more than a near-death experience for me. Although, in truth, can there ever be such a thing as *only* a near-death experience?

It is the day after my father poisoned me.

I am starting to come out of a deep, foggy place in my head. A woman's voice is calling to me from somewhere very far away. It seems to me almost like I've been having a nightmare—only not. The memory of red flashing lights— lots of them—swirls around in my brain. I remember seeing open rear doors of a large van and knowing that it was an ambulance. Blurred images of uniformed men. Then someone was picking me up. Then nothing.

"Sandy, Sandy," the unknown woman's voice continues to call to me.

I am aware that my body is stretched out, face up. Someplace. I don't know or care where. My eyes stay shut. I don't think I could open them if I wanted to, which I don't. I just want to stay wherever I am in this far, far away place. I can't feel anything here. I can barely think here.

"Sandy, can you hear me?" It is the same lady's voice.

I am so tired. Why is she bothering me?

Maybe she'll go away.

"Come on, Sandy," she coaxes again, "wake up, Sweetie."

Darn it! She is not going to leave me alone.

I feel a gentle nudge on my shoulder stirring me even closer to consciousness. I become aware of my fingers touching crisp sheets. I am in a bed. But not my bed. My bed never feels this way. It never feels fresh.

No, oh, no. Everything in my body hurts. Please don't make me feel again.

That woman is relentless. But she is not mean. I can feel her next to me now.

She shakes me, still gently but firmer. Her voice is kind but so much closer than before. "It's time to wake up now, Sandy. Open your eyes."

There is no escaping her. I struggle and finally pop them open as she had asked.

A youngish-looking woman is leaning over me. At first I think she is Miss Drew, my second-grade teacher. I am both startled and relieved. Then my eyes clear, and I see that I am mistaken. With her short, dark hair and pretty face, she only looks a little bit like Miss Drew. I recognize the long-sleeved white uniform she is wearing. She is a nurse.

She smiles at me. Her concerned blue eyes look down at me. "Sweetie," she calls me that again, "there's someone here who has been very worried about you." Her soft hand pats my cheek reassuringly, and then she steps back from my line of view. Another head bends over me. The heavy, almost black eyebrows that frame his dark brown eyes grab my attention first as they often have. His eyes go right through me. His hook nose flares, growing larger and larger until it shadows over me like a giant hawk about to pounce on me. And then his upper lip curls up in his trademark snarling fake smile.

"It's daddy, honey," he says for the sake of the nurse.

A soundless scream from a pit so deep within me, so ancient within me, wells up and catches in my throat. It is an abyss. An endless, endless abyss. I am being sucked into it. I can't catch myself. I can't stop myself. I am falling into the horrifying bottomlessness of it, caught in its violent, swirling eddy. Hurling and tumbling helplessly like a limp rag doll. Down, down...drowning in my own terror.

I can't get the scream out of my throat. My heart stops. It just stops. Then everything goes black....

Eventually, I wake up again. I don't know when. Three days pass during which time people in white coats take turns asking me how I am feeling. I say fine. Then they ask why I had swallowed all those pills? Was I worried about my mom's health? Did it make me sad that she was in the hospital? Was I missing her? I say I dunno. They finally decide I should go home and do what I was apparently already doing—forget about it. I say okay.

So, that's what I do. I go back home to my unfresh bed, to my father's painful, humiliating assaults, to my mother's hysteria, constant criticism, and cruel anger.

I also went back home to an altered reality. To repress, as a diagnosable condition, is subconsciously to force ideas or experiences too painful to endure or remember into the unconscious mind. That's what happened to me. Post-Traumatic Stress Disorder. From the time I fell into what was essentially a deep, mental chasm—a primal scream, if you will—my world split completely in two. Maybe even three.

World #1: School. My salvation was now, more than ever, my world at school, where I continued to be alert, intelligent, even popular. In my daytime school world I had absolutely no awareness of my nighttime Nightmare on Elm Street life. In this world I was like all the other ten-year-olds I knew. My daytime self had never seen an adult penis and, since sex was neither taught nor discussed among socially correct people at that time, I was completely in the dark on the subject. While at school, I could reference certain mundane happenings in my home, like what I had for breakfast that morning, but even those types of things were often fuzzy and sometimes completely eluded me.

World #2: Home. At home, when I was alone and knew I was alone, I was okay. A child in the blind. When the family was there, I would become more the observer—the watcher of myself and the others. But I was still protected by the way my mind segregated my life—as though different parts of me were keeping secrets from me. It wasn't that I had different personalities. I did not. It was more like there were different subdivisions in my head that didn't communicate with each other very well—and sometimes not at all. Still there were other times in which I would be physically detached and yet very aware while enduring those long, intense, cruel, and demeaning assaults in which my father stole my body and my dignity. But while that was going on, I never consciously thought of myself as a fifth grader. During the times of assault, my school world—my world of what for me was rational reality—was not available to me.

World #3? Non-existence…or maybe just completely uninvolved, unfeeling observational being. Not really alive but not dead either.

The interesting thing about the levels of split I experienced is that when I was in one side of the split, I had no idea that another side of me co-existed. The division that overtook me was an involuntary form of survival. This serious denial offered hope to me in my unremitting trauma. For without that protection, the stress, isolation, pain, and fear with which I was living could easily have broken my mind, then my body and my spirit.

I am twelve years old, in the early part of the seventh grade. It is a Thursday morning. I am feeling odd and sickly today, but I can't quite pinpoint what it is. It leaves me so uncomfortable that I have decided not to go to school. I need to stay home. It is an instinct that something inside of me tells me to listen to. So I do. I tell my mother I am sick. She yells, of course, and basically calls me a stupid bitch. I understand—she likes to have the house to herself during the day. But I prevail and, instead of going to school, am back in my bedroom with the door closed.

I breathe deeply and feel safe for the moment, surrounded by these four walls and two narrow windows. My father is at work, so I am safe there. My mother hates it when I stay home from school, but I have learned that when I'm ill, if I stay very quiet in my room with the door closed, she won't come in. She won't stay out to give me my privacy. No, that would never happen. But I think she won't open the door because she wants to pretend I am not here.

I sit on the floor cross-legged and reach for a box that I have kept under my bed undisturbed for the past two years. I pull it toward me and blow the dust off the lid. I carefully lift the box and hold it to me as though it were some kind of fragile flower. I sit there for I don't know how long until I become aware that I am rocking back and forth. I rock some more, still cradling my box. Then I set it in front of me and gently lift the lid.

There she is, just as I had left her so long ago. My dream doll. Her blue eyes stare straight up at me from her flawless face. Her close-cropped brunette hair still has every strand perfectly in place. Her spaghetti-strapped pink tutu frames her shapely figure, and her open weave pink tights cling to her long, perfectly contoured legs. Her pointed toes are delicately shod in pink slippers with silk pink laces that crisscross up her ankles. She is my ballerina doll, twenty inches tall and gorgeous. My grandparents, aunts, and yes, even my parents, had given me dolls on Christmas throughout the years. She is the last doll I ever asked for—and miraculously got! I got her three years ago when I was nine, the only doll I chose to keep.

I know I am way too old to play with dolls anymore, but I stare at her longingly. Finally, I carefully lift her out of the box, raise her graceful arms over her head, posing her in a pirouette, and escape into my make-believe world. For a few timeless hours I am her. It feels good.

Then the high of my fantasy begins to wear off, and I reconnect to my body. There is something wet and squishy between my legs. I set my ballerina down, get up, and risk an encounter with my mother. But it can't be avoided. As quietly as I can, I slip into the bathroom. I wipe myself with toilet tissue and then look at it. I am shaken and distraught, but I don't know why.

The tissue is covered with red blood. I have started my first period.

I cram a wad of toilet paper between my legs and return to my room. I toss the doll into the box and shove it under my bed, vowing never to look at her again. I don't know why I am taking it out on the doll, and I don't even know why I am mad. I wait 'til later in the afternoon to tell my mother about my period. I have to tell her because I need to find the sanitary napkins, and I don't know where they are. Her response to me is loud and angry. "Goddamn it! Shit!" she storms. "I didn't think I'd have to deal with this so soon."

It is later in the evening, and I spy both of my parents sitting in the living room talking—at least my mom is talking, gesturing emphatically with her hands. I can't hear her words, but I know she was telling my father about my period. My cheeks get hot and turn red with embarrassment.

Then something odd happens. My dad actually leaves me alone for almost two weeks. Unprecedented since the first time he raped me two long years ago. His usual pattern was at least three to four times a week. Arduous assaults, more often than not with me being stripped of my clothes and him remaining fully or mostly clothed. He could spend hours playing doctor or little boy—you show me yours, I'll show you mine, but first you show me yours—or a myriad of other warped games, all of which involved humiliating exposure and always ended in rape.

So he gives me this little hiatus, then suddenly he reappears with a vengeance. He is on me and in me nightly, sometimes two or three times a night. It is an onslaught that overwhelms and almost breaks me.

It is now almost twelve weeks since my first period. Things with my father have returned to their normal horrible status. It is late in the day when my mother calls me into the kitchen and asks me about my periods. She has noticed that the stash of sanitary napkins in the linen closet is not dwindling the way it should be. I tell her I have only had one period. She gets hysterical. I mean *really hysterical. She calls my grandfather and asks him to come right over. My mother and father sit at the kitchen table with my grandfather, and I am off to the side on the white painted stool where I have been instructed to sit. My mother tells her father that I was raped by a stranger and she is afraid I am pregnant. My grandfather—a man about town with all kinds of contacts—says, "I'll take care of it."*

A few nights later, he picks me up at my house and, without any discussion, takes me to a medical office. I don't remember anything after that except waking up several times during the night. I am on some kind of cot-like bed. My grandfather is sitting on a chair next to me. He stays with me through my fitful night and brings me back home in the morning.

I have no idea and little memory of what had transpired the night before. I am feeling heavy and weighed down inside of myself and in a not-too-unfamiliar daze. I go to the bathroom and am surprised at what I find when I wipe myself with tissue. I am filled with blood. I remain sitting on the toilet seat, staring at the blood-stained tissue in my hand for some time, too disconnected to feel anything but lonely.

All of these incidents happened in the fifties, a long time before Roe v. Wade. And I was a chaste little girl from a good Christian family. So, although I had always had a facility for words and language, I never would have thought to call what I had just experienced an abortion. It was definitely not a word in any of my spelling bees. Nevertheless, in the bathroom the morning after my grandfather returned me to my home when I was twelve years and five months old, I discovered that my first abortion had produced my second period.

Later on that same day, Ginny, without preamble, placed a wad of condoms in my hand. I was clueless. I had no idea what a condom was or what it was for. "Your father is a sick man," my mother said to me, noticeably leaving herself out of the picture. "Make him wear these." With that she promptly left the room.

As a twelve year-old, I looked at the milky-colored, slithery rubber worms in my hand and threw them in the trash as quickly as I could. I grabbed the bar of soap that always sat at the edge of the sink. I turned on the hot water full force and furiously scrubbed the palm of my hand. I scrubbed and scrubbed and scrubbed until at long last I looked down at my scalded hand and saw that I had drawn blood.

11

―――――――――――

COSMIC CAFÉ

Choice has built-in paradoxes. On the one hand, it appears that we have choice, at least mental choice, over everything. On the other hand, overwhelming circumstances seem to give us no choice at all. Nobody consciously chooses to be raped, murdered, tormented. That's an insane idea. So what, then, is choice?

The power of choice is the recognition that we have the right and the ability to perceive any circumstance or condition any way we want. That recognition does not come instantly or without going through a huge learning curve—a huge choosing curve. In the end, though, we get to choose whether what did happen, what is happening, or what might happen determines what we are and our worth. On this point, I was not exactly an Einstein. Seriously remedial was more like it. It took me years of trial and error, forwards and backwards, triumphant moments tramped down by huge mudslides, to get in sync with this process of learning to find something greater in me and about me than just the sum of my experiences. And the sum of my mistakes. I struggled to find the presence of life, that divine spark of intelligence within me, and organize it in three primary compartments: spiritual, emotional, physical. Only to find, what *was* I thinking? What part of me would *not* be spiritual?

It's all God; it's all us. It's all the same thing.

I was in my early thirties, in denial about what I had hoped was a semi-adequate marriage and the mother of three if I didn't count my husband. In addition, I spent each day trying to pretend I was okay. It was like a virtual football game going on in my life, and I kept trying to run with the ball—to live a decent life—while the enormous linebackers

74

of tension and anxiety chased me relentlessly. In hindsight, I understand it was the result of living so many years without being able to find a place of emotional safety that frequently made me feel physically unsafe. But, in all honesty, where the hell is hindsight when you really frickin' need it?

I was living in Denver at the time, and, spurred on by the pounding feet of the uniformed giants, which were always only half a step short of a full-body tackle, I decided to stop frantically looking over my shoulder and reach for the stars. Yep, I sought out the counsel of a well-known local astrologer. She read my chart, looked at me, and said, "Honey, you need a treatment."

"*What?*" A strangulated sound with just a hint of indignation slipped out of my mouth.

"No, no, my dear," she said, gently patting my hand. "It's not *that* kind of a treatment. It's a form of prayer and affirmation that people who are well-trained in the Ernest Holmes school of thought can do for you."

She wrote out a name and phone number and pressed it into my hand. "This is Bea. You don't have to be involved with Science of Mind or Religious Science or any of that, but trust me, she will help you."

I looked over my left shoulder (and felt inside my body). The linebackers were still in hot pursuit, so I called Bea, completely unaware that years later this grandmotherly, gray-haired stranger would be the conduit for introducing me to the man who would become my true life-partner. But long before my future revealed itself, Bea worked her "magic" with me, doing her treatments of prayer and affirmation, insisting on looking at me and my life as healed, visualizing me in harmony and joy. For me, Bea was a bottle of holy water come to life. She never over-explained what she was doing or tried to sell me on it. Her ability to see me as whole and the force she put into it had a powerful effect and did for me what no amount of therapy could. I started to get lighter from some place deep within me, and slowly it began to bubble out into my world.

The years and years of study I had spent searching out alternative philosophies, religions, and perspectives began to coalesce. And my point of view about myself as a result of my earlier experiences began to change. The victim thing—the concept that I was the sum of what had happened to me and how I had been treated—loosened its vice-like grip.

It occurred to me that the more difficult life had been, the more important it was to connect with one's sense of spiritual presence. It was essential to connect to a bigger picture—a point of view greater than pain and suffering, greater than fearful and hellish memories. As a child, my spiritual background came from the parochial school I attended, which provided its own proverbial kettle of dualistic fish. School, as in a place to be other than home, was my personal savior. But the parochial part—the religious part—hardly saved me from the horrors of my home. For me, organized religion was a bust. It was not going to be the bridge to connect with my spirit. And for a long time I had "attitude" about it. Even after I was well into my twenties, if someone said the word, "God," I would follow it with, "Damn!" Or to be more accurate, I probably would have said, "Fuck God."

Ultimately, my bitter attempts at agnosticism proved to be utterly useless. Hard as I tried, hating God wasn't helping. It was just making it worse. Then, as I drew into my thirties, I entered a court of last resort. Blaming the church wasn't working, although it wouldn't have hurt them to have been a little more astute. Blaming my parents and every other asshole I had encountered in my young life wasn't working too well either. My options for finding comfort through finger-pointing were rapidly narrowing, so, mostly because I couldn't think of what else to do, I began the long journey of contemplating choice. What if I really did choose? What if I chose my parents, my environment, my experiences? What if in another space and time the part of me that is forever—my spirit—had conversations and made plans with other souls that were not yet in bodies.

I played with this idea in my head and, these being pre-Starbucks days, began to visualize a little outdoor European café in the sky, preferably in a setting that resembled Provence, France. Might as well think big. I doodled with a mental script, picturing the spirit of my father there, without his trademark sneer. I pictured my mother there, without the henna hair. And I pictured the essence of me there with a twinkle in my eye and laughter in my voice.

In my fantasy, the three of us would sit around a celestial wrought-iron table covered with a red-and-white checkered cloth and a bottle of the finest champagne we could conjure up. We would lift our glasses. "To life in all its forms," we'd say with good cheer.

Then, down to business.

"Well, I'm getting ready to go back in," I'd offer up, referring to my impending return to the planet Earth. "My management team over here has been working hard with me, teaching me. I feel like I've been in training for a marathon. It's as though my coaches have been standing by with their little stopwatches, making sure that I am sufficiently prepared so that when I get into a body and the friction hits, I don't make a catastrophic error and have to quit the race prematurely."

I could see myself taking a deep, non-oxygen-oriented breath. "I think I'm ready," I would say to the others around me. "I want to go for it. But this time I want to finish the job: I want to feel the truth of all that we are while I'm in a body. I've gotten past the place of just "lumping" my way through life—remember that last Irish peasant gig in which I managed to accomplish absolutely nothing? And I'm doing a lot better on the victim/tyrant thing." I shook my head. "Some pretty awful three-act plays...."

"Yeah, well, it's all God," my old soul friend, Angelo, would murmur as he pulled up a chair to join us. He would look at me with amusement and add, "Don't forget, it doesn't really matter where you've already been in whatever lifetimes you think you've had. Everything you need to help you fulfill your intention for this round will be recreated in this new life you're entering. I'm not coming with you this time, though. I'll be your coach from here. You'll recognize me in your dreams. I'll be the one running along the sidelines in yellow gym shorts with a whistle hanging around my neck and cheering you on. You won't be able to miss me."

"Just remember, girlfriend," he would slap my back playfully, "it's all God."

"I know, I know, Angelo." I'd hold up my hands in mock surrender. "Just make sure you blow that whistle loud enough so I can hear you when I'm in my new body. Leave me plenty of markers to stimulate my memory of this conversation and my awareness of something greater than a limited physical reality. You know when I'm in a body, I still get caught in the 'I've failed God' routine."

My spiritual cohorts would roar with laughter. Preposterous!

"You mean you still get caught in your 'I'm not worthy' soap opera?"

"Right on, Ang," I would laugh.

"I know that you know it's not actually possible to fall short of the glory of all that we are. It's only possible to forget."

"Right. But I could get caught in the firing—or actually misfiring—of the synapses and ganglia of the human nervous system, and from that point on it's as if, as they say on earth, all hell breaks loose. I'd get separated from myself, stuck in feeling like the bad guy, but desperate to be the good guy."

Nods and chuckles would surround me.

"In the body I get convinced I've committed the unforgivable sin," I'd say, sticking my light body finger down my throat and imitating a human gagging sound, "and then, of course, I look for love in all the wrong places."

"Well, not to worry," the spirit who would soon become my mother would chime in. "I'm needing a service project. We know how this game works. If you're really going to accomplish this level of healing in a lifetime, you'll have to get all your earth plane issues triggered first. Otherwise, there is no mastery. Without friction we all stay on the repeat and repeat circuit. I'll go in before you and be your trigger. I'll be the thorn in your side, the pain in your ass and heart that won't let you go. *You* will have to be the one who gets rid of me. But let me warn you, you are going to hate me," she'd say laughing.

"I'm not quite where she is," the entity who was volunteering to be my father would say. "On the human plane I still swing on a regular basis from victim to tyrant, submissive to dominant. The issues I have with women, power, and authority once I'm embodied, well, quite frankly I don't even want to go into them."

Actually, this is turning out to be a hell of a play.

The father-to-be guy would look at me without guilt or self-judgment, pause for a thought, then say, "As long as I need to get more experiences under my belt, I might as well go in before you and be another part of your trigger."

The deal would be set.

And just like in my mental screenplay, true to her word, never once during my lifetime with her did my mother break character. Not even for a split second. And my father, just as he foretold, became the monster he promised to be.

As for me, by the time I was in my early thirties, this self-authored, sensory theater resonated to my core. It so captured a potential for empowering me and adopting a new interpretation about the meaning of what happened to me that I began to change. For the first time in my life, I could feel the empowerment of "they didn't do it to me." For the first time in my life, I knew what not being a victim felt like.

Victor Frankl wrote, "The last of the human freedoms is to choose one's attitudes."

Is it possible that I'm wrong about the existence of my wonderful cosmic café?

Of course.

Do I care?

No.

Because whether I've lived a kazillion times or not, this is the only time I will get to be Sandy. This is the only now that I, as Sandy, have.

12

OH, HOLY NIGHT

Music is like a mystical shape shifter, only it's a frequency shifter. It's a gift for all ages. It can soothe a weary soul, energize, inspire, and make us tap our feet even if it's the only part of us we feel strong enough to move. It can change our whole energy field, for better or worse, depending on what we connect it with.

Let's high-five it for music!

My first chance to participate formally in music came when at long last the Lutheran church I belonged to allowed me to join the children's choir in September of the fifth grade. I was ten. My deep, throaty voice qualified me to be an alto; my age qualified me to wear the choir robe.

Did it get any better than that?

Not in my world! With music I could create a space that was not reminiscent of my past or invested in my future. I could create that rare, timeless moment of now. I began singing and connecting with the songs of my church so deeply that, even well into my adulthood, if I woke up with a hymn in my head, I knew it would be a good day.

But the anthems from my church were not my only bastion of musical solace as a kid. And timeless moments were not the only ways I used music. Sometimes it was more like a drug, helping me to feel special, like I belonged somewhere or to someone, even if it was only to an anonymous audience in a make-believe theater. In my pre-Elvis days there was Judy Garland. Judy, live at the Palace! As a child, I would go to the basement when I was sure no one else was around, put one of her 78 rpm records on the old Victrola phonograph, crank up the volume, hold a hair brush to my mouth, and belt out "Stormy Weather." What a team!

When it came time for the bows, I took multiple ones, closing my eyes and reveling in the adoration the audience was showering on me. They loved me; they really loved me.

The attraction/addiction I had to this fantasy lasted into my late twenties, when I realized it was becoming a problem that I consciously had to break. I would slip into it too often, always ending up feeling worse, not better, for the experience. I would succumb to the desire to escape for twenty or thirty wonderful minutes, pretending to be somebody else in another time and place, ripping out my great solos. Too soon the moment would pass, and I would end up feeling like one does after eating too much ice cream. It was great going down, but then you just feel like shit. So, I made myself stop it. It wasn't a process. It was a choice. I realized, when that feeling to escape into the singing fantasy came up, I was really trying to avoid a pain I didn't think I could handle. I was trying to fill a seemingly empty space and to pretend I belonged and mattered.

With determination, practice, and will, my Judy Garland fantasy fell to the wayside, leaving me with a love of singing and just a tiny little secret remnant of a desire to sing—no longer because it would take away my pain but because I wanted to see if I could.

It was in my forties when, in the midst of the world of motivational speaking, I got a chance to play out my songbird fantasy in real life. One spring morning, after just returning from a speaking venue in Atlanta, I went rushing excitedly into my office. The words tumbled breathlessly out of my mouth as I greeted my office staff. "I was in the middle of my lecture and the audience was so with me and I was using a hand mike and I don't know what came over me but I was feeling so good and you know how I've always wanted to sing so I opened my mouth and I just— sang." I whipped an audiocassette out of my brief case. "And it's on tape!"

We huddled around a portable tape player and listened expectantly....

And that's when I knew why I spoke for a living.

Even as a child I was a good speaker, but on one Christmas Eve, so very many years ago, it was the music that held center court. But the melodies on this eve were not a cause for celebration and joy. They were, instead, a portent of the shadowy, murky depths lurking within the music of the night.

It is 3:30 in the afternoon on Christmas Eve. I am thirteen years old.

I have spent the last hour rummaging through my mom's stuff, searching for the blue beaded necklace she gave me as an early Christmas present a week ago. I thought it was odd when she gave it to me. Not the necklace—it was very pretty. But it was not like my mother to do nice things for me. Caught by surprise, I had gushed with thanks. I don't know what I could have been thinking! But it did go perfectly with the white blouse and blue wool flannel jumper I will be wearing tonight.

Then, of course, the necklace disappeared a few days after it was given to me. When I asked my mother if she had seen it, she answered, "What necklace? I never gave you any necklace."

I am so angry with her, and I am really mad at myself, too. I had let her sucker me in again. She has been pulling stunts like this for the past year. It began last Christmas when she gave me a heather gray suitcase as a present. Samsonite. A few days later the gray suitcase turned into an aqua blue one. When I asked her where my gray suitcase was, she said, "Gray? I don't know what you're talking about. It was always blue. What's wrong with you?" It took me several months and several incidents to figure out that she is running a campaign to convince me—and maybe even others—that I am crazy.

It didn't hurt my feelings, but today—especially today—it pissed me off. Christmas is my favorite time of the year. I think it's because of the music that I love to sing and be around. It makes me feel warm inside. And happy. And special. Yet today I woke up feeling cranky and bloated and belching for absolutely no reason. I almost threw up for Pete's sake.

And that necklace kept sticking in my craw.

So, I've been on a mission determined to find it. My mother left earlier this afternoon to go drink and gossip with her sisters at my grandmother's house under the guise of helping prepare for the family celebration tonight.

I have seized the moment and gone through her night-stand and her entire closet. It takes time because I have to make sure every single thing is put back exactly as it was or old eagle eyes will notice. I don't even want to think what she would do if she thought I was going through her stuff.

So far I've turned up nothing unusual—some abandoned lipsticks and an almost empty tin of loose powder. And this stupid rat-tail thing she used to put in her hair. But I know the necklace is here. She's too cheap to throw it away. Plus in some odd way, I think it's a trophy for her.

I am in the second drawer of her dresser. I push her girdles to the side and reach deeper into the drawer. And then there it is, shoved in the left rear corner covered by some old nylons. MY necklace! I am on fire with fury. My eyes narrow as I picture myself wearing my necklace and staring her down later tonight.

Another belch escapes my mouth as I cradle my bloated tummy. What is this all about? It seems like I haven't been feeling really well for months and months.

I am still rubbing my belly when I look over at the clock on my mother's nightstand.

Oops, it is getting late. I have to get ready. I grab my necklace and slam the drawer shut. It is no longer important if my mother sees her things disturbed. She'll know soon enough that I am on to her.

Miraculously, my mood shifts as my thoughts shift, and I forget about my mother.

Tonight is the most special night of the year. I will be singing with the children's choir in two services. I am in the eighth grade, so this is my last time to sing with the choir on Christmas Eve, but I don't really want to think about that. I have been a member since I was first eligible as a fifth grader. One of the best things about attending Lutheran school all these years—maybe the only good thing about it—is the music. We began practicing for tonight early in October, and I loved every single practice session. I don't want it to be over. Being an alto makes it even better. I get to sing all the great harmony parts.

It is five o'clock, and I am in the choir room. I search excitedly for my choir robe with all the other kids, and quickly slide it over my head. There is a thrilling buzz in the room. I race to get my penlight flashlight and make sure the batteries actually work. Many of them don't. On the third try I hit pay dirt.

In this moment all is well in my world.

I wonder: Is there any way this feeling can last? Is there any way it could stay this way?

Well, "not really" would be the answer to the question I pondered on that December 24th in 1956.

What I didn't know and couldn't intuit as a child was that there were good things lying in wait for me and my life. But as a thirteen-year-old trying to find triumph in her newly recovered necklace and joy in the music of the season, I had no idea that one day I would take my own four-year-old daughter with her huge blue-green eyes and lush, sandy-blonde hair to a Christmas Eve pageant and re-engage my love of this special night. Just her and me, hearing the Christmas bells peal and the music soar. Savoring the specialness that all kids, even the grown-up ones, relish.

And that's exactly what happened. My daughter, proudly sporting her new blue velvet dress trimmed in white lace, with matching white tights and shiny black Mary Janes, tucked her little hand in mine as we left the service. I breathed out into the cold night air, looked up at the starlit night and clear, brilliantly-etched moon, and thought not about my past but about Apollo 8, where astronauts James Lovell, Frank Borman, and William Anders were circling the moon and reading from Genesis. *"In the beginning...."* It was a wonder that stirred my soul, and for a brief moment I felt connected with that little space capsule and the men in it. I was one with them, one with the people on the other side of the globe, and one with my beautiful daughter. For a brief moment I forgot about all the things that had transpired in my twenty-five years of living. My life had not ended in separation and pain. In the beginning there was creation, and it all came from one source. In the beginning there was me or at least the potential of me. Hearing the voices of men in a gravity-free reality, in what was almost another time and space, opened my heart and stirred my soul. I was not alone. I was part and parcel of the One that connects all that is.

Little did I know on that magical night, when I got the briefest glimpse into a new possibility, that my desperation to understand my past and find surcease from the pain would ultimately drive me into new frontiers and to make new choices that were outside of the box, choices that would one day open up an entire new life for me and would support the idea that we are all one and all belong to each other. The thought of no separation among us couldn't truly become a reality until the separation inside of me was better healed. The perspective that we all come from the same universal gene pool—that in essence we all belong because we're here—was still embryonic within me. How could I have known that these concepts would soon drive the very core of what would become my life-long passion for learning and living?

At the age of twenty-five, the distant drumming of this future of mine was so faint that I could not yet hear or envision it. Just as on that Christmas Eve of my thirteenth year, I did not know that my final participation in my choir was going to be so startlingly and frighteningly different....

The lights are dimmed in the hallway outside of the choir room, which is our cue to line up. The director signals us to turn on our penlights, and we begin our procession into the darkened cathedral dimly shadowed only by the array of candles on the altar. The organ heralds our arrival with a resounding rendition of "Joy to the World." Goose bumps are all over my skin. With penlights aglow, we march two by two up the wide middle aisle of the packed sanctuary and at the head of the altar move to pre-assigned places to form a large, cross of lights.

The pageantry of it all never ceases to stir me. It is my favorite moment.

The organ cues us, and then I get to do my next favorite thing. I begin to sing a cherished carol with my fellow choir members.

"Oh, holy night…." I belt out the words with gusto as my penlight joins my choir mates in dancing off the high-pitched ceiling. "The stars are brightly shining. It is the night of the dear Savior's birth…."

My voice cracks embarrassingly as yet another belch, unbidden, bubbles out of my mouth, replacing the musical note I intended. I get myself back on track, but now I am feeling very, very strange, like I am somehow disembodied. I am having trouble with my vision. I blink several times to try to clear it, but it continues to blur.

"Long lay the world in sin and error pining…." I continue to sing, but I am feeling weirder and weirder.

And then I am not at the altar anymore. Suddenly, the sanctuary disappears from me, and I disappear from it. I am in an unknown place where I am giving birth to a beautiful baby boy who will help save the world.

"Fall on your knees…." Oh, God. I am back in the church again. Beads of sweat pearl on my brow although it is actually cool in this massive sanctuary. I drop my voice automatically to sing the harmony. "Oh hear the angels' voices…."

I am out of the church again—in this strange, other place that appears backlit with a soft glow. A baby is in my arms. A son. I am not scared but oddly drawn into a sense of peace. I will be the mother of someone special. Everything will be okay. And for the first time in my thirteen years I will have someone to love. How I have ached for someone to love.

And then with a jolt I am back, singing at the altar again.

"Oh night, oh night divine."

Through my early adult years I developed a Norman Rockwell-esque fixation on what Christmas was supposed to be. At least what it was supposed to look like. I was certain that if I could get it to look a certain way, it would also feel a certain way—as in healed and loved and happy. Home and hearth. *Saturday Evening Post*'s finest. Well, nice try, but as they say in the Old West—or maybe Cuba—no cigar.

A multitude of horrific events had happened around the holidays, like the Christmas Eves my father would wake me, take me into the living room to show me my stack of presents, and then rape me under the glow of the tree lights. And, of course, the Christmas when, as a ten-year-old, I knew my folks were planning to kill me was a double whammy. Thank God my mind was able to protect me so well—to segregate the trauma and allow the other parts of me to join the collective excitement of the holiday that flooded my school, city, and church. It was the music that carried me along its wavelength frequency to greater possibilities.

But as I grew into a young woman, the sights and sounds of Christmas I so treasured became enshrouded by a melancholy I could not shake. I was only twenty-three when I estranged myself, for the safety of my two young children, from my parents. I didn't know it at the time, but with that one move, I also gave up my entire extended family, which included a large array of cousins and aunts and uncles—and great-aunts and second cousins and their children, too. From the point of estrangement on, Christmas consisted of my children and former husband, alone in the unfamiliar cities to which we moved for his work. Perhaps it should have been enough, but it wasn't.

Would anything ever be enough?

Not the way things were going. My life was way too isolated, way too deficient in Norman Rockwell values. Or so I thought. No parades of loving human faces or even angry human faces. No faces, period. No helium-filled, brightly colored balloons, no huge crystal bowls brimming with frothy, somewhat disgusting eggnog. None of the longed-for, familiar pictures materialized.

But mostly it was that nothing could fill the emptiness that lived so deep inside of me. On Christmas Day I could succeed in having all the accoutrements. My good china and crystal would be on the table, a golden brown turkey roasting in the oven. Terrific, brightly wrapped presents managed to find their way under the tree for the kids. And the tree itself was always perfectly trimmed, except for the time when my toddler son and six-month-old puppy ate the bottom two rows of hand-strung pop-corn off it—but that's a story for another time…. Call me. We'll talk.

As a younger woman, my Christmas successes met only with failure. I could get all of it to look perfect, but I cried myself to sleep every Christmas night anyway.

"Why?" I cried, "Why can it look so right and still feel so wrong?"

The questions only pierced my gut deeper and sank me further into my depression. Slowly, I began to understand that when trying to figure out what was going on inside of me, "why" questions led nowhere. They only pushed me deeper into my internal box canyon. "Why" was a painful loop I needed to avoid.

"Let's try another type of question," I eventually said to myself, trying to command my legs to come out of their curled-up fetal position.

Forget about why. Begin with what or how, not why.

Okay, what? Trying to make things look right is obviously not the answer. What intangible thing has escaped me? There's got to be something else I want to get out of Christmas besides the whistles and bells? Something else has to be driving me. What is it? How do I find it?

And then, of course, my stomach would start to hurt worse.

I moaned. With all this horseshit, there's got to be a pony here someplace.

What was my hidden agenda? *What* did I want the re-creation of a Norman Rockwell painting to do for me? Almost by default, I came up with my own version of sacred geometry. Although, to put it more accurately, it was closer to semi-sacred algebra. My formula? What am I really thinking when I think I'm thinking X? In the case of Christmas, what was I really thinking when I thought I was thinking that all I wanted was to have a room full of loving people around me? What was I looking for?

The second coming? Hare Krishna? Woodstock? I had *never* had a room full of loving people around me, for God's sake.

What I was really thinking was that I wanted the presence of all those people to fix me. I wanted their presence to validate my worth and to fill my sense of emptiness. It wasn't the actual room full of people or family that I needed. What I thought I needed was what they would do for me by being there.

Now that's a hell of a pony.

Through the years I learned to make friends and include them in our celebrations. Nevertheless, especially at Christmas, it was family—or more accurately the sense of acceptance and belonging that the idea of family represented to me—I longed for. It went on like that until I put myself through the long process of teaching myself how to choose a point of view greater than my past, how to choose an identity that didn't hinge on pain and suffering as a personal truth. I'd like to tell you there was a magic wand that whipped me into shape, but there wasn't. It was mental discipline, teaching myself through relentless practice the ability to be in charge of the focus of my mind. I had spent the first three decades of my life pretty much letting my mind lead me. Now it was time to take charge and lead myself where I wanted to go, to search deep within me to find the answer to what am I really thinking when I think I'm thinking X? Did the bozo across the street really upset me this much? Or am I playing and replaying some perceived slight because that experience triggered some sense of worthlessness in me? Am I this stirred up because I think some nameless guy is an asshole? Or has my brain cross-referenced with my own history? Is my fear of my own lack of value, my own shame, and self-judgment the "X" that I'm really thinking?

The hard work and repetitive, consistent practice paid off, and I was able to retrain my mind and the connections in my brain.

Among many other things, Christmas tears are long gone; Christmas aches are a thing of the past. Although we never became the Waltons, my children, grandchildren, husband, and I are a loving family. I adore them! So, I did accomplish what I set out to do at eighteen. I broke the back of abuse. That insane, evil legacy stopped with me.

Through the years, I've held onto the happy memories of singing with the children's choir, so naturally I still start playing and singing Christmas music in October. Or earlier. There is no holiday song that rekindles pain or longing. I look now into the clear, crisp night of a winter's eve and feel the music within me. "Oh, holy night…." For me, this beautiful song is not even a hymn about religion. It's a note—a harmonic—that lifts my heart with compassion and appreciation for myself and all mankind. It's good to be alive, and it's good to be able to feel both the positive and the negative, the difficult and the easy, the light and the dark—and to know that in the end it's all the same energy, expressing the multitude of variables and potentials that lie within our grasp.

It's not the Phantom's "Music of the Night." It's the music within.
If we choose it.

13

THE LITTLEST TEACHER

Years ago, before I became a counselor for real, I had a friend who was feeling traumatized by one of his employees. He was a pretty self-aware guy with an international reputation who understood the concept that the people and circumstances that create friction in our lives are often our very best teachers. He practiced this idea; he taught this idea. But the woman who managed his organization was driving him bonkers. He was lamenting his situation to me one afternoon. "I know she's my teacher," he sighed, "I'm just ready for another teacher." His uplifted hands appeared to be beseeching the skies. "Any other teacher," he added.

I laughed, and I understood. Friction and contrast—although helpful and even necessary in the scheme of life and personal evolution—frequently suck. Sometimes they do more than that. Sometimes they hurt so badly that it makes one double over.

That's what happened to me with my greatest friction, which also turned into my greatest teacher. No, it wasn't Ginny and Tom, although God knows they were in line to qualify. A tiny, little boy who lived only a few short days became my greatest personal teacher.

It is early February, about six weeks since I weirded out at the altar on Christmas Eve. I think I've been okay, though, since then. I am sitting at my desk looking outside the window of my eighth-grade classroom. Everything is bleak. Dirty snow and dark, naked tree limbs. I don't really like February or even January for that matter. Once Christmas is over, I'm ready for April. Ev-

erything in between feels stale and uninteresting. Now I'm just waiting for spring. I sit here suffering through the most incredibly boring geography class ever invented. Mr. Fredricks, the student teacher who is conducting the class, is standing in front of the room reading from a book in a relentless monotone. Ugh! This is not going to end. So far the only thing interesting is the big red-rimmed, white-headed pimple blossoming on the end of his nose, which he has apparently decided not to pop. It's been ripening for days. My friends and I have been making bets on what day we think it will explode. But after a while even the pimple becomes boring.

I am feeling yucky again today and very tired. To top it off, I am still nauseous and barely able to control my belching. It's more disgusting than the tip of Mr. Fredricks's nose. A yawn sneaks up on me, and I stifle it. I wonder if I can fall asleep and still keep my eyes open.

"Yeow! Ow!"

I cry out loud before I can stop myself. Chaos is suddenly imploding inside my body. I double over and grab my cramping gut. It almost knocks the breath out of me. My alarmed teacher stops his droning and helps me down the short hallway to the nurse's office. Within minutes my parents are called, and the nurse rushes me home in her car.

Doc Stevenson is already there when I arrive. I am disoriented to the point that I don't even think I resisted his examination. But everything is fuzzy, and I'm not sure. The next thing I am aware of is the sting of a hypodermic needle being plunged into my hip. Then I hear my mother's loud voice, and for a few brief seconds I am coherent. She says to the doctor, "She's been in trouble like this before. We didn't want to tell anybody. My dad took care of it last time. She's been gaining weight, but who could have known?"

I am horrified. And ashamed. I have never been with a boy. I have never had sex. I am, of course, a virgin as all good girls my age are.

"There's a place right over the state line you can take her to," says my doctor. "There's plenty of time. I'll make the arrangements.

Then I become even more disconnected, and I melt into a gray netherworld. Nothing is well defined here. Nothing makes sense.

The next thing I know, my father is pushing me and shoving me harshly into the back seat of the car. He is furious. I feel him slapping me hard as I fall over on my side, sprawling across the seat. He slams the door then takes his place in the front seat behind the steering wheel. The car begins to move, but I am too out of it to know or care where we are going. I come to a couple of times during the trip only to hear my father having a conversation with himself in an unusually high, frantic pitch, but his words scramble in my ears and remain a blur….

The room is bright. Too bright. Please, can somebody turn down the lights? And it's cold. Surgically gowned people are around me. A gas mask is pressed down over my nose and mouth.

The lights and noise that were around me are no more. But the hallucination—or whatever it was—from Christmas Eve keeps coming back. I am to be the mother of a son who will make a difference in the world. And, as a by-product, I will have someone to love. I desperately need someone to love. I desperately need a reason to live.

But I am aware that I am very sick. I know that my body is raging with fever, yet I feel cold not on my skin but deep within my body. The cold is in my blood and in my organs. I cannot get warm. Sometimes I shiver uncontrollably. I am all alone. There are no familiar faces around me. Whenever I am awake, my head throbs. I drown in how sick I feel, until once again I am blessedly released into unconsciousness.

Out of focus strangers drift in and out of my awareness for who knows how long. They try to get me to eat something, but I keep moving my head away, which only makes it hurt worse. I cannot eat anything. Not even a bite. Then I slip away again.

I finally awake. For the first time in days my head feels clear enough for me to think. I am in a single bed that has the sidebars of a hospital bed, but the rest of the room, with its yellow dresser and filmy curtains, feels more like a small bedroom than a hospital room. I touch my face with my hand. I am not so cold inside my body anymore, but my forehead is still burning up. I reach for the glass of water next to my bed with a straw in it. It is an effort to swallow a few sips.

A short time later a harried-looking middle-age woman with stringy brown hair and no waist walks into my room. She is wearing a long-sleeved, high-necked white blouse and a dark, straight skirt and carrying a clipboard, so I know she is not a nurse. She marches briskly up to the side of my bed. I am weak and find her intimidating. Without addressing me by name she shoves her papers in front of my face.

"Sign here," she says, pointing to a blank space.

"What?"

"It's the law. You have to sign this."

I look up at her blankly.

"You have been here three days already, and this should have been signed when you first got here."

I am still not connecting the dots and am slow to respond.

"You have to sign this," she says sternly, impatiently tapping on the clip-board she placed in my hands, "so that the baby can be adopted."

"Baby?"

I begin to read the paper she wants me to sign. It refers to a baby boy. And then the world I am in becomes clear. I remember now. I was pregnant. Nobody knew. It was my deepest, darkest secret. But I had a plan. I was going to run away with the baby and build a new life. I would love it, and it would love me. It would not be the end of me. It would be the saving of me.

But now it isn't an "it" anymore. It is a boy. I have a son.

"I can't now," I shudder. "My head hurts." I hear my words slurring as they come out of my mouth. I close my eyes and deliberately let my hands go slack. The clipboard slips to my side.

"I'll be back," the lady bristles, grabbing her papers. I peek, surreptitiously watching her backside as she leaves the room. I keep my eyes closed just to be safe. I hear someone enter the room and draw near to my bed. A soft hand checks my forehead for fever, and I open my eyes. A uniformed nurse is looking down at me.

"How are you feeling?" she asks in a mild voice.

"Sick."

She checks my pulse, then pats my hand.

"You rest," she says. "I'll ask Miss Miller to wait until tomorrow to come back."

And then I am alone in the room again.

I wait for several minutes to make sure no one is going to come back in, then I sit up in the bed and dangle my feet over the side. Wooziness almost drives me back under the covers. But I have to get out of here. I steady myself for a minute, looking down at the back-tying smock I am wearing. I slide carefully off the bed and, still wobbly, head for the doors on the opposite wall. The one to the left I already know exits to whatever is outside my room. The one on the far right turns out to be a tiny mirror-less lavatory with a stack of sanitary supplies on a shelf above the toilet. I rinse my face in cold water, which makes me shiver all over, and try to smooth down my hair, hoping I have made it sufficiently presentable. I sit heavily on the toilet. I may be only thirteen, but I feel older than the oldest person I have ever met.

There is one more door in the room that opens into a narrow closet. In it are the clothes I wore when I came here, an overnight bag, and my full-length beige winter coat, which has always looked a little too much like a shag carpet for my taste. I slip out of the hospital smock and dress as quickly as I can, wincing at the discomfort when I twist around to step into my underpants. My arms struggle into my coat. I stagger dizzily and head toward the door that leads to the unknown.

Carefully, very carefully, I crack the door open a few inches. The only thing I see is a white wall aged to a dirty ecru across the way. My heart pounds in my chest. I open the door wide enough to poke my head out. No one is in sight. To my right I see what some part of my fuzzy memory thinks is an opening for a broad stairwell. A picture flashes from the night when I had first entered this building: a large foyer with an attendant present and what, in my drug and pain induced stupor, seemed to me to be an enormous curved staircase. No, that was not the direction to head toward.

I look to the left at a rather long hallway ending with a narrow door. That's the direction I take.

Adrenaline pumps through my body like a leaking faucet suddenly exploding into Old Faithful. The surge makes me forget about my fever, pain, and fatigue.

He has to be here somewhere. He has to be. I am not leaving without him. He is my lifeline, my saving grace. My only hope. I will love him, and he will love me, and everything will be okay.

But I have to hurry before anyone comes along. Stealthily, I push open the first door I come to and peek in. It is a duplicate of my room, but thank God it is empty. The next door has a glass window in it. Inside the room are four rectangular infant cribs. Only one of them is filled.

It's him!

Relieved, I rush into the room and lift the sleeping baby out of his bassinet. I glance at his tiny face. It is perfectly formed. He lies there, quiet and serene, swaddled in a light blanket. He is just as I pictured him. My heart skips a beat. Maybe he will be my savior.

Quickly, I tuck him under my coat, hurry out of the nursery, and move toward the door at the end of the hallway. It opens onto a back staircase. I close the door behind me quietly and descend to the first level. I can hear but not see people somewhere down the hall to the right. I opt for the only other choice, a door in front of me at the base of the steps. I slip through it, still clutching my baby close to my chest. Mercifully, he remains silent.

The door closes automatically behind me with a loud, clicking noise that makes me jump. I am in some kind of an oversize garage with large, open bay doors at the end of it. I scurry to them, and then suddenly I am free. I have escaped the building and everything in it that was going to steal my life from me.

I am out in the cold February afternoon with the brisk air biting at my face. I cross the street, pass a few small-town shops and a diner, and head west. My arms remain folded across my belly, cupping my hidden infant to me. I walk for what seems like forever through the increasingly rural area into the setting sun, until I come upon an old outbuilding. A rickety, empty barn of sorts.

I feel neither hunger nor thirst. During my long walk, I had times when I knew that I was very ill. And then there were other times when in my delirium I knew almost nothing.

I huddle now in a corner of the abandoned building trying to keep my baby and myself warm. I bend over him as I squeeze him to me and drift off. It is light when I come to, shivering and burning with fever.

I open my coat and look down at my little boy. My father's son. I begin to rock with him. But something is amiss. I nudge him. Gently at first, then with more urgency. My cold hand touches his face.

Oh, no! NO! NO! NO!

I am holding the still, lifeless form of an innocent infant.

I don't know that any one individual's death justifies the survival of another. It seems like an odd equation. But I do know that it happens, and if my projected coffee house in the sky is even remotely real, then the beautiful soul that inhabited this little body for so brief a time gave me the greatest gift of all.

Through the years that it took me to put all the pieces of my past together, the one pain I couldn't live with was the crippling guilt I felt from having inadvertently caused my baby's death. That guilt drove me to seek answers, to find surcease, and eventually to understand love. In some ways, then, he really did become my savior, because my memory of him became the force that pressed me through the darkness and ultimately into the light of my potential. Without ever knowing or realizing love, I had been given it.

Yesterday, the raven that often visits my home stopped by again. I was actually writing this chapter when he landed outside my window. In his beak, he carried what appeared to be a large walnut. I smiled, remembering the many times I've seen the symbolic picture of a raven carrying the sun in his mouth. Was he carrying a reflection of light for me?

My raven visitor dropped his treasure into the small hole he had just dug and covered it lightly with loose dirt. He lingered for a magical moment....

His wings fluttered as he lifted off the ground, and with his wingspan spread to its fullest, angled north to south, he flew up majestically directly in front of my window. I couldn't have literally reached out and touched him, but he felt that close just before he soared up and away, leaving his buried bounty behind. A metaphoric sun? A stale walnut? A lumpy stone? I opted for the sun thing and definitely took it as a sign.

My thoughts returned to my work and to when I was only thirteen, in the midst of the darkest night of my soul. On that barren winter day so long ago, alone and distraught, cold and sick, holding a dead infant, there was no hope. And there sure as hell was no sun—in any form. I knew that it was all my fault. I had caused my son's death and my own downfall. Any hope that tomorrow could be better than yesterday vanished. Any life I might have fantasized or longed for lay dead in my arms.

A wood sculpture of a laughing Buddha sits on the desk in my office. During the long years of my recovery from the guilt and loss of the innocent baby who ultimately taught me so much about life, I often wondered if perhaps on some days even the Buddha cries.

Then again, probably not.

For how could the Buddha cry when, in the end, even the darkest night has the potential to uncover the gift of an amazing sunrise.

I shiver violently, holding the body of my dead baby. Eventually, I do the only thing I can think to do. I make my way back to the phone booth in front of the diner I passed the day before and call my mother. She is hysterical. She screams into the phone that she had been notified that I was missing. She continues to yell that a few hours later she covered my tracks (and hers) by calling Miss Miller, the director of the girl's home, and telling her I was already back home with the baby. I should be goddamn grateful! Miss Miller is closing her file.

"And for Christ's sake," finishes my mother, "stay out of sight!"

I hang up the phone and wait in the shadows of a side street.

My mother arrives in less than two hours, driving grandmother's pink-and-gray Kaiser sedan. She does not take me home but to the home of my aunt, who lives across the street from Doc Stevenson. He treats me daily for the massive infections and pneumonia I contracted during my ordeal. I do not know what my aunt was told, but the subject of the baby or his demise is never mentioned to me by anyone. My mother comes over most days and drinks beer and gossips with my aunt but never talks directly to me or asks me how I am. I try to stay as far in the background as I can.

I am slowly moving back into my daytime world. My only awareness is on getting well and getting back to school. When I do return, almost seven weeks have passed, and I am quite changed. I am at least thirty pounds thinner, and as I found out this morning, whistle-bait curvaceous. My face is different, too. It has aged. Although I am still only thirteen and rarely even wear lipstick, I am told I could easily pass for eighteen.

It is springtime now at last. The principal of the school has called me out of class and asked me to come to his office. I sit across the desk from him, more curious than worried, because I haven't done anything wrong.

"I have some very sad news for you, Sandy," he says sympathetically. Tears are already forming in my eyes, but I don't know why. "I'm sorry to have to tell you this," he continues, "your grandfather died this morning."

My grandfather's funeral takes place on a gray Chicago day. I find myself sitting in the church, biting my lower lip and staring at my grandfather's open casket. I am not yet fourteen. Three lifetimes have passed since I was a five-year-old, calling him daily via Ma Bell's operator, just to say, "Hi." Just to make sure he was still there after his bout with tuberculosis and the removal of his left lung.

My eyes are riveted to my grandfather's lifeless body. I can't look away.

The service begins, and the lip biting no longer works. Unexpectedly, I start to sob. I cry in a way that I never have. Deep, heaving sobs. I am no longer able to stifle the sounds of my tears. I hear murmurs from behind me. Cousins, second cousins, aunts, and uncles have never seen me like this. But the sobs continue convulsing out of me uncontrollably.

I cry for my grandfather, who had showed me decency and respect. I cry for the hidden memory of a lost baby boy, who should never have been born, and having been born, should never have died. I cry for a guilt inside of me I don't understand and can't fix. I cry for my life, a life so painfully without promise. I cry for a grief that has been in me so long I can't remember life without it. I cry for what might have been.

For the first time in my life I cry and cry and cry for me.

14

ANALYZING THE UNANALYZABLE

You know the one about the guy who shot both his parents then threw himself on the mercy of the court because he was an orphan?

Well, that doesn't really have anything to do with this chapter, but since we're not in love—or even like—with Tom and Ginny, and it's been kind of heavy, I thought I'd start with something light.

Not every moment as a child in my house was about torture and trauma. I mean, they had to take time out to eat, drink, pee, and catch up on whatever in the world *did* the neighbors think. So, yes, there were pauses. Brief and disconnected, but they were there.

Although I cannot remember a time when my parents and I laughed together, that's not to say Ginny didn't love a good party. Getting ready for it was half the fun. As a child, I watched her preening ritual. She sat in front of the huge oval mirror atop her vanity, leaned forward, closely checking to make sure her roots weren't showing, and then instinctively tightened her neck until the veins bulged. Isometrics 101. The make-up brigade followed. Lots of blush—or rouge as it was called then—lots of loose powder, red lipstick, and drawn-on eyebrows. Then, of course, the hair meticulously wrapped around those infamous dyed-cotton rattails to create the effect of a reverse page-boy. She struggled into a corset and nylons, which all good women did, and topped it off with shoulder pads that made Linda Evans's *Dynasty*-era shoulder extensions look like amateurs.

Yes, indeed, my mother was determined to be a woman of her day.

And my father? Sicko that he was, he hid his anger at being the long-suffering, emotionally-martyred prisoner of two dominating women, namely his mother and his wife, in the false disguise of the bon vivant—a fun-loving, magnanimous fellow. The saintly good guy to Ginny's alcoholic bitch.

Many were the times when my mother's cousins, second cousins—maybe even thirds—aunts and uncles, siblings and their spouses, along with an occasional friend or two would gather. Loud voices filled the house as everyone endeavored to talk above each other. And there was laughter as they stood or sat around with cigarettes in one hand—except for my father who went for disgusting cigars—and drinks in the other.

So, yes, there were pauses, along with their false façade of normalcy. And I, smart cookie that I was, used the breaks to escape. I read addictively. I ate addictively. And whenever possible, I fled from the house to be with my friends. Addictively.

In my childhood home it was pretty much every man—well, screw the man—it was every kid for herself. There were clearly no connections, and any interaction only risked the rise of my mother's voice or the slimy possibility of accidental eye contact with my father. I chose to be un-aligned, was, in fact, raised to be unaligned. Experience had taught me that any attempt to connect to anyone within the encaging walls of my home almost always led to something bad.

My thoughts when I was not being abused were usually simple and relatively disconnected from the trauma. Because when you're getting raped nightly, verbally skewered daily, there's little room for contemplation. My life was about survival, a compelling, consuming, full-time job. Self-awareness was a luxury that had to wait 'til I had a bit more time. It's not that I never thought about a little girl's equivalent of the "orphan defense," but I didn't ask myself or anyone else a lot of questions. I don't remember ever wondering why these things were happening to me and not somebody else. It just didn't occur to me. It would have been like thinking that someone who was being swept away in a tsunami wonders why this is not also happening to his or her neighbor, when really the only thing you can think about—if you have any thoughts at all—is which way is up, finding a way to breathe, and praying to God that when the storm is finally over (assuming it ever ends), you will still be alive.

Through the years people have asked me, "Why?" Why were my parents the way they were? What made Ginny so willing to sacrifice her own daughter? What made Tom such a perverted predator? Cafés in the sky notwithstanding, how did my parents actually manifest their perversions and distortions into such an ugly reality? How did they, as human beings, fall so far over the edge of humanity?

Thirty years of private practice/workshops/teaching/speaking/mentoring/coaching later, my honest answer is, I don't know. Not for sure.

The ordinary, everyday choices anyone makes in life build like a kinetic energy source, gathering impetus as they travel along, funneling toward a pinnacle where each person will reach his or her tipping point. In which direction will one go? Personal choice. It's a self-made summit, with self-propelled momentum carving out a pathway that will dominate one's life, joy (or lack thereof), and potentials. If an individual, like a Ginny or a Tom, has been sufficiently self-indulgent, ignorant, and completely unwilling to take personal responsibility, then that's like living within a contagious virus. Put two of those people together and the damn virus mutates, which is how the sum total can become more dangerous and destructive than the individual pieces.

Vis-à-vis Ginny and Tom.

Not that either one of them had such a great time in their early years. Ginny grew up in that difficult family of hers. Mean, alcoholic mother and philandering, emotionally unavailable father whose attention she could never quite capture.

And the obviously depraved Tom was also the result of a messy union. A harsh, moralistic little snip of a woman for a mother and a weak, submissive father. It wouldn't surprise me to learn that Tom had a dark side emerge when he was very young. I can't prove it, but his pleasure at other people's pain, his need to control, dominate, and truly demean and humiliate his prey—well, it makes me think of a boy in the deep south torturing squirrels, rabbits, and cats.

Were either of my parents severely physically or sexually abused? There was never any mention of it. But, if I had not spoken up as an adult, there would never have been any mention of what I had experienced, either. So, I'm back to "I don't know."

Here's what I do know. Both of my parents had mothers who were real pieces of work. Tom's mother lived to be ninety-three. I only saw her in the blistering Tennessee summers, but never did I see her wear anything less than layers and layers of long, dark clothing. An armored truck would have had trouble getting into her "personal places."

Ginny's mom was no better. She was a hide-the-bottles-wherever-you-can alcoholic, heavy-handed and mean to the core.

Tom's male role model, his concave-chested dad, always looked sunken in on himself. And much like his son, my paternal grandfather scurried around in obeisance, awkwardly trying to satisfy his demanding spouse. But he did live to be eighty-nine, so if my father has left me anything besides a fierce will to survive, I'm hoping it's his parents' longevity genes.

Perhaps Ginny and Tom's greatest downfall was that neither of them was willing to become self-aware or responsible. They were not willing to ask the most fundamental and primal question: Will we keep striving to discover within ourselves something greater than what we've known, or will we become bottom-feeders?

Nobody really likes bottom-feeders, not even the bottom-feeders themselves.

What I really think happened with my parents is that two underdeveloped, emotionally stunted, immature and wounded people connected and together found a way to sink lower than where they had individually come from. They found a way to bring out the worst in each other. They took lousy role models, weak wills, lack of character development, and, with a little help from alcohol on my mother's side, turned themselves into pure amorality.

The launch point for our potentials begins and ends with us, for it is not what happens to us in life that is the greatest challenge. What we decide to do with it will determine how we lead ourselves up the mountain.

15

AN ENDING

My six-year-old granddaughter spoke animatedly one afternoon several years ago as she and I rode in my car. Her hands flailed emphatically in the air while she explained how her classmate, Gretchen, was being mean. Gretchen had apparently gone on and on about my granddaughter's lousy drawing, rotten singing, crooked walk (whatever that means), and stupid tardiness for arriving late to school that morning.

"I'm so sorry, honey," I lamented. "I'm sure that wasn't easy for you." And then I added, "Gretchen must have been having a really bad day."

My granddaughter looked at me like I had two heads and said, "*She* was having a bad day? What about *me!*"

Good point, Babe.

Never was there any doubt in my mind that my wonderful granddaughter had an intact sense of self. She had been raised knowing she had the right to her own voice. Finding voice means to find the birthright of self-expression, self-awareness, and self-identity. It means I have dominion over not only who I am, but also how I am. It's my right to have a thought, a feeling, a perspective. An action. Governments may try to steal voice from their citizens at any time; circumstances often try to do the same thing. But, as long as I know I have the right to choose my own thoughts, then I will be connected to an awareness of self that no one and no thing can ever take from me. My voice is the expression of an inner sense that it's okay, even good, for me to be me.

My voice is my passport to freedom.

Sometimes people confuse their voices with anger. Anger certainly uses one's vocal chords but rarely is it a true use of one's voice as an indicator of self-awareness. Mostly it's just a long, loud temper tantrum. In my younger days, temper tantrums I was able to do. Voice, not so easily. I could flaunt an opinion—sometimes not a very well-thought-out one—in front of anyone if (and this is a very big *if*) they didn't intimidate me. Like the time when I was fifteen and had just transferred, along with my best girlfriend, Glenda, to a new high school. I stood on a street corner hotly debating with a group of five or six girls who were the core members of the most popular "in" clique at the school why Glenda and I should be allowed into their group. Finally, they relented just enough to crack the door open, and I slipped into their inner sanctum, grabbing Glenda's hand and sliding her in with me. We all became fast friends for the next three years, until college and life parted many of us. Ah, sweet, ballsy memories of old.

But if I was scared or insecure around someone, if I thought I needed his or her approval in order to be okay or safe, I would quickly turn into a bobble-headed ass-kisser.

Daaaaaamn!

Still, if it's all God, then someplace in the Universe, it's all good. But it ain't all fun.

It's possible, even advisable, to find confidence and a sense of self as the result of a direct intention. I took a more circuitous route. My confidence and awareness of my innate right of self-expression came about as the result of facing fear. For it was fear that held me back, fear that strangled my voice. It goaded me into defending myself with temper. It controlled my life.

As I did in almost every step of my journey out of darkness during my twenties and thirties, when I realized that fear was the cause of my self-suppression, I faced the fear by first reaching for an idea greater than whatever I perceived had power over me. It had to be greater than my mother's evilness, more powerful than my father's cruel tyranny. It had to be greater than my overwhelming guilt, shame, and unworthiness. And stronger than my anger. Trust me, that in itself was a stretch.

I kept returning to the concept that at some level of consciousness there exists a pure field of Infinite Intelligence. And some-how, some-way I belong to that divine field. I am part of it, and it is the very core of me. That is the foundation upon which I built my healing. The perspective of universal oneness combined with the decision that I am worth my own effort are the sands upon which I carved out the pearl I wanted to become.

Well, of course, I threw in some psychology, psychodrama, lots of transpersonal communication exercises, reams of learning, boatloads of trial and error. And many were the times when I got lost in a tantrum. But underneath it all, there was an idea that prevailed above all else, an idea that carried me through the darkest night and grayest day. Whatever it is that I perceive God to be—It and I are one.

My granddaughter found her voice at a very young age. Not everyone is so fortunate. Young or old, finding one's voice ultimately becomes an essential part of life and of the ability to thrive in life. The suppression of oneself simply means that fear is at the helm. It creates the illusion of the loss of choice.

As long as one has the ability to form a coherent thought, there is choice. Think Mary Richards, a.k.a. Mary Tyler More. Just because she's a fictional news woman from Minneapolis doesn't mean she's the only one who can throw her hat up in the air and "make it after all."

That level of freedom, which, put another way, is simply the law of attraction in action—the light of one's desire magnetizing itself back into form—doesn't kick in when fear is the focus. When I was willing to trade a piece of myself in order to keep the status quo or avoid an outcome—the end of a relationship, job, social position, whatever—that fear was actually drawing me into the reality I was trying so hard to sidestep. Just making do or keeping up appearances in order to fake being okay and acceptable—or because it's too scary to rock the boat—is, in the words of George Carlin, as effective as rearranging deck chairs on the Titanic. Baby, that ship is still going down.

Finding one's own voice and the courage to follow it, whether it comes about as a result of a situation that catapults an individual into a new choice or the result of a well-thought-out process—or anything in be-tween—is a required course in the school of life. It is at the core of personal freedom and the beginning of personal power.

I am going to be fourteen very soon now, but I feel so screwed up. I have just awakened from another weird dream. In fact, last night I had two of them, and they've been coming more frequently. In the first dream I'm lost in a strange town and can't find my way home, and I don't get to graduate with my class.

How silly. Of course I'm going to graduate. I'm an "A" student. But, still, I find the dream unsettling.

The second dream is even scarier. A robber with a gun breaks into my house when I am home alone. He points the gun at me, and I know that he expects me to say something. To talk him out of shooting me, I open my mouth to speak, but nothing—absolutely nothing—comes out. I am paralyzed, speechless with fear. He pauses for a few more seconds. I still can't move or speak. Then he pulls the trigger....

Well, the good news is my first dream was wrong, because it's June now and I am graduating with my eighth-grade class tonight. I am very excited. I pull up the back zipper of the white, narrow-waisted, full-skirted dress I am wearing for this great night. It's the best dress I've ever had. I bought it with my baby-sitting money. It has a scoop neck and cap sleeves and an extra layer of lace that forms a wide cummerbund around my waist. I look in the mirror with satisfaction. I'm having a good hair day, and I even snuck a little make-up on to bring out my eyes more. Not bad!

After the graduation ceremony, there is a family party at my house. I have fun with my cousins and other extended family members, especially Clark and Joey. Then it's time for people to leave. My mother insists that I go with my father to drive my great-grandmother home. In an instant my elation comes crashing down. My happiness disappears with a violent, shuddering thrust. I walk heavily to my room. I take off my beautiful dress, wad it into a crumpled ball, and discard it into the corner. There is no joy in Mudville. Whatever that dress meant to me is over.

I put on an old shirt and Bermuda shorts. My mother is hollering outside of my door for me to hurry. I am keeping people waiting.

Half an hour later, my father, great-grandmother, and I arrive at her house. I thank her for coming to my graduation. My father sees her to the door. Then he drives me to an isolated area, and I once again become a rag doll for him to do with as he pleases. When I get home, I toss the Bermuda shorts on the heap with my graduation dress. I know I will never wear either one of them again.

It is July now. I am staring at a small, reddish-brown spider coming out of its hole to check out those unfortunate catches already spun-hung out to dry, who will undoubtedly become tomorrow's dinner. The spider watch, yucky as it is, helps me ignore my mother's voice. She is yelling at my dad about having to make another trek down to my paternal grandparent's primitive homestead in rural Tennessee. Mother doesn't want to go, and, quite frankly, neither do I. It's very hot down there, and they still don't have indoor plumbing or running water. They do, however, have yet another mean old rooster who viciously tries to spur anyone who dares to walk through the fenced chicken yard on the way to the outhouse. Maybe he's dead by now. My grandfather had threatened to cook him last time we were there, but my grandmother, railing with her iron cane, which she wields with black belt precision, vowed that he'd be way too tough to eat. I'm hoping old age or coyotes got him.

My mother finally agrees to this trip, providing she has a real vacation first. She wants to go to a resort town at the foot of the Great Smoky Mountains. She berates my father for his rural roots, the "goddamn outhouses, chewing tobacco, filthy spittoons, wrong-height washstands…." Her laundry list of complaints seems to grow exponentially with each passing moment. You name it, she's pissed about it.

The harangue ends. We pack our suitcases, and off to the Smoky Mountains we go.

It is dusk, the bewitching hour. I am swimming in the pool of the motel we are staying at. Luxuriating in it, actually. Unexpectedly, an uneasy quiver goes through me and causes me to look up at the second floor. My father is standing there, leaning against the outer railing, staring at me in an odd way. A sick feeling stirs inside of me. It invades my stomach and my pelvis and makes me want to recoil. I am troubled and uncomfortable, but I don't know why.

I awake with a start. He is straddled on top of me with his hand clasped firmly over my mouth. "Be quiet," my father hisses in the dark. The next thing I know, he has removed his hand and slapped wide, sticky tape over my mouth. The distinctive smell of adhesive travels up my nose. I gag. Panic tailspins me into claustrophobia. Then he uses the tape to bind my hands to the posts of the metal headboard of the twin bed on which I lie. A minute later my panties are gone, and my feet are spread-eagled and likewise bound.

"Can't risk any noise out of you here, girlie," he sniggers in my ear. The restrictions of the tape convert my panic into rage. If I could get free, I would kill him. He takes his time with me, enjoying my trauma, as I wiggle fruitlessly trying to get away until I collapse into submission. When he is sated, he leaves me as I am, bound and tied, and, like the spider, he goes back into his hole—the full-size bed in the adjoining room where my mother sleeps.

I lay here exhausted, drained and frightened. I'm sure he's planning to come back. That's not the problem. I can survive that. But I am panicked once again by not being able to free my limbs. I realize I am drenched in sweat. Instinctively, I know I have to slow down and try to breathe. My father's snores resound from the adjoining room, and my mind begins to clear. I am no longer in a rag doll mode. Nothing in me feels robotic anymore. Submission is out of the question.

"I don't care what it takes," I vow to myself, "this is NEVER going to happen to me again. I will NEVER be his spider's prey—all wrapped and tied up, waiting to be devoured, again. NEVER!"

My anger crystallizes my mind even more. Instead of frantically pulling against the restraints, I begin more methodically to twist and turn my right wrist and hand to work it free. I start to fret. What if he gets here before I am done? And for just a moment I panic again. Then I make myself breathe. Just breathe.

My father, thank God, remains in his loud slumber, and I remain singularly focused on what I am doing. It is already light before I finally succeed in securing my freedom. But during this long night a cold clarity has dawned on me. It has created a detached, blindly fierce fervor inside of me. I finally, FINALLY know what to do.

As soon as I am able, I march through the open door into my parent's room and go swiftly up to my mother's side of the bed shaking her harshly. She starts to yell, but she looks at me, and in a rare fit of wisdom she shuts up. I am vaguely aware that I have cracked, and I know that makes me dangerous. Given half a chance I will make Lizzie Borden look like fucking Snow White!

A voice comes out of me from someplace inside of me that I don't know. It is a cold sound and feels disembodied. I glare at my mother.

"If he ever touches me again," I say, "I will kill you. I don't care how long it takes for me to do it. I am younger than you, and I can outlast you. You won't be able to keep your guard up against me forever. I swear to you I will watch you, and I will stalk you, and when your guard is down, I swear to God I will kill you."

I hold her eye for a moment, and without another word I turn and leave the room.

A little fear turned out to be a good thing for Ginny—and for me—because my father never touched me inappropriately again.

Once the abuse stopped, the nightmare reality of my night world descended completely into the abyss of the deep emotional and mental compartmentalization I had fallen into shortly after my father poisoned me. A lot of time would have to pass before my mind became strong enough and I became courageous enough to begin consciously to integrate the horrible reality of my life at home without collapsing into a clinical split. So far, while I definitely was seriously fragmented in my personality, I still held a firm grip on my own sanity. It's the difference between a hairline fracture of a bone and a full-out jagged break.

So, sanity relatively intact, on that early summer morning in the Tennessee motel, at the tender age of just barely fourteen, I found the beginning chords of my true voice. And when I confronted my mother in a way that held no room for dialogue or negotiation, I was actually taking the first step in what would become a long journey to understand another essential truth.

I can only be a victim if I give someone else my mind.

At the time when I was so vigorously shaking my mother awake, I had become fully aware of the hierarchy within my natal family. Although in that moment I believed it was my mother who had the power, in the end, of course, it was I who held it.

16

KISSES SWEETER THAN WINE

So what happens to kids who have been put through the meat grinder of predators? Do they have an unconscious, compelling need to play out the abuse scenarios with others? Do they become promiscuous? Do they end up seeking love and attention in all the wrong places? Are they a magnet for other creeps?

The answer to all of the above is, usually. Unless…unless there's some intervening circumstance that gives them another option, which helps them to hang on to a thread of normalcy. Then they get to experience both sides of the coin: the devastating reality of the "night child" and the typical ups and downs of an everyday normal child.

So it was with me. It has been said that in order for children to survive psychologically after passing through truly dire straits they must have at least one "somebody" to help them. I don't agree. Although having a warm body to assist would truly be a gift, it is not a requirement. I feel certain that there are, and always have been, amazing individuals in our world who completely on their own have found the courage, the stamina, and the spirit to bring them through the dungeon of a hell on earth into the promised land. I am not one of those people. For although I did not have the support of another individual to help me, I did have a substitute, a thing. That thing, of course, was school.

In school I could be the other me. A fifties, all-American, everyday girl. Doris Day, Sandra Dee, pink poodles on felt skirts, sweater sets, et al. I could gossip with my girlfriends, flirt with the boys, excel, and be praised for it. I could pretend I was normal, and for several hours every day, I could believe it.

Bless those hours. They gave me the space to have fun at sock hops, enter a few local beauty contests, and wear the class ring of a first-string basketball player during my junior and senior years in high school. And on one unforgettable late summer night, those beautiful hours provided the space that gave me Witzy.

Witzy kissed me.

Really. The handsome, affable prize of last year's senior class, renowned for his James Dean sexy smile, looked down, cocked his head to the side and turned that coy little smile on me. And then he actually kissed me!

Right there as we sat parked on the side of the road in his—well, more precisely his father's—1957 fire engine red Ford Fairlane Convertible. I was fifteen years and four months old, but who was counting?

We'd been driving around my neighborhood for the past half-hour, being silly and flirtatious, while he did the steering with his left hand and kept his right arm firmly draped around my shoulders. I was in charge of the gears.

My fingers snaked around the gearshift. I nudged it forward, cringing at the nails-on-chalkboard sound of the gears grinding loudly in my clumsy attempt to move the stick from first to second. "Oh, shit!" I mumbled under my breath. Witzy gulped. I tried again, and we both winced. Finally, in a protective bid for the survival of his pop's transmission, Witzy, a.k.a. Ronald Jefferson Witzman, abruptly pulled the car to the side of the road, revved the engine once, then turned it off.

Our paths had crossed the previous year when I had been a lowly freshman, way too insecure to know that with my short sandy-brown hair, large blue-green eyes, and almost flawless skin, I was actually quite pretty. Witzy, on the other hand, was gorgeous. He had a slender build, even features, that killer grin and boyish charm. Of course, he was a boy, but what did I know. I was only fourteen when I met him, and he was an exalted, extremely popular senior. I had an instant crush on him. I looked for him daily, swooning inside as I watched him walk down those hallowed halls of our high school with his slightly bowed legs and easy, self-assured gait. Alas, he, who had his pick of upper classmen—I mean women—was always pleasant to me but clearly uninterested in the biblical sense.

He graduated in June. I nursed a mournful ache in my heart, certain I would never see him again. I had lost the love of my life.

Then three months later, out of the blue, Kismet! We bumped into each other at a party. I was wearing the black-and-red light wool plaid skirt that fit snugly around my hips and the long-sleeved black blouse unbuttoned at the top to form a sufficiently deep V at the chest, which I had purchased two days earlier with my baby-sitting money. I had just checked myself out in the bathroom mirror, thinking my investment had gone to a good cause when, upon reentering the basement rec room where the party was underway, I ran into Witzy. I mean literally. He grabbed my arm to steady both him and me. I laughed and looked into his smiling eyes. The blue crew neck sweater he was wearing set off the blue whirlpools of his eyes. For the first time ever he held my gaze. I was standing there trying not to whimper from sheer excitement and at the same time thinking that had I known that almost knocking him over was the best way to get his attention, I'd have tried it when we first met a year ago.

I flirted, he responded. He flirted, I responded. I kept the giddiness I was feeling under barely concealed wraps and pretended to be trés *cool. Just another party; just another Saturday night. And then, he asked me out. I heard my voice calmly say, "Oh, sure. That sounds like fun," while another voice in my head was shrieking, "I've got a date with Witzy! Oh, my God, I've got a date with Witzy!!"*

And that's how I ended up with him almost a week later in the front seat of a parked car cocooned by the darkness of a mild, late September night in the suburbs of Chicago. A Friday to be exact.

He caressed my face and turned it gently toward him. I looked up at him, drinking in his eyes and the little crinkles around them, the lock of hair that fell over his forehead, his sensuous lips. Elvis Presley could have driven up at that moment and I would have ignored him. I was exactly where I wanted to be. On the radio, The Everly Brothers were crooning "All I Have To Do Is Dream"..."Dre-e-e-e-eam, dream, dream, dream...."

Witzy bent his head toward mine. He was inches from me when his breath caught in his throat. He paused, still caressing my cheek. He pulled my head to his and placed his lips on mine. Sweetly at first, then with more hunger.

My heart fluttered, and I melted into a slice of heaven.

Obviously Witzy was one of my adolescent coups. Thank God for the good times. But the angst and stress of the abused child in me also had its forum. While Witzy, and a small succession of teenage beaus, held kisses sweeter than wine for me, I also had the "creep factor" to play out. Take Rudy Farmer for example. Please, do take Rudy Farmer.

The Rudy journey began when I was about four-and-a-half. My father was at the wheel of his Hudson sedan, driving a car load of folks including me to the last stop of a round-robin potluck dinner involving at least eight adult couples and an unwieldy cache of pre-birth-control-pill kids. Dessert was at our house.

I had been stuffed into the back seat of the already overcrowded car and placed on the lap of Rudy Farmer. He was a thirty-something guy with a swagger. Medium height, medium weight, average looks, but an above-average predator in waiting. He had a thing for motorcycles and little girls. Everybody knew about the motorcycles.

My mother twisted around from the front seat talking loudly, trying to get Rudy's attention. Ginny, still suffering from a severe case of spotlight-itis, as well as desperate-to-get-male-attention-itis, flounced her newly freshened henna hair in Rudy's direction. Her version of a red flag in front of a charging bull. But his focus was on the cute little girl sitting on his lap.

"Gimme a kiss, honey," Rudy whispers into my ear as I sit quietly on his lap. His breath smells of whiskey. It's a familiar smell and doesn't upset me at all. Everybody in the car is being happy. It makes me feel happy, too. The car is so cold I can see my breath. My dad is fiddling with some knobs in the front, trying to get the heater working. I snuggle deeper into my warm blue coat.

I feel Rudy's hand brush up against my hair. With his other hand he gives my arm a little squeeze. I first met Rudy when it was still warm outside. I ran down the stairs of my grandparents' house, and there he was, leaning against the doorframe of the apartment my grandparents were building in their basement. He was nice to me, and I liked him right away. The apartment is finished now, and Rudy and his wife, Mary Alice, live there.

My mom stops looking at Rudy for a moment and says to me, "Go ahead, Sandy, give him a kiss." Her cheeks are flushed, and her eyes are bugged out again. I think she thinks that makes her look pretty. It gives me the creeps.

I like Rudy, so I pucker my lips and touch them to his cheek.

Mom whinnies loud and high, like some kind of crazy horse, and once again looks at Rudy. I wince. The sound hurts my ears. I can tell that my mom wants Rudy to talk to her.

But he doesn't. He nuzzles me instead. Then he turns my face to him and says softly, "Give me some more sugar, hon." His lips are wet when he puts them straight on my lips and keeps them there for an extra second or two. My stomach feels like it just dropped all the way down to the floor, and I want to rub my lips to get any part of him off me. But I sit there unable to move.

I watch a spider that somehow survived the frosty weather as it hurries to retreat to the crack between the window and the metal of the car. Who will he eat tonight?

I am no longer okay. I no longer like anything about being in this stupid car. An icky sweet taste comes into my mouth. I've had it before, sometimes after I've thrown up. I want to scratch wildly at my tongue and rip the taste away. But I sit like a stone, like my arms are too heavy to move them. I want to scream, and I am doing so inside my head even louder than my mom's voice, but no sound comes out of my mouth.

Something is terribly wrong. I don't know what. It has a familiar feeling. But I can't place it. I just can't.

We are almost home.

My dad pulls the Hudson alongside the curb by our house. I bolt out of the car and dash into the house. I don't want anyone near me. I don't want anyone to touch me. I hate them. All of them. I don't need a reason why.

I run into the tiny room I have slept in since I was two, slamming the door behind me. My closet is directly across the room from the door. It becomes my fort. Nobody will get near me tonight!

I am keeping the closet door open just enough to peek out and protect my territory. I am the Lone Ranger. I look around at my weapons of shoes, boots, skates. Oh, look, there's a baseball. But there is no Tonto. I could really use a faithful Indian companion in here with me.

Oh, well….

The bedroom door creeps open, and Aunt Esther pokes her head inside. I wind up my right arm—the one holding a black boot, stand up, and hurl it at her head. She slams the door shut quickly. Then she tries again. The door re-opens slowly. I can see her head but not the rest of her. "Why don't you come out, Sandy?" she says. I respond with the baseball I found in the back of the closet. "Hi ho Silver, away!" I almost nail Aunt Esther, and she closes the door rapidly. I think the tic in her eye is getting worse.

Uncle Benny tries next. The door opens, and his large frame fills the door-way. With the speed of light and a cloud of dust I greet him with an ice skate tossed as hard as I can. The door bangs shut. Uncle Benny does not try again.

I am left alone for a while. I become the Lone Ranger's narrator. "Return with us now," I practice saying the words out loud in a low voice, "to the thrilling days of yesteryear." I try to remember the Lone Ranger's Creed, but I can't. It's all gobbledegook. It never made much sense to me anyway.

I hear the handle on the door to the room jiggle again. Oh, no. It's Aunt Rooshe. She must be a hundred years old. I always hate when I have to go to her house. It's dark and stuffy, and there are all those awful white lace doilies everywhere. I toss the other black boot at her. She gets mad and leaves right away. Other adults try popping their heads inside the bedroom door, but not my parents or Rudy Farmer. I eye those who try to take over my space fiercely and immediately pelt them with the remaining weapons from my arsenal. Finally, Aunt Clara knocks on the door and asks if she can come in. I am sure Silver must be getting really tired by now, and so am I, so I say okay. She comes in and starts talking to me in a soft, kind voice. I can't really make out the words, but whatever has kept me going this past hour isn't inside me any more. It has disappeared. I can't even remember why I got so mad. All I feel is tired. I don't think I have the energy to throw something at Aunt Clara if I wanted to. I surrender my closet peacefully and accept her peace offering of chocolate cake.

I enter the living room where glasses and ice cubes are clinking as the adults refill their drinks and talk loudly. I join my equally noisy cousins and do my best just to blend into the wallpaper.

Who knows for sure when my father began his campaign for ultimate power over me? The only thing I'm certain of is that, at the age of four, I found Rudy's behavior had a nasty ring of familiarity and left me feeling both paralyzed and assaulted.

And for a little girl, it was all pretty confusing, trying to figure out why certain behaviors that happened at home were not a good idea for elsewhere. There were things that apparently could and could not stand the test of polite company. Learning the rules of this rocky road of dueling environments was not without its pitfalls, as poor little Kenny Valendar was about to discover.

I am in the first grade. It is the noontime break, and our teacher, Miss Reynolds, has just stepped out of the classroom. It is an open period, so although

we have to stay in the room, we are free to move about. I am talking with my classmate, Kenny Valendar. He is nice and usually pretty quiet. We are friends. He is a little shorter and skinnier than I am, but I think he's kind of cute. Kenny is leaning against a bookcase, showing me the little comic strip that was wrapped around the Bazooka bubblegum he just opened. I am standing in front of him.

"Here," he says handing me a piece of the gum he has just broken in half. I start to reach for the gum when some demon or something takes over me. I suddenly push into Kenny, trapping him against the bookshelf, and force a long kiss on his lips. I feel him struggling to push me away, and finally he is able to come up for air. He wipes his mouth with the back of his hand and something that sounds like "Aarrgh!" escapes his lips. I do not know what possesses me. I am only aware of Kenny and me as I go in for the kill again.

"Stop that! Stop that now!"

Miss Reynolds's loud voice pierces the air and the fog in my brain. I am aware that every child in the room is staring at me. I look at Kenny, who looks like he wants to die. I want to die, too.

"Get back to what you were doing," Miss Reynolds commands the class as she calls me up front to her desk. I am aware of the hushed voices of my classmates and their secret glances as I stand at the side of the desk where my teacher is seated. I fight back tears as she sternly tells me that only bad girls do what I did and that I have created a bad reputation for myself. She says that I am never to do that again; if I do, I will be severely punished.

I return to my seat. I am so ashamed. I am so embarrassed.

But I have learned my lesson. I now see the difference between home and school. At school there are rules for behavior. I realize that if I obey the rules, I can control what happens at school. At home it doesn't matter if I'm good or bad; I have no control. At home, my parents control everything. At school, I can create an effect.

I secretly watch my classmates and start to copy how the most popular ones behave. Good academic work gets a lot of praise. I buckle down and excel as a student. I earn the right to clean off the blackboard, pass out papers, and collect the crayons. I am becoming a good example. My teacher now thinks I am a good girl. I am on my way. By the end of the year, even Kenny is talking to me again.

When I was almost eleven, Rudy Farmer resurfaced in prime predator form. He decided to mentor me by teaching me how to kiss. Like I didn't already know. But because of the split that existed inside of my head, I didn't know that I knew. Complicated.

As a child, being fractured into two distinct worlds didn't stop me from still wanting to be special in the eyes of an adult male. I wanted to be—needed to be—important to a father figure, so I was pretty easy bait.

Rudy and his wife, Mary Alice, were still living in my grandparents' one-bedroom basement flat, only now they also had two young children. Mary Alice was not much better than her screwed-up husband. When I would stop in at their apartment to set up a baby-sitting gig, Rudy would be openly seductive with me. One night I arrived while Rudy was taking a bath. He bantered with me through the door and teased me about coming in and washing his back. Mary Alice, sitting at the kitchen table, invited me to do so. And I did. Little wonder that this wholesome couple were friends with my own psycho June and Ward Cleaver wannabe parents.

The night Rudy ejaculated into my hands, he whined, "My God, if your father knew, he would kill me." Which turned out to be the ironic joke of the century.

It's true that by the time Rudy Farmer re-imposed himself on my life I was already in what felt like a freefall descent down the long, hopeless staircase into an exit-less hell. Rudy, in spite of his perversions and the toothless old duck he would one day become and in spite of the fact that he stood shoulder to shoulder with my father as one of the world's serious assholes, was in truth the least of my problems and did minimum psychological damage to me. The same cannot necessarily be said for the other innocent children he undoubtedly pursued. Rarely does a predator in the course of his or her lifetime have only one target.

So, the kissing sojourns of my youth had their ups and downs—in truth more downs than ups. But the ones in my outside-of-the-home world had sweet moments. And some sweet kisses.

And that's how it was for me all those years ago on one priceless end-of-summer night in 1958 when I was fifteen, with my past securely blocked in a hidden compartment in my brain. Life's precious coping mechanism allowed me to be fully present when Witzy kissed me.

Time stood still, and for one brief moment, caught up in the passionate thrill of living life as a normal teenage girl, I had the perfect fifties experience. In the arms of my boyfriend, I died and went to heaven.

17

RECONNECTING

Clinical repression is the inability to recall consciously experiences that one's system finds too shocking or painful to endure. It is a deeply rooted survival mechanism. The body invokes this level of separation when it perceives the organism to be in dire straits or true, all-consuming danger. It is an automatic intervention, abruptly triggered immediately before the overload is about to blow all the circuitry. And because it's this level of primal response, the individual is not, for that time, in charge. It is completely, totally involuntary.

The involuntary compartmentalization that occurred someplace deep within my brain between the ages of ten and twenty-three was more than a band-aid, more than a walking cane that helped me limp along through those very rough years of my life. It was, instead, like the world's finest pair of golden crutches, helping me to walk with a fair amount of fluidity, metaphoric breaks in my legs notwithstanding. But even the best crutches become impediments once the crushed "legs" begin to heal. Then, those old crutches actually impede walking. Eventually, they have to go. Eventually, in order for me to thrive and to heal, the inability to access all of the compartments within me was going to have to release its protective hold on me.

But before it did, before I could become strong enough to stand on my own, I had to have a little more practice exercising my voice. Exercising my own authority, especially with my mother.

Oh, yes, Dad was there, too.

I like to think I had my last physical fight at the age of eight when I tangled with my cousin Billy the Bully. It was during that battle that my eight-year-old mind was confronted with a serious dilemma. Which direction was I going to choose? Which way was I going to climb my mountain?

Billy was the son of my mother's brother, a hot-headed, bombastic alcoholic. *Sans* the drinking, Billy was taking on a lot of his father's characteristics. And he liked to pick a fight. As a kid I, too, had a lot of rage tucked inside of me, so when Billy's path crossed with mine, it was not a pretty sight. Billy and I tangled for the last time on a warm summer morning. We rolled around on the ground punching and hollering until I got the upper hand. I pinned him unmercifully. I had him on his back, with me straddled across his chest holding his arms down, sweating into his face. I looked him in the eye and pulled my little fist back intending to imprint my superiority on him. And then I saw it, the look of utter defeat in his eyes. It was a look I understood from someplace tucked deep within my young body. It tugged painfully at my heart. It stopped me cold. Without a word, I got off of him and walked away.

From that point on, except for the initial skirmishes with my father when he was attacking me, and—oh yes—that sincere threat of imminent mortal danger against my mother when I was fourteen, which in hindsight I'm relieved she didn't press me on because the "Burning Bed" defense didn't exist in the fifties, I was pretty much violence-free as far as my behavior toward others goes. Not anger-free, of course. Let's stay real. But definitely violence-free. Until, that is, I slugged Ginny shortly after my twentieth birthday.

I had managed to slip through the years of fourteen to twenty in a quasi-normal fashion, thanks primarily to my continuing inability to remember the specifics of my childhood. I was reasonably popular in school, had a steady boyfriend (not Witzy), listened to Johnny Mathis, drooled over Paul Newman, danced The Twist along with Chubby Checker. My parents pretty much ignored me, and I returned the favor. By the time I was twenty, I was living on my own in a studio apartment in a suburb neighboring the one in which I had grown up. So, it came as a surprise to me that in the midst of a pleasant summer Saturday afternoon, completely out of the blue, I got a gnawing urge to go see my parents. To this day, I have no idea what triggered that compelling feeling, but compelled I was. Within minutes I had hopped on a city bus and was headed toward their home.

My relationship with my mother had been overtly tense ever since my close encounter with her in the Tennessee motel as a Lizzie Borden stand-in—although at twenty, conscious awareness of the incident was still blocked. The awareness of intense verbal and emotional mistreatment was always there, but as far as the sexual and severe physical abuse, it remained hidden behind the massive protective firewall of repression locked in my brain—which made what was about to happen one of the great unconscious *coups de grace* of the century.

I am aware of the soft breezes flowing through the open kitchen window as my mother, father, and I sit at the small square table with one side pushed up against the wall. Mom is, as usual, drinking and edgy, which in turn makes me edgy without the benefit of the booze. My edgy is verbally aggressive and strident. Sorta like hers, without quite as many personal attacks. She tends to go for the throat with comments like "YOU'RE an idiot," "YOU'RE a whore." I'm more inclined to attack the dastardly deed, as in "That was a really stupid thing to do," or "That was an idiotic idea." Of course, I pepper my insults with a few "YOU'RE an obnoxious asshole" comments, too, so, what can I say? I'm here now. My father is sitting across the table from me like the lump that he is while my mother and I are talking. Actually, it's not a real conversation, 'cause we're just yapping at each other.

Oh, God, there it goes. She's starting to screech. About what? Who the hell knows? It's not like she ever makes any goddamn sense.

But now I'm pissed, too.

The noise of her voice escalates even more, and I raise my voice immediately to equal it. Like I'm going to let her best me in the volume department? I don't think so.

She gets up to fix herself another highball; I match her step for step. Before I even realize what is happening, we are squared off with each other in front of the sink, and I hear myself yelling back at her. Our "he said, she said" pissing contest is peaking to its familiar finest.

My turn.

(Drum roll for the impending coup de grace)

"Don't tell me what I do and do not know!" I bellow wickedly. "You know damn well I have a really good memory [which I do], *and I remember everything* [which I didn't].

"EVERY. SINGLE. THING!"

"You remember EVERYTHING?" My mother's eyes bulge, and the veins on her neck stand out. But I am too much on a roll to pay attention to the glint of fear that registers in her eyes. "Just what do you remember, missy?"

"You have no idea, lady," I shout. "I remember SO much more than you think."

I watch her face as anger turns to shock.

I am clueless as to how I have scored such an obvious victory, but as they say in the trenches, "Never look a gift horse in the mouth."

Not that anyone has ever offered me a horse or anything.

"How dare you talk to me that way in front of your father," Mom, stuck on an irrational binge, shrieks, pointing to my fake-goody-two-shoes dad, who is still sitting at the table, mostly because he doesn't know how to escape the kitchen. He's an idiot. "HIM?" I say incredulously. "HE'S a pathetic marshmallow."

"You will not speak about your father that way," she shouts. And with that she hauls off and slaps me full across the face.

Well, I don't know what comes over me, but without the slightest hesitation I draw my right arm back as far as I can and, like a pitcher ready to throw out the first ball of the season, I wind up and release one right back at her. Bull's eye!

She wails mightily, crying and cursing. Tom knocks the chair over in his rush to get up and console her. Finally, he has something to do. They tell me to get out. I look at them in disgust and leave, unaware that it will be months before I will speak to either of them again.

***

And that, truly, was the last time I ever had a physical altercation with anyone.

As far as unlocking the tightly locked compartments in my head that I pretended to have access to when I was so angry with my mother—which really was a pretense because you can't remember what you don't know is missing—that would be one marriage and two babies away. All of which I managed to sandwich into a scant three years.

I was already dating Leo when I had the big fight with my mother. Seven years older than I and equally limited, Leo was available, and I was needy. I was too scared and too insecure to live my life on my own. I didn't have a clue, yet, about the splits in my emotional reality. I was just a girl of my era, doing what girls did: looking for a husband, getting ready to have kids.

Work? Career? Independence? No way. I was busy looking for the proverbial white-picket fence.

Ugh!

This was years before I had truly connected to my own voice or discovered my little algebra formula: What am I really thinking when I think I'm thinking X? Years before I had taught myself to believe in and carve out my own path—long before I would teach other women how to establish their awareness and their expression of self.

Yep. Years before the happy years.

But, fortunately, it was also a few years after my commitment at age eighteen to breaking the cyclical abusive connection with my parents. It was a commitment I stayed conscious about, a commitment my stubbornness enabled me to cling to.

Leo seemed to be a nice enough guy. He went out of his way to be supportive of me, and I was—well, still needy. So we got together. We were careless, I got pregnant, and ultimately we got married. My daughter was born, and then less than two years later my son came along. And that's how it came to be that before I was twenty-three, I had a husband and two kids. I also had a state of mind that made me nervous and driven, but I didn't have much of a clue about either condition.

I was committed to living out the "young couple in the suburbs/everything is beautiful" fairy tale. In my ignorance I didn't even know I was pursuing a fantasy.

It is a Saturday night in September of 1966. I am four months into my twenty-third year, and my son is four months into his life. I have hired a sitter so that Leo and I can go to a movie and dinner.

We are sitting in the middle of a long row in the center of a large movie theater. On screen a mega-sized Elizabeth Taylor is screeching her guts out at a besotted but rather ineffective Richard Burton. George Segal, minus the banjo he usually shows up with on Johnny Carson's Tonight Show, *watches with his paramour from the sidelines. Liz continues to blast away.*

Who's afraid of Virginia Woolf?

I am.

I squirm with barely controlled panic as my eyes stay riveted to the screen. But it isn't the visual that has gotten to me. It's the audio. Elizabeth's on-screen discordant histrionics are taking me on a collision course with some unknown terror inside of me, crashing me into the seemingly ancient chords of Ginny's voice, pressing me all the way back to when I was a little girl. Everything is jumbled, and I have no idea what is happening in my head. But something is. A cacophony of terror and horror is for some ungodly reason building in my brain.

My breath catches in my chest. I look from side to side with urgency at the row upon row of people seated all around me. I am trapped. If only I could close my ears!

I consider plowing over the massive collection of knees that block me from the aisles, but I can't rouse myself out of the seat. It is as though a g-force greater than anything I have ever known is holding me in place. Stinging bile spews up into my throat.

I, who don't vomit as a matter of principle—no way am I going to mimic my mother's fainting and regurgitating skills—almost puke all over the bald pate of the elderly gentleman seated in front of me. Had I been a woman with a weaker stomach, the guy would have been a goner.

I settle into a cold, clammy sweat accompanied by a brain fog and somehow make it through that damn movie.

After the movie I tell Leo I am not up for dinner, so we go straight home. I sit in the overstuffed, inexpensively upholstered mauve chair in the living room with my knees held tightly to my chest while Leo dutifully takes the babysitter to her house.

My head is reeling. My body is numb. Leo returns.

We sit in silence, me on my chair, him on the matching sofa across from me.

"I think I've been raped," I finally say softly.

My husband looks at me for a moment; then, Leo being Leo, he gets up and goes to bed. Later, he will tell me that he hadn't heard me, and that may be so. But for this night I remain in my cushioned chair in the otherwise empty living room, slowly rocking myself back and forth until dawn.

Unknown to me at the time, Elizabeth Taylor's brilliant portrayal of brittle, piercing shrillness actually created a crack in the steel vault of my heretofore invincible inner separation.

I've been asked how that feels. The answer is simple. Repression doesn't feel. It is the involuntary process of distancing oneself from things too overwhelming to feel. But when the waters part abruptly, opening an immediate pathway for clarity and conscious awareness, as they did for me, it is unnerving—shocking—to the very marrow of one's bones. And on that *Who's Afraid of Virginia Woolf?* night, as my long-term repression began to crumble, I knew with every fiber of my being that what was being revealed to me now was absolutely true and real. I recognized it from the deepest pit in my stomach, the harshest thud in my chest. The pictures, unbidden by me, revealed themselves so fully, so acutely, that I had no doubt. The fortress that had supported the world in which I had tried to hide—the world of "I'm a normal young wife and mother and everything is just fine"—was like the walls of Jericho. The trumpets sounded loudly, surrounding the walls of my denial, and they were forever felled. On that first night, the shock of it left me totally, abjectly numb. And so, in my stupor, I rocked. And rocked....

Yet, even in the hollowed-out vacuum of my head space, I knew that what had been hiding, locked away for so many years, could no longer be shoved down. The tip of the iceberg had popped through the surface of my reality, dismantling my carefully constructed and desperately desired cover of normalcy. The tip, having been exposed, would pave the way for the depth and breadth of the rest of the iceberg, which would rapidly follow.

As I rocked myself through that long night, all I was really trying to do was keep at bay the heretofore unbearable feelings that had been harbored just barely beneath my conscious awareness for twelve long years. All the challenges and changes that would accompany my journey of dealing with the harsh truths of my past were still in front of me. Except for one.

From that night forward, I refused to allow my parents to have any contact with my children, and, therefore, I did not allow my parents to have contact with me. I was a Mama Bear who had suddenly realized that her cubs were at risk. Nothing on this planet—or any other one—could have convinced me to allow Ginny or Tom even the most remote possibility of being in a position to harm one hair of my children's heads.

And they never were.

18

DISCERNMENT

The discernment of what is historically real and what is only emotionally real can sometimes be a very fine line—especially in the process of recalling difficult incidents from long ago. That's why it's so important to make sure that you are hearing only your own voice—your own sense of things—from within. And you have to be able to know the difference between when you are hearing that inner voice of truth and when you are listening to a reaction involving a current circumstance that emotionally connects you to your unresolved past.

Feeling unworthy, inferior, rejected, unlovable, ugly, unredeemable, victimized beyond recovery? That's not truth talking. The hooks for identifying yourself from the point of view of those emotions are in the past.

I sat behind my desk in my office in the Executive Building at Denver Tech Center, staring out through the long, broad windows on the wall directly across from me. This was my first real office. I had almost leased the one down the hall recently vacated by former astronaut Wally Schirra, which I thought was quite cool because, like most people my age, I was very into the original Mercury Seven. But in the end, I chose this one. It was a bit bigger and would accommodate my clients better; plus, there were those great floor-to-ceiling windows.

I'd come a long way in a few short years. I had finally mustered the courage to put an end to what for years had been a dead-end marriage, but not before I had one last child. So there I was, thirty-eight with three kids, a divorce from Leo, and now a real office counseling/coaching practice with a receptionist et al. A far cry from when my first clients would come to my little home and have to wait in my bedroom while I finished with the person I was talking with in my living room. There wasn't even room for a chair in the bedroom. They had to sit on the edge of my bed and wait. I thought for sure they would never come back. But they did, and they sent their friends.

Joanna, my shared receptionist, who also worked for several office holders in this wing of the third floor, buzzed in, breaking my reverie.

"Elena Nelson is here," she said.

"Great. Send her in, please."

I opened my door to a statuesque woman in her early forties with long, very straight coffee-bean brown hair, alabaster skin, and huge amber eyes. It was her first visit to my little domain. We sat across from each other in the high-backed cushy chairs I used for sessions. Elena spoke haltingly as she recounted the details of a horrific childhood involving the physical and sexual abuse inflicted on her by her U.S. Army Captain father and Austrian-born mother. I listened closely. I knew she was telling the story accurately, not just intellectually, but also—for lack of a better way to describe it—by the energy or frequency she was transmitting. It hit the truth button in me, which I had learned to develop acutely in my own process of healing. So, I not only heard, but also felt the truth of what she was saying.

Then Elena recounted a story about having been involved in ritualistic abuse and putting a baby in an oven and killing it.

Suddenly my truth-o-meter fell off the flat edge of the earth. It wasn't that I didn't feel that her father actually did bring in some of his army buddies for his version of a sick party with her. But when Elena began talking about the baby, what she was saying no longer rang intuitively true to me. It isn't that it wasn't possible. I had worked with ritual abuse cases before, so I knew anything was possible. And it wasn't that she didn't believe her story. She did. But it no longer resonated with my truth button.

"Tell me more about the incident with the baby," I said kindly. "What do you remember about it?"

"Well, I.... There was a whole group of people around in a circle or maybe a semi-circle, I think," she said crying. "They handed me this baby and told me I had to put it in the oven. And then they crowded in on me and then.... And then I did it." By now she was sobbing.

I passed a box of Kleenex to her.

"I killed a baby," she moaned. "How could I have done that?"

I gave her a moment while she blew hard into the tissue.

"Odds are, my dear, that you didn't."

Her head shot up. "What?"

"When did you first start to remember about the ritualistic abuse?"

"Well, my former therapist said she believed I had been abused in that way. And I thought about it, and then after a while, I remembered the baby and that whole horrible scene." She was crying again.

I suppressed a sigh. Great. Fine. Her therapist said so; therefore, it was.

"What gender was the baby?" I asked calmly.

"Uh, I don't know."

"Do you remember who handed you the baby?"

Elena looked at me, confused. "You know, I don't know."

"Was this little baby clothed or unclothed?" I kept my voice deliberately soft so Elena would not feel interrogated or accused.

"Well, uh, clothed," she answered. "I think."

"How old were you when this happened?"

"Maybe thirteen or fourteen, something like that."

"Elena, when you think about the things your mother and father did," I asked, "and then you think about the experience with the baby and the crowd pushing in on you—does it feel the same inside of you or different?"

"The stuff with my parents is really clear." She paused for a moment. "The stuff with the baby is pretty vivid, too," she added, "only maybe it's a little bit like looking through wavy water. But it *feels* real."

"I understand, Elena." I paused for a moment as she wiped her eyes and shifted in her chair.

"I would like you to consider a possibility," I continued. "Don't jump on it and make it yours right away, unless it really is. Do a 'let's pretend' with me. Let's pretend that we're basically a bunch of energy, non-visible frequencies, housed in a physical form called a body. Sometimes we have experiences in which we and our bodies have suffered greatly, like when we've been abandoned, wounded, and betrayed by those who are supposed to help us live and grow. When that happens, the body retains a specific frequency, which is like a chemical or energetic message that connects it not only to the field of pain within itself, but also to corresponding fields of pain within others. That's how our historic memories can sometimes get blurred with our emotional vulnerability. The un-healed wounds consisting of our own pain and guilt can set up a cross-reference with other stories and situations that energetically corre-spond with our hurt and unprocessed guilt.

"Discernment is the key here. Discernment is the ability to know the difference between your inner voice and someone else's suggestion—the ability to know the difference between your true inner awareness and something that might merely be an emotional response to a collective thought. It's as though a greater truth, a greater awareness, comes from something that your personality is not consciously authoring. It's a fine line sometimes. But the more you're willing to unfold self-honesty, the more you're willing to explore self-discovery, the easier it is to discern the unflinching truth of both your emotional reality and your factual his-tory."

Elena nodded and seemed to understand what I was saying.

"Prior to your therapist's suggestion, did you have any sense of ritual abuse or of having killed an infant?"

Elena looked a little stunned as she contemplated. "You know, now that you mention it, I don't think I did. But I always have had so much pain and a sense of terrible things around me. The thought of it felt real."

"One of the ways you can help yourself to know the accuracy of a memory—or something you think might be a memory—is to check to see if you can corroborate it with any other crystal-clear experience. For instance, with the remembrance of the baby, can you remember what you were wearing or what you felt like afterward? Did you look at your hands in horror? Did you hold the baby close or away from you? Was the stove hot? Did it burn your hand? Was the baby crying or quiet? Heavy or light? Never be afraid to examine a memory completely, unabashedly. If it gets dismantled, it gets dismantled."

I understood Elena's mental dilemma. Picking through surfacing memories to unfold the tapestry of a troubled cloth of truth is a rough road that I knew all too well. I had experienced my own difficult years of dealing with recovering the painful, segregated segments of my mind. Only I was more fortunate in my choice of therapists. I picked an analyst, John Taylor. A very caring, middle-aged, portly man with the kindest blue eyes, but an analyst to the core. No prompting—ever. For the process of reuniting with the parts of my life that had been blocked to me, he was exactly what I needed.

I force myself to stay in control, the aching pressure in my chest notwithstanding. I am twenty-three and feel old beyond time. It never occurs to me that I am still young.

I wrestle with the uncomfortable silence that hangs in the air on this Tuesday night in late January. I have nothing I want to say tonight. With the exception of wanting me to write a book, John Taylor never coaches or leads me. He is, after all, an analyst, and he stays super-glued to that protocol. So I know he is not about to help me with the conversation.

I lean back in the brown leather recliner opposite John's straight-backed swivel chair and stare at him in silence. He has that goddamn pen poised above his notebook on the off-beat chance that I might actually say something. The whirring of the small tape recorder busily documenting a litany of dead air is the only sound in the small office. The tape is mine; the request was his. John had asked if I would be open to taping the sessions in case I would one day want to write a book.

Whirrrrrr…

Thoughts swirl in my head. I cannot do this. I cannot. And I don't want to! I can feel my face harden in anger as I lean back into John's recliner. If I could throw the goddamn cut-glass candy dish sitting on the table next to me through the window right behind his friggin' head, I would. If I could disappear from this room—if I could disappear from this planet and never have to deal with anyone or anything again, I would. If I could take my nails and gouge them across my cheeks, I would. But he's right there watching me, with his pissant little ballpoint perched and stupid-ass notebook at the ready. I'm stuck here in this son of a bitching goddamn chair with no way out. I cannot stand it, not one more second.

Whirrrrrr…

I want to scream. I want to take that goddamn tape recorder and shove it up somebody's ass. I don't care whose. But he's still watching me. Unflinching, without criticism, without judgment. Without comment.

Spider to the fly?

No, no. Kindness is still on his face, in his eyes.

I close my eyes and try to relax. It doesn't work at all, but I am not about to lose control in this office. I am not about to let him see what is really going on in my head. What good would it do? I'd only embarrass myself.

Besides, I don't think I could actually talk even with a gun held to my head. Everything is too deep. Everything is too hard, fossilized in an ocean floor I can't touch, can't reach. It is impossible.

I keep my eyes closed and reflect on the past few hours—the drive down here from my rented townhouse in Milwaukee to John's office in Chicago. I've been making this ninety-mile trek three to four times a week for the past several months, ever since the Virginia Woolf debacle. Leo walks in the door at 5:00 P.M., dinner is on the table, and I race out. Tonight, I once again got impatient on the freeway that seems to connect, almost as a straight line, my home to John's office. Driving my yellow Dodge Charger as though it were some kind of armored tank, I had tailgated some poor bastard to the point of recklessness. Riding his ass at 80 mph! And all I could think was that he was the asshole, and he was making me late. Thank God, he finally had the good sense to get the hell out of the left-hand lane. Jesus! What was I thinking?

A sigh escapes my lips before I can catch it. I open my eyes. John is in his usual relaxed posture, watching me.

"Do you want to talk about it?" he queries.

"No."

Whirrrrrrr…

In spite of myself, I am starting to find safety with this good man who doesn't hurt me or press me or lie to me. In fact, he feels like my only hope. That's what keeps me coming back. Sheer desperation. But I've been protecting myself all my life, and there was never anyone I could trust. How could I explain this to anyone? How could I possibly explain to anyone that I cannot open up on demand? It's impossible to share me at that level. If I did, I would…well, it doesn't matter what I think would happen because it's impossible. Doesn't he get it? I simply cannot—I cannot do this!

Whirrrrrrr…

Evenings of driving in to see John turned into weeks; weeks became months. Once the Pandora's box within me had been sledge-hammered open in the movie theater, the memories came flooding back to me pretty quickly. I was able to get through that part okay by finally opening up and addressing it with John, but only on an intellectual level. The other stuff— trauma, abandonment, pain, rejection, guilt—I was only able to talk about as if I were reading a geography textbook. All mental. John's Kleenex supply is safe when I am around. Unless it's hay-fever season, I rarely use them. My emotions remain sequestered behind my own personal moat. But the mounting depression with which each new memory leaves me is becoming overwhelming. The resounding ache that I am trying so hard to control seems to be on a collision course with the part of me that is crying out to be a happy, okay, normal woman.

Memories continue to resurface in hodgepodge order and often at inconvenient times.

Like tonight. It is a dark and stormy night. Really. Rain and hail slash across my car, pounding on my windshield as I endeavor to maneuver my car north to Milwaukee. It is already past 9:00 at night, and I have just finished a session with John Taylor in Chicago. I fight the howling wind to hold my car steady and in only one lane. The defroster is blowing full force to keep the inside of my windows as clear as possible. Outside, the windshield wipers, flopping back and forth as fast as they can, are rapidly losing their battle with the elements. And I am still a good hour from home.

I check the rearview mirror to see if anyone is even remotely close to me. Not a soul in sight. I am alone in the middle of a brutal storm. I look over to the right to make sure I am not edging too near the shoulder of the road.

"Oh, my God!" I yelp out loud. A nausea-inducing shadow is sprawling across my own right shoulder. It is moving! My flesh crawls with panic. On a good day I do not do well with the insect kingdom, and this was not a good day. I brush frantically at the creepy-crawly monstrosity on my shoulder.

Nothing was there.

But the sense of it grows. I slap at it with greater ferocity and almost fishtail my car across the median.

"Come on, Sandy," I say to myself sternly. "It's not real. Hold on to the steering wheel and breathe. You can make it home. You HAVE to make it home."

The sensation of something on my shoulder intensifies. It will not go away. I flip the rearview mirror down, pop on the dome light, and check it out. And that's when I really scream. The shadow of a huge, tarantula-sized spider is perched on my shoulder, inching its way toward my neck.

"It is NOT real," I repeat, only this time I say it out loud. Still, I cannot stop myself from slapping at it again.

For the next fifty minutes I somersault between my "it's not real" affirmations and my hysteria. At long last I pull into my driveway. I don't even notice the drenching rain as I run into the house. Water drips from my shaking hands as I fumble with the lock and safety chain, finally securing the door behind me. I drop my rain-soaked coat on the floor and, holding on to what feels like my last shreds of sanity with every ounce of will that I have, I head straight for the phone. It is late, but John Taylor, God bless him, takes my call. Within an hour I remember it all. The Thanksgiving Eve when my father had inched a large, black spider up my naked body to terrorize me.

Although I was completely frazzled on the phone with John on that storm-filled night, it turned out to be a good thing, because it made me too broken to stay in control, too broken to protect myself by resisting the natural flow of emotional release. For the first time in my adult life, I cried about the pain of my past in the presence of someone else. It was like an inner rain, cleansing away shame, cleansing away fear. Making room for a little more sunshine.

I continued to see John, but I was never able to replicate with him the emotional breakthrough I experienced on the "spider" night. It isn't that I didn't want to, but I wasn't able to. For the most part I addressed my issues and memories in an intellectual manner with few emotions and even fewer tears.

On occasions in the privacy of my home I would have breakdowns. But they were so fruitless. I would cry and cry and cry until I was drained and exhausted. As a young woman, those crying times left me feeling completely threadbare and hopeless, like I had dropped myself into a boiling cauldron of emotions from which there was no way out.

By the time I was twenty-six, I had put most of the factual pieces of my life together, letting them slide into place like an interlocking jigsaw puzzle. The full tapestry was clear. I understood intellectually what had happened to me physically, knew at some level that I was deeply wounded emotionally. But I had no idea how to stem the flow of pain leaking out of me like spurting blood from a severed vein.

The inner pressure that had once galvanized me into the multi-weekly trips to see John began to wane—not because I was feeling any better but because I wasn't getting anywhere. I wasn't sure how much longer I wanted to keep making that long, tedious trek down to Chicago.

One night, as my time with John was drawing to a close, I woke up in the middle of the night and was able to re-see with my mind's eye the large, brightly lit foyer and broad staircase that I had first seen as a thirteen-year-old in labor. And then, of course, I was able to remember the baby. His fate did not resurface so easily.

For a few months I fantasized that he was alive and I would find him. With time, the recognition of the baby as a reality became less and less threatening to me. I could stay safe, sane, and still remember. Then, at long last, I became strong enough to allow myself to know the end of the story as it actually happened. The child—*my* child—was dead.

I was devastated, soldered to my guilt. I didn't think of me as having been a brutally traumatized young girl. I thought of me as being horribly at fault. Through my ignorance and stupidity I had destroyed a human life. The fire and brimstone of the Christian hell I had been instructed about so often as a child in parochial school burned through my abdomen. I had committed the unforgivable sin from which there could be no redemption. I understood why God had abandoned me all those years ago. I knew that He was right to do so.

My baby was dead. I was guilty.

Could anything be worse than being responsible for another person's death?

It was a gut-wrenching, seemingly unbearable truth.

Then I discovered another horrible truth. Knowing what happened didn't take away the pain. It didn't heal.

Now I was really screwed.

I stopped seeing John Taylor, threw away the boxes and boxes of tapes I had collected, and set about trying to find a way to live with the pain that tore at my gut and imploded in my head.

Eventually, I would come to learn that there was no truly effective way to live with the pain. Oddly enough, it was that very awareness that a few years hence would drive me to re-explore my past in search of healing one more time. One more time was all that I would need.

I left the security blanket of John Taylor's office when I was twenty-six, not yet realizing what an important role he had played in my journey. His kindness, generosity, and impartiality gave me the landscape I needed to rediscover the historical facts of my life. Although knowing them didn't heal me, I'm not sure how I would have gone forward in my life if I hadn't found a safe place to remember. John Taylor was my safe place.

19

GOD'S A BRIT?

I had not expected to grow up to be a counselor/teacher/coach/lecturer, which is what I've been for more than thirty years now. A singer would have been nice, but that would have required a talent for singing. A princess would have been okay, but that sets up the lineage problem. I probably would have settled for a happy housewife, but then again I had Ginny for a mother, and in the early years, really bad taste in men, so the odds of becoming the female half of an "Ozzie and Harriet" cloned couple were remote.

I certainly did not expect to grow up and discover the level of intuitive awareness I've developed. It's not that I'm always psychic in the more traditional sense of the word—that's assuming that anything about "psychic" can be put in the context of what's traditional. It's unlikely that I will be able to tell you that your lost keys are under the left side of the dresser in the purple bedroom—although occasionally that will pop out. For me, especially when I'm working, my extra-sensory awareness is expressed through recognition of the energy field or frequency of the person with whom I am speaking. It lets me "see" the person's journey and patterns so much more quickly and to feel in my body what the other person is feeling in his or hers.

That's a gift, but learning how to use it—especially when I was younger—has provided me with a few dicey moments. Like the time in 1981 when I was flying back to Denver after a successful speaking engagement in New York. Everything had worked great. I boarded the plane content, tired, and happy to be going home. I relaxed into my aisle seat and closed my eyes. The plane pushed back from the jet way and slowly headed toward the runway. Suddenly, completely out of nowhere, I started to panic. We're talking *panic!* It took every drop of self-control within my shaking being to contain the urge to demand that the crew return to the gate and let me out. Images raced through my head. Pictures of explosions and debris and the plane erupting on takeoff. And body parts.

We were surely doomed.

Yet, at the same time, some part of me echoed a distant awareness that this inner hysteria wasn't real. But it felt damn real, and my pulse raced with the booming force of a battering ram.

"My God," I thought, "you can't have these thoughts when the plane is getting ready to fly." I quickly reached for my purse, which held a heretofore untouched bottle of "just in case" pain meds that my doctor had given me for a little medical procedure I had done right before my trip. I popped two of those untested babies into my mouth and swallowed them dry. I made myself lean back against the seat again and tried to breathe. Then, I opened my eyes. My glance fell on the lady to my left. Her face was frozen in a mask of terror; her hands, white-knuckled, held a clawing, death-like grip on both armrests.

"Oh, shit," I said to myself. "I took her pills!"

I doubt that my taking the drugs my seatmate certainly could have used helped her one bit. But I don't know for sure. I was out cold for the rest of the trip to Denver.

Fortunately, I can't even remember the last time that I confused the emotions and physical realities belonging to other people with the ones that are mine. Good thing. It keeps me drug-free and much more rational.

Nonetheless, especially when I work, I do let the awareness of where other people are in their bodies and minds flow through my body and mind. It helps me see the world through their eyes and understand their patterns so much more quickly. And it helps me follow their trail of when they are connected to their truth or unconsciously lost in their story.

As a child I had glimpses of this intuitive awareness within me. I would sense something, and, on occasion, see things and know what was coming. But it made me feel even more odd, and I quickly shut all of that down. I already felt sufficiently weird without adding any voodoo stuff to it. Instead, I held to my thought that perhaps someday, provided, of course, that I lived past the age of eighteen, I just might become a teacher. I never really believed I'd make it to adulthood, a thought not too uncommon for abused kids. Once I did, though, I thought I'd be long gone before thirty. Finally, I decided to quit worrying about my longevity and focus on trying to live.

Intuitive proclivity went even further out the window during the difficult decade of my twenties when I regularly swallowed up to thirty extra-strength Excedrin daily just to keep the headaches at bay. And to keep my voice from shaking when I spoke. That's the kind of constant anxiety with which I lived. It was an anxiety that oozed from the past and flooded my present.

Finding any real quality of life in my twenties was difficult. I educated myself, formally, whenever I could, but often informally, in a quest to find some way to learn enough to live with the pain I felt. Ultimately, the combination of classes, personal study, seminars, workshops, and life experience led to a degree involving a lot of credit for what used to be called a university without walls curriculum. Today it would be called distance education. But, still, the most impactful and wisdom-producing education I've ever had, and continue to have, has been under the auspices of the school of life.

During the rocky road of my twenties, I also tried—I mean really tried—to be an agnostic. I never attempted atheism. That was a little too extreme, even for me. But I did think that if there was a God and he let children get hurt the way I and so many others have been, then fuck him.

Angry as I was, and try as I might, I just couldn't get the agnostic tag to stick. So, one day after entering my thirties, I threw my hands in the air and said to whatever I perceived God to be, "I give up. Every time I try to figure out how to make sense of what happened to me, I go crazy. Yet, I see trees growing out of rocky mountainsides and dandelions growing through cracks in sidewalks. I see planets, stars, even galaxies that manage to avoid colliding into each other on a daily basis. If order and a quest for life are the nature of existence, then those elements must also be the nature of me. But I'm stuck. I can't figure out how a divine order—or any other order for that matter—could possibly apply to my life. So, I'm just going to have to trust that one day you'll explain it to me."

I pictured the "one day" I was referring to.

It was a balmy, summer morning in my version of heaven. I don't know how long I had been dead, but it felt like I'd been around this new place for some time. I was wearing a little *Happy Days*-type cinch-waist, full skirted, boat-necked, sleeveless summer frock. A blue print. No pillbox hat—wrong season. Anyway, I was primly puttering in my window-box garden when God came strolling by. I don't know how I knew it was God. I mean, he wasn't wearing a sign or anything. And he definitely wasn't wearing a scraggly beard or long, badly-in-need-of-a-trim, gray hair. He was actually fairly attractive.

"Jolly good to see you, Sandy," he saluted, cheerily.

"Hello, sir," I called back.

He drew closer.

"Splendid day. Sorry I haven't gotten over here sooner. If this were a ranch, I'd tell you I've been busy on the North Forty." His eyes twinkled with a smile.

I laughed.

"But, seriously, old girl, there's something I've been meaning to talk to you about...."

Whoa! Wait a minute!

Jolly good? Splendid? Old girl?

God's a Brit?

And so my vision went. Filled with humor, filled with color, filled with potentials.... In the end, I had to do what I had been so resistant to doing. I had to surrender the need to know, the need to understand, and accept—without doubt—that the spirit or core of my very existence would literally explain it to me. One day.

In the meantime, while I was still in my late twenties and still in the throes of my quest for pain relief—which my trusty old super-sized Excedrin was no longer capable of providing and my stomach lining could no longer handle—I read and studied voraciously. I tore a page out of Buckminster Fuller's book and became my own lab rat. I was searching for a way to live with the pain I felt, but in the end it became obvious that there was no living with it. Through the "science" of ignorance and the application of a hit-or-miss strategy, I stumbled into a combination of a spiritual perspective and a pragmatic approach to life and pain relief that bounced me into the spiritual surrender of "someday you'll explain it to me." It was my first real release of my attachment to my story of pain and suffering.

I was shocked. It really was starting to work. I was actually beginning to feel better.

Long before any of the books were out and popularized, I made up exercises to teach myself the process of transpersonal communication—talking to the wounded part of myself. Initially, it seemed to make things worse. I would try to talk to the child I had once been and end up falling into pit after pit of swirling morass and wounded victimization. Then it would take me days to climb back out of that level of seeping emotional trauma.

One day, almost by happenstance, I saw this wound within me as though it were a large deeply-bowled tower. I realized that I had been going into the tower through the same door every time, getting caught in the same bitter, murky swamp in the center of this hollowed-out tower of pain and exiting the way I had entered. It left me drained and leaking wounded-child insecurities into all areas of my life.

Finally, I focused on the idea that, if I entered that tube of pain again and kept looking with my mind's eye straight ahead, I would see another exit. I would find another way out.

And that's what I did.

I started another internal dialogue with the wounded child stuck in the darkest recesses of my mind, only this time I didn't merge with the pain of my experiences as a child. I remained the woman I was, reaching out to the part of me that had been so hurt, gently lifting the girl I used to be up to my now instead of collapsing into her reality. The wonder of all this is that it didn't leave me feeling desperate, aching, and alone. I began to discover that the woman who was capable of reaching to the child was me. My litany of wounds—that I wasn't enough, wasn't even redeemable—loosened its grip on me. I was more than the pain, greater than the memories. It had never occurred to me that there was any way I could actually be enough, yet I found that I was. I learned that the pain that had been a part of me almost all of my life wasn't really stemming from the woman I had become but from the point of view of the child I had once been.

Revelation about the inner child notwithstanding, the most powerful experience I had at that time was based on a spiritual awareness. I began to contemplate that within each being, no matter how large or small, exists a full-grown soul that knows exactly what it's doing. What if there was some part of me that chose my parents? Some part of me that had a say in this life experience? A part of me that chose! Not that I as a personality caused or wanted the abuse, but some part of me understood my own personal book of life and was willing for tough times to produce an evolution that one day just might be worth the price of admission.

A surge of energy flooded my body. There truly was another way to frame my past. I was not a victim.

It was exhilarating. And then I thought, "If at the end of my life I find that I was wrong, that life really is just the luck of the draw, what then?"

"Well," I said to myself, "if I'm wrong, I'm wrong. But right or wrong, by choosing a point of view in which I am not a victim, I'll live a happier life. For sure."

So, I chose to believe that I chose. I chose to believe that my soul, the essence of my being, knows what it is doing here. I chose to believe that my life is not just happenstance and, in that choice, I felt empowered.

It's still okay if I am wrong. But I was right about one thing. The awareness of personal empowerment changed my life and became a cornerstone in helping me ultimately create a joy-filled life.

20

THE MOTHER OF ALL DEPRESSIONS

Humor is a pathway for light, hope, and healing. "We have to laugh," wrote noted poet Rosario Castellanos, "because laughter, we already know, is the first evidence of freedom." For whatever reason—maybe it was the absurdity of Ginny and Tom—I have always been drawn to satire and irony, and they have been a windfall for me throughout my life.

Let freedom ring.

I was in my mid-thirties and, in my efforts to make peace with myself, I realized I was also going to have to endeavor to make peace with my world. So I took on the concept of the sacredness of all life. Forgetting that my early spider sagas had taken me one step short of entomology phobic, I began with the insect kingdom.

I know, I know…. It's a head-scratcher.

As I sat one afternoon on an easy chair in my living room, trying to absorb what I was reading, I looked up and noticed a big black ant zigzagging its way along a wall in my foyer. I ripped a small square of paper off the upper right-hand corner of the article I had been studying and marched over to the intruder. He really had nothing to fear. If I had wanted to squash him, I would have smashed him with my loafer. But here was my opportunity to practice my connection with all life. Why the paper? God forbid I should have to touch the darn thing.

I gently scooped the ant invader onto my swatch. He gently fell to the floor.

On my hands and knees I searched the tiles until I found his scurrying little form and once again scooped him onto my paper. I opened the front door carefully, balancing him on his make-shift raft, and placed him on the concrete slab of the covered front porch. I straightened up, proud of my success and at the same time knowing full well that had Mr. Ant been Mr. Spider he would never have made it out of the house.

I felt my three-year-old son brush past me. I had been so caught up in my own field trip into oneness that I hadn't realized he had followed me outside. He noticed the big ant in front of me, raised his cowboy-boot-clad foot high, and stomped Mr. Ant into kingdom come—or wherever it is that thoroughly squished ants go.

Which pretty much made my attempted inroads into the practice of unity with all life a bust. All these years later I'm still not very good with the creepy, crawly world of bugs, but from the ant incident forward, I did make a deal with them. When I'm outside, unless they're attacking me, I won't interfere with them. Come into my house, and it is so over.

More importantly, though, I found there was a moral to the ant-stomping story. A good one. You can't save that which doesn't want to be saved. I couldn't make the decision for the ant to live, and I can't make the decision for others to reach beyond their pain to find a greater goal, to pursue the light that letting go brings—and no one else can make the choice for me.

On the other hand, there are times when people might look like they're jostling to be next in line for squishing, but what they really want is a helping hand. What they're really hoping for, perhaps praying for, is another point of view.

"Hello…," I answered groggily into the phone.

"I'm sorry to wake you, and I hope I didn't make a mistake on this one," said a familiar female voice. "This is Martha from the exchange. I've got a Wendy Ann Brae on the phone. She says it's an emergency and that she's your client. She sounds really messed up."

"Hold on for a minute," I said as I tossed my legs over the side of the bed, forcing my body into an upright position. I turned on the light, glanced at the clock and groaned—1:35 A.M.

I yawned into the mouthpiece. "Sorry, Martha."

"Do you want me to put her through."

"Uh, sure. Okay. Thanks."

A few clicks later and I had a heavy breather on the other end of the line. "Wendy?"

Silence. Well, not quite silence. There was that heavy breathing going on. This time I stifled the yawn. "Wendy, come on. You got me out of bed. Tell me what's going on."

"Sandy," her voice sounded thin and reedy, "I'm going to kill myself."

"How are you going to do that, Wendy?"

"I'm holding a loaded gun to my head. I can't take it anymore. I'm going to shoot myself."

Now I was wide awake.

"Can we talk about it?" I asked.

"It won't do any good."

"I understand. Tell me, did anything happen in the last few days to bring this to a head?"

"My boyfriend won't call me back. My mother's…asshole…." Her voice broke off. "I don't want to live anymore." She was almost whispering now.

"Sweetie, that's a very rough place to be," I said quietly. "I know that when you feel that way it's awfully hard to find a reason to hold on. But I know what I would choose if I were in your shoes."

"What?"

"In my life one of the things that helped me stay alive was that I didn't want to come back and have to start over. I never wanted to have to do the whole diaper set again.

"Wendy, I don't have any moral thing that says you can't take your life if you're hell bent on doing so. But what if you do that and you get to the other side and it's not nirvana? What if you don't even get to go into a numbed nothingness?"

More heavy breathing, but at least she was still breathing.

"What if you destroy yourself and find that it didn't release you at all? You might find that you get to wherever it is we go after we die and you still have to deal with all the crap you're going through now. So you get there and go through a little review of your life—the one you just took, by the way—and you find that you have to come back here and go through the whole damn process again only in another body."

"How do *you* know that's what happens!" she demanded, irritated.

Good, I thought. Mad is better for her right now than hopeless.

"I don't," I replied.

"Then what if you're wrong?" she shot back.

"I could be," I said evenly. "But what if I'm right?"

I understood Wendy's plight. It had only been a little over a decade since I had been in shoes similar to hers—minus the gun.

I am twenty-eight, living in what for me is the dead-end town of Phoenix, in a going-nowhere marriage, isolated and alone. And then, suddenly, it rolls in. A foreboding as intense as any I've ever known is building inside of me, a sense of doom that doesn't seem to be founded on any crisis currently going on in my life—well, at least nothing I am aware of or willing to cop to. But the doom is here and with it a premonition. It is like knowing that a sun-blocking meteor is on its way and there is nothing that can be done to intercept it. It's almost here. I know it is. I am driven to go through the tiny condo Leo and I are renting as though I were child-proofing the house. Only I am trying to disaster-proof me. I toss any old medications that we have lying around. I toss the bullets to Leo's gun, and I even toss my precious stash of Excedrin. Knives are okay. I am as squeamish about blood and guts as I am about insects, so I know knives can't hurt me. I'd never use them on myself.

And then, it descends on me—an enshrouding, black, heavy, consuming morass. Hell. I am being re-burned alive every day, but I never actually die. Instead of flames licking at me, it is as though an alien fungus is consuming me, spitting me out and then consuming me again.

I have no idea what is actually happening to me, only that I am hanging on by the thinnest thread. I cannot possibly try to analyze anything, although some part of me thinks it may be imperative that I do so. But I can't. Whatever this storm is, I am already way too caught up in it and way too broke to seek help for it. Every weekday morning I barely hold myself together while the children get themselves ready for school. It's not as though I can help them. I can point and give directions. Sometimes.

After they leave, I draw the drapes and take the phone off the hook. I sit in the straight-backed chair, looking at those layered sea-green drapes. No radio, no television, no distractions. Stuck here in this gold upholstered chair as though I am held in place by some kind of all-purpose Velcro.

I look at the clock on the wall.

And I give myself an order. It's nine o'clock. You will live 'til ten.

It's not as though I am aware of feeling lonely and abandoned. I'm not aware of feeling much pain or much of anything else for that matter, except the heavy force of unknown origin that keeps pressing me down, down, down into some kind of mind-numbing abyss. Sometimes I rock myself in my forlornness.

Other times I just look from the clock back to the drapes—not because they are interesting, but because they are there.

Tick, tock…tick, tock….

The clock ticks away the seconds. The seconds turn into minutes.

It's ten o'clock. You will live 'til eleven.

I leave my chair on occasion to use the bathroom or have a slice of bread. Food helps, but only a little, and only briefly, because in no time at all the intense doom once again enshrouds me.

Tick, tock…tick, tock….

It's two-thirty. You will not let your children come home to a dead mother.

The school bus drops the kids off around three. They bound in the door. I tell them what to get for a snack and send them out to play without ever leaving my chair. When Leo shows up from work around five, I get out of my safety net— my velvet gold-colored chair—and trudge up the stairs to my waiting bed.

Seeking medical help is not an option. We are flat-ass broke. But even if money were not a hindrance, I don't know how I would get the energy or courage to do it. Up to this time, John Taylor has been the one and only exception to the rule of thumb for my life. Before and after him the bottom line has always been the same. If I want to survive, my life has taught me, time after time, that the only one I could count on was me. How do I know this? By the simple fact that there was never anyone around who, with any consistency, covered my back. No one to whom I could turn. No one but me. I would have to find my way out of this dark, dark hole myself.

I had tried reaching out one other time after John. I went to see a psychiatrist I had heard about. I sat across from her desk and followed her request to tell her the story of my life. That was such a very scary, awkward thing for me to do. So, I looked away and, in fairly rapid detail, revealed to her the painful, sordid, abusive events of my life as succinctly and detachedly as I could. When I finished, I looked at her. Her first words to me were, "Are you lying?" Shades of Ginny. Shades of the no-name cop when I was ten. Shades of everything that I, as a kid, feared if I told anybody.

Shades of hell.

My shoulders sagged. Can this be happening? Pen in hand, the woman I had so hoped could help me reached for her prescription pad and asked, "Are you taking any pills? Let's start with Valium and something for sleep, then we'll see what else you will need." I knew without a doubt that if I let myself have a drug-induced way out of my pain, I would never find my way back. I refused the scripts, left her office, and never returned.

No, in my twenty-eight-year-old world, there was, once again, no place to turn for help.

Tick, tock…tick, tock…. Day in, day out. Just me, the gold chair, and the clock.

It has gone on for almost three grueling months.

This morning is different, though. I feel the slightest glimmer of something inside of me that is not quite a light, but more like a little sliver of space. For the first time since this began, I have a sense that, if I really work at it, I might be able to move myself. Just the fact that I can contemplate an ability to do any-thing is extraordinary. It is a hairline fracture in the relentless armor of my doom. A crack in the paradigm of my pain.

This morning I was able to force myself to leave the phone on the hook for ten minutes. This afternoon I cajoled myself into opening the drapes for a full fifteen minutes. It is a huge accomplishment.

Slowly, oh so slowly, this dark night of my soul—the mother of all my de-pressions—is lifting. Within a month I am functioning at about seventy-five percent of my norm, relapsing into a mind-numbing state only for short periods of time during the day. I am on my way to a total recovery.

It took me a long time to understand that I'm only a victim if I give someone or something else my mind. For several years I held the thought that if people only knew what had happened to me, they would care. Then I realized it isn't that they wouldn't care, but whether they care or not, they're busy with their own lives.

The world outside of me was not going to be the answer.

Ultimately, I learned that the choice to identify myself as a victim and two bucks—not at Starbucks, of course—might buy me a cup of coffee. In other words, being a victim has no market value.

It also took me a long time to understand that I could be what I choose to be, that I am indeed that which has the capacity to look fear in the eye and dissolve it. No problem can be resolved from the point of view of the problem. The point of view of the problem is the point of view of the wound. That's a victim. That's a story. I had to learn to recog-nize when I was making victim statements and perceive the world from outside of the box of pain and suffering. To ask myself, "What's another way of looking at this?" I had to self-educate and spend every day, not only choosing, but re-choosing. Every day, all day, choosing again and again. What's a new point of view? What's my intention for this day? I can either focus on peace or anger (war), but I can't do both. They're antithetical. I can immerse in love or hate. But not both. I can even choose pain or joy as a state of mind I keep bringing myself back to.

But not both.

I have to pick one and stick with it. Writing is rewriting, and I was rewriting my life, my choice. Choosing and re-choosing once again. When students and clients ask me why I was able to do things that they have so much trouble with, I tell them there is no difference between us, except I was desperate enough to practice more. That's the key. Practice. Choosing your intended thought instead of the habit of pain and victimization and practice, practice, practice.

The practice paid off. It empowered me and enabled me to begin to discern a new "voice"—a new awareness—inside of me. The voice of truth and self-direction. That voice, that amazing self-awareness, is so powerful that it can move a mountain and open up a life.

And, finally, I had to learn not to resist any part of where I had been or where I was. To let the journey be what it is and what it was.

To get out of a hole, you have to be able to reach for something greater and stronger than that which got you into the hole. Something that *you* believe to be greater and stronger than your wound. It can be self-esteem. It can be a blue butterfly, a mighty oak, a night sky. It can be a magic wand or a great religion. It can be whatever you choose, whatever lights your fire. My choice—that which made the most sense to me and stirred my passion—was that I'm one with the core of everything that life is, one with a Divine Forever. It was the point of view stronger and greater than the trauma I had clung to. To this day, it is the beacon that I follow. It works for me. It makes sense out of my life and of our chaotic world. It brings to me an awareness of belonging, a passion for peace, and the experience of a promise fulfilled.

Oh, by the way, Wendy Ann Brae, my suicidal client of so many years ago, put her gun down the night we talked through the wee hours of the morning, and she lived. Last I heard, she had four sons and two dogs.

21

ROSALYNN'S STORY

During my years of self-exploration I have had moments—sometimes really long moments—of great density, ignorance, and pride. The type that precedes a fall. On occasion, I still have them. But I've also been blessed with extraordinary moments when I have pierced the simple veil that appears to separate us from all the other dimensions, realities, and possibilities that coexist in this time and space. Times when I have felt that I could reach out to the horizon and touch the setting sun with my bare hands. I have had dreams that are so lucid I know I have been transported to an alternate reality. I have been blessed with moments of such great clarity that, in this body, I have merged with the part of me that is forever and then a few seconds later popped right back into the illusion of separation.

What if it's all God? What if, in the end, it's all just one great adventure?

"Please let me be wise." This silent prayer pressed into my mind late one night as I spoke on the phone with Rosalynn, a dear and long-time client.

"I'm losing it, Sandy," her voice quivered. She was calling from New York. Rosalynn, a very attractive, successful, full-of-life woman in her early fifties who could easily have passed for being a decade younger, had been a single mom for a good part of her adult life and my client for several years. Just eight months earlier my husband and I had officiated at the fulfillment of her dream—her wedding to her beloved partner.

Now, through no fault of her own, Rosalynn was in serious trouble. She was calling from Sloan Kettering Cancer Center a few scant hours before going under the knife for a complicated three-surgeon, ten-hour plus process to remove a very nasty, multi-tentacled cancer. They were going to open her up first from the front and then from the back, and then, "if she was doing okay," they would also snip out a few extra tumors around her lungs. This part of her courageous journey was coming to a head. Had it been me, they'd have had to put me in restraints and knock me out a week ahead of time. And then I still don't know if I would have had the guts to go through with what Rosalynn was facing.

I held the phone close against my ear, endeavoring to be aware of every nuance in Rosalynn's shaky voice.

"You're not going to die," I said into the phone. And I knew she would not die on the operating table the next day. Her life force was too connected to her body. I could feel it. "You're almost there, Sweetie. You didn't spend all those years hiking up all those mountains and sweating through all those spinning classes for nothing. You've trained your body to be resilient and your mind to be strong. You'll get through this night, and the surgery will be over in the blink of an eye."

"Could that blink start now?"

We laughed.

"You'll be with me, right?" asked Rosalynn.

"Tomorrow, while your body is lying asleep on the operating table, our spirits are going to soar together. I've already put in the order at that great coffeehouse in the sky—a latté for you, a brevé for me. We'll hold hands and chat it up among the stars, and, before we're even done with our coffees, you'll be back in your body.

"Every hand that touches your physical body tomorrow will be God meeting God. Every energy that surrounds you will be the energy of love and healing. Your whole being will be cradled in the palm of all that you are, all that is forever."

"I'll see you tomorrow," she said.

"I love you," I replied and reluctantly hung up, wishing I could physically hand her the powerful cord that I so viscerally felt was connecting her to her body.

I rose early the morning after my conversation with Rosalynn. Holding my intention of oneness, I began to meditate on her around 4:30, the time I knew she was checking into the hospital. At 6:00 A.M. I felt with her in the pre-op process. At 7:00 I knew that she was close to falling asleep and then learned—not via the ethers, but through her daughter—that shortly before going under anesthesia Rosalynn had decided against the coffee and instead opted for a carrot/apple juice thing. Our celestial Starbucks had to be morphed into a fabulous juice bar. So be it.

Starbucks, juice bars—it matters not. The details don't change the principle of the great "café" in the sky—that alternate reality "room" from which we perceive and plan for our soul's journey in this lifetime. This is where Rosalynn and I are meeting, spirit to spirit, soul to soul, while in my body I write these words and she in her body undergoes surgery.

I mentally ordered Rosalynn's juice combo and instructed my taste buds to relinquish their hold on the brevé for which they had already watered up. Coffee can wait for another day. After all, Rosalynn is the one having the surgery. It's only fair that she gets to choose.

I hit the "fast backward" button in my mind and remembered when I had first embraced the concept that I, not chance, circumstance, or other people had created a game plan for this life, story-boarded to perfection on another but concurrent plane. Just as I had felt my spiritual team—my "angels"—rallying around me, I felt Rosalynn's team keeping watch over her.

Whoa! I jumped at the piercing sound of my office phone ringing, jerking me out of my reverie. It was Rosalynn's daughter. Four hours into the surgery and it's going well. They think they'll be able to get to the cancer-damaged area around her lungs today, too. One stop shopping and then healing—that's the prayer for today.

I told Rosalynn last night that this was a marathon for which she was trained and was ready. That's my truth about her life. That's my truth about my life.

You know, this carrot/apple juice stuff doesn't taste half bad.

22

A BRIEF REVIEW

Let's have a brief review.

No true change is going to happen without choice. And no true choice is going to be implemented without will, heavily laced with more than a little courage. One of the gutsier choices has to be the willingness to give up one's story. A story is: My mother plotted to kill me, and so I am screwed forever. Too dramatic for our daily lives? A story is: The clerk in the store was rude to me but not the skinny blonde next to me, so it must be because I'm fat or drab or that the wart on my nose hasn't fallen off yet. Or maybe all three. A story is: My partner just yelled at me and now I have to be a victim because, after all, people always yell at me…. Nobody *ever, ever* treats me right. I never get *any* breaks. It always *rains*.

Basically a story is anything we get attached to—and play and replay—in order to validate that we don't have any worth. It's the addictive drama—the head noise of inner war. Even if everyone is doing what we think they're doing, we still have to detach from the story—the idea that our value is on the line. It's not. So, our persistent three-act plays, with all their good guy/bad guy dialogues, have got to go. I know that doesn't seem fair. And it's probably not. But it's required anyway.

These are the choices necessary to achieve change:

Take a moment, breathe deep, and remember this is only a list. Do with it what you will.

1. Adopt a living-philosophy/point of view/passionate belief system that is greater than your history and/or pain. Mine is: God and I are one.

2. Make the choice that you are not a victim. I don't care who did what, when, or where. There's a good chance I've got a story that can top yours, and, trust me, I am not a victim. You, too, are not a victim. Not unless you give someone else your mind, and you are *always* in charge of that. No excuses. Adopting the consciousness and lifestyle of a victim is a choice. It is not a result over which you have no power.

3. Let go of your attachment to drama. It's theatre, and not very good theatre, played out on a stage in a cluttered attic. Change your mind. Constant drama is a way of trying to be special; it's a way of trying to validate that you are alive and important. It's based on the perspective that you don't feel special and don't really feel alive or connected in your core. If your life is a freakin' soap opera, then chances are that you are compensating for a shit load of unworthiness. You're really not unworthy, but you're building a life based on your fear that you are.

4. Do unto others…. Life is in many ways a mirror. The ways in which you repeatedly, both overtly and covertly, criticize/judge others are *always* a reflection on yourself. If criticizing and judging others is a reflection back to yourself (and it is), that's not a kind way to treat someone with whom you're supposed to be falling in love—namely you.

Well, I think that's enough listing for right now.
Is this list doable?
Absolutely.
If you haven't already done it, can it change your life?
Indubitably. In the doing is the undoing.
Will it take devotion, commitment, effort, and work?
Yes, but we are all worth our own effort.
Is the list simple to understand?
Relatively.
Easy?
Not on your life.
But don't forget, it's very, very doable.

If we have the courage to reach for change, life will find a new way to dance with us, leading, gliding, tripping, and bumping us into new pathways. New lights. New potentials that let us unfold a life greater than the stages of our past. Greater than the stories that keep contracting us into the limitations and darkness of our fears.

23

THE VIRGIN AND THE WHORE

It took me quite a while to quit trying to make my journey look like I was the main character in Swan Lake, prancing around in a pristine little tutu trying to look like I've got it all together. The part of me that doesn't have it all together is as important as the part that does.

Not that there's anything wrong with prancing, but one has to spread a little mud on the canvas of self-growth in order to get the job done. If it's too pristine, if it's too neat and tidy, it's probably also "tutu" fake.

"No prancing," the voice inside of me said. "It doesn't work that way. Real growth doesn't happen that way."

LuEllyn was a beautiful woman in her early thirties with long blonde hair and a penchant for chain-smoking. Not a natural blonde but a gorgeous one nonetheless. Toni was an athletic, attractive brunette with shoulder-length, naturally-curly hair in her late twenties. Kimberly, a bottle-dyed-to-perfection redhead, was a cosmetically-enhanced, perfectly-tanned fifty-two-year-old who lived on the beach in tony Malibu. Caroline was a smart, successful actress from New York who just happened to be a lesbian. Christianna was a sweet, kind school principal from the Midwest in her late thirties who adored her three dogs and vegetable gardening. Single, but still looking.

Not a Jerry Springer candidate in the bunch.

And there have been so many more.

What do they all have in common? They either are or were clients of mine who were sexually abused over long periods of time by the men in their family. And they each held the same guilty, hard for them to comprehend, secret. At some point during their long years of being held hostage to abuse, they actually became sexually stimulated. They were guilty for that, and they were guilty for not having found a way to stop the abuse sooner. They held within them the terrible fear that at the age of eight or ten or twelve their bodies had betrayed them and they had become whores. Sullied ladies of the night.

In actuality, of course, they were children of the night. Children who had separated from themselves sufficiently to survive their environment. Children who had to divide themselves, surrender to their attackers, and, through absolutely no fault of their own, become a part of their hostile world. They were young ones who had been stripped of their innocence and emotionally enslaved by their predators. They were not seductresses although they were often afraid they had been.

They were little girls who, in order to survive emotionally and/or physically, had to let their bodies—and therefore themselves—engage in the arena they had been forced into against their wills. So they developed compartments in their heads. When they were in one compartment, they behaved a specific way; when they were in another compartment, they behaved according to its mandate.

They had been manipulated, seduced, used, and assaulted—stripped of their free will—and their survival mechanisms embarrassed and confused the hell out of them.

They were not whores. They were simply unintegrated little survivors, split into two or more parts. And they felt guilty about it. Only one was dealing with recovered memory. The others had never forgotten. But they all had the same piercing question. How could they have been stimulated?

Well, they were definitely talking to the right woman.

What these women didn't realize when they first came to see me was that if some part of them had not, consciously or unconsciously, chosen to accommodate the betraying and painful situations in which they found themselves, they very well might not have survived either physically or emotionally.

There's a lot of writing, presuming, and thinking in our world about unity—finding that oneness within. And it's my goal, too. But unity includes duality, and duality serves a purpose, especially for anyone who has survived—or is in the process of needing to survive—war, trauma, or abuse. The ability of the brain to compartmentalize or organize itself into separate units is a primal but essential resource for most people in the heat of battle. If one survives, the shelling (literal or metaphorical) stops, the immediate peril ends, and the process of endeavoring to stitch oneself back together begins.

As a survival mechanism, my duality gave me breathing room. I morphed into a "night child" after I slipped into repression when I was ten. Although I never wanted to go with my father to the places he took me in the dark of the night or the light of the day—not that it would have made me wrong if I had been willing to go—once he started his assaults I found a switch in my brain. Instead of enduring the unendurable, I became a part of it. I could click that switch and flip pretty quickly from the good girl at school to the bad girl at night, from the virgin to the whore.

Of course, no child goes into the world of the whore because they have nothing better to do that day. It is strictly an autonomic survival mechanism that shows up in what at first glance would appear to be a Machiavellian way. In truth, it is a gift, backwards to be sure, but a gift nonetheless, which allows individuals, especially children, to endure, like those precious children of the night, those treasured women who sat before me and who had instinctively chosen to survive.

How, therefore, in spite of my past, was I able to have healthy sexual relationships with boyfriends, lovers, and husbands? It was the "untainted" part of me at play. I was one of the fortunate ones. I was so deeply rooted in the world of school—the world that for the most part I could control—that it anchored me to the promise inherent with the good girl, the promise of a happy ending.

Not everyone who experiences these levels of trauma is so fortunate. Some simply shut down and are never able to touch and be touched in a healthy, loving way. Others addictively replicate the aching loneliness, isolation, and low self-esteem with which sexual abuse left them by becoming promiscuous, thus deeply etching themselves to the script of the bad girl or boy. Still others become so broken and weak in their will that they align themselves with their weakness and perpetuate the cycle of abuse by becoming perpetrators themselves.

By being so heavily invested in my school world, I caught a break. Add to that the era in which I was born, and it was a veritable boon. Few drugs, little sex. Good girls of my day didn't engage in either, and I was definitely a good girl.

I was in my thirties—an attractive, seemingly secure mother of three—who, in my daily inner life, was secretly still fearful that I was barely one lit match away from total implosion. I realized that my only way out of the pain I felt was to start stitching the two parts of me together. My mission, assuming I chose to accept it, was to learn how to integrate that more dominant good girl part of me with equal caring and acceptance for the wounded, muddy swamp part of me.

I wasn't sure it would work and was even less sure how to begin.

"Yes, Virginia," I thought to myself as I saw the snow-capped mountains on Denver's western horizon for the first time, "there is a God. It's birth place surely is in Colorado."

I was thirty-three, and Leo and I had packed our kids—there were three of them now—and our meager belongings and finally gotten the hell out of Phoenix, to be, in the words of John Denver, homeward bound to a place I'd never been before: Colorado. I drank in those first scenic views like a woman dying of thirst who suddenly comes across an oasis. I had a feeling deep in my chest that I had come home at last.

I had recovered fully from the excruciating depression of my late twenties, and I was doing so much better, especially since the birth of my youngest son who was almost eighteen months old already. But the ache inside of me was still there, deep, penetrating, and on a bad day downright brutal.

I looked up at the mountain tops again. As a child, I remembered lying on my stomach on my bed, reading an article from the Sunday paper about Denver. Something about the way the author wrote the tale of the mystique and beauty of this part of the West always stayed with me. Maybe Colorado would hold magic for me, too. Maybe here I would find my peace and my dream.

I loved the Denver of the mid-70s and quickly set about rebuilding my life, raising my kids, and searching for ideas and answers. Searching for relief.

I was productive and capable, but in the privacy of my own being, my heart still throbbed with pain, and the pit in my gut would not let me go. I continued in my quest for personal healing and freedom from within—but to no avail. I couldn't find any modality or philosophy that took away my grief and pain.

In the end it wasn't conscious wisdom but a default position that goaded me forward. I would read something or get an idea, sometimes a harebrained one, and practice it on myself. I fell on my face a lot, especially at first, but then I'd pick myself up—a bit tattered and torn—but wiser for the experience.

There was the time I crouched in the cramped space between my bed and dresser and saw myself dangling over two worlds, that of the sane and insane. For some reason it didn't scare me but fascinated me. The fine line between the two worlds was so thin, with each side perceiving itself as totally rational. And I realized what a precarious division and narrow choice opting for sanity could be. I observed the world that we call insane, but I did not identify with it and was never tempted to do so. I knew that I could choose—and in fact had already chosen—and that made all the difference.

There was the day I felt I couldn't go on anymore. I lay on my bed, losing my battle with hopelessness. And then I felt myself leaving my body. I was up in the corner of the room at the ceiling ready, even wanting to leave. Then I had a vision of another place where endless lines of people were sandwiched in with each other robotically moving through colorless lives. I knew that if I left, I'd be doing the same thing, punching in and out of another pointless life. With a thud I plopped back into my body.

I knew that if I wanted tomorrow to be different than yesterday, I was going to have to change the way I responded to things today. Through hours and hours—and then more hours—of contemplation, it became clear to me that I was still so deeply rooted in the pain of my past that there was no way I could go forward. As a last resort, I decided to explore the depths of my past one more time. But I swore to myself that after this I would never open myself to the pain of it again. And I meant it. One more time but never again. We're talking eternity here.

My commitment was made; my intention was set. I began the journey of trying to deal with the mountain of pain still buried inside of me. It was not an easy ride.

I had help along the way. Lovely, gentle, and good to the core, Bea was a major gift. Well into her sixties and grandmotherly in appearance, Bea stood by me. She pulled me through a night when in desperation I called her, crying that I knew who I was but I didn't know where I was, and it terrified me. Bea told me to get quiet and she would do her treatment for me—a prayerful, empowering affirmation. It worked. A few hours later I had traveled through that dark, treacherous canal of my mind and emerged into the light.

Lucille was significant. She was an assertive, powerful woman who had a strong bead on transpersonal communication—namely, how to talk with wounded parts of oneself without becoming joined at the hip with the pain of a past experience. Her ideas made sense to me and inspired me into action.

I began to visualize myself standing on the side of a pit, throwing a rope down to the child I had been, who in my mind was caught in a time warp of sorts, and pulling her up. Frequently, I fell in it with her, and then we were both caught in a world of hurt, a no-way-out pity pot.

I started to understand that it wasn't what happened that still plagued me. The problem was, of course, the conclusion that I had drawn about myself—the fear that I had committed the unforgivable sin—the fear that I deserved all the terrible things I had experienced.

I began to think of myself as a spiritual godmother to the child I had been. I thought that perhaps no matter how severe my wounds were, if I had simply had a spiritual fairy godmother who had come to the head of my bed every night, things might have been quite different. I envisioned her stroking my hair—and every hurting child's hair—for a moment. Then I saw her opening the big book of life she held in her lap and saying, "Honey, let me explain to you what happened today...."

Well, if that had happened, I think we would have all been all right. So, now it was my job to role-play the godmother with the part of me that was still psychologically stuck in the past.

It was my job to re-parent myself.

I thought about the child I had been and knew that she absolutely needed the imprint of three emotional realities:

- To know that she is loved.
- To know that it is not her fault.
- To know that it is over.

It's basically what every child needs.

Through practice and then more practice I continued to teach myself how to communicate with my inner child, and I continued to learn that it doesn't work to identify with the pain of the past. That left no one holding the fort of potential and healing. Becoming one with the wound wasn't the answer. It only left me drained and wrung out. So I practiced staying in the point of view of a woman reaching for the child—the point of view of a woman who wanted to help the child and saw the child as whole. As long as there were still two of us, I figured I might as well let it work for me.

I found that when I could align a picture of the child I had been with a feeling of compassion and caring for her, my brain responded differently than when I saw the child as a victim. I realized that the little girl I'd been wasn't a victim and wasn't just a survivor. She was a hero. She was the part of me that held the flame of what I might become and kept it alive.

By the time I was thirty-six, I was doing okay. I had learned to love and even integrate the four-year-old, the eight-year-old, and the ten-year-old I had once been. But I had not gone beyond that. There was a part of me that was aching and still missing. I didn't know where to find it. I didn't know how to find it.

Unknown to me at the time, intention carries the day no matter how long it takes to manifest itself. My intention was so firmly rooted in my desire to put the Humpty-Dumpty I had become back together again. It drove me with the same fierce force that drove me to succeed at the talent festival when I was eight, to jump into the deep end of the pool later that same summer in order to teach myself how to swim, and to threaten Ginny with certain death if she didn't rein in Tom.

It worked, too. I did find my way home to myself. There's no "she and me" inside anymore. It's all just "me." The age of eight metamorphosed into ten as it was always meant to do. Twelve became fourteen. Fifty-eight blessedly turned into sixty.

It's not that I did anything momentous or special to get there. I just kept trying to put one foot in front of the other. Quantum leaps are like that. They're achieved by everyday practice, practice, practice, and then, as if in the twinkling of an eye, a new awareness dawns. And it is as though what has just been revealed has always been known.

I am thirty-six when I discover her. The forgotten child within me. She is just an adolescent buried deep in the recesses of my mind's eye. Pubescent and old all at the same time. She is emaciated, skeletal, barely alive. Every fiber of my being wants to turn away from her.

But I can't.

She is helpless, hopeless. Desperate. Her hair is stringy, her complexion sallow. I look at her, and I want to be disgusted, repelled. I want to do what I have always done before. Reject her, hate her. Reject her, hate her.

But I can't.

Her terror pierces my brain, reflecting back to me the sub-surface mortal terror that is always present within me. Alone in my bed, I throw the sheets off and toss and turn—one small step away from total hysteria. Emotions from every angle collide violently in my head, cascading me into the chasm of certain death. My skin is on fire, every inch of it screaming with a burning itch.

For sure I am going to die.

I can't cry; I can't breathe. I can't get rid of the picture of her face. It looms grotesquely, hauntingly before me. I would sacrifice a decade of my life for a way out. Anything to get away from her.

But I can't.

In the wee hours of the morning I finally turn toward her. The wounded adolescent child within my own being. I look into her hollow eyes and see what I have been afraid to see. The anguish, pain, and suffering of the guilty. She judges herself cruelly, as have I. This child who has just given birth to her father's baby. I feel the raw brutality of her pain. Of her regret. Her relentless hopelessness.

It wrenches my heart. But I know better than to become her pain. That would leave both of us in a deep pit with no way out. One of us has to stay on solid ground and lift the other one out.

It is my turn to be the adult; it is my turn to be the parent of that which has never been parented. This part of me that I have spent so many years rejecting is now reachable.

I know this. I say this. I pray this. But, God forgive me, I still want to push her away. She is reachable, but I can't reach out to her. I cannot! She is an anathema to me. Soiled goods. She is rejection held together with a thin layer of rotting skin.

I lay there, distraught in my bed, torn in so many directions.

And then I catch the look in her eyes again. It is the look I had seen in the eyes of my cousin Billy the Bully so many years ago. It is the look in my eyes when no one else is there to see.

Reject her, hate her. Reject her, hate her.

I try to turn away again, but her eyes….

They stay with me. They will not let me go. They are the echo of me.

"If you want to reject her," I say to myself, "you do that. But when you do, you look her square in the eyes and see what your cruelty does to her."

I cannot. I can't look her in the eye and be one of her brutes, her Tom or her Ginny. I cannot look her in the eye and be one of her enslavers.

My heart softens, and then I feel as though it is breaking. In actuality, though, my heart is simply cracking wide open. For the first time I want this self-rejected part of me the way a mother craves a lost child. For the first time I can feel, not just think, my caring for her—my longing for her.

I am overcome with compassion for the war-torn child she has actually been.

This inside part of me is a ravaged child whom I have finally found after searching for so many years. I feel that I have crept through every nook and cranny of my world looking for the part of me I have been missing, and here she was all along, deep, deep inside of me. What I needed had never been somewhere else.

I began to speak softly to her. "I am so sorry for all the years you have suffered. And I am so sorry for all the years you have been alone. I swear to you, it was not your fault. I've tried all my life to find what was missing, what kept me empty. I didn't know that it was you I was searching for. I'm so sorry that I didn't know how to find you.

"I promise you, now that I've found you, I will never abandon you again."

My arm slowly reaches out to embrace her. In reality it is only a pillow I am holding; in my mind's eye it is the emotionally emaciated child. I whisper into my pillow child.

"I love you."

I hold her tightly. The healing sobs of love lost and then re-found pour through my body, releasing my spirit from its isolation and drenching my pillow.

24

FINDING FORGIVENESS

If life is about fairness, we're all screwed. Taken at face value, circumstances in life are frequently not fair. Harsh and despicable as the inequities of life situations might be, the unfairness and inhumanity that we can encounter in life is not what takes us down. The way we identify ourselves—as in good or bad, right or wrong, guilty or innocent, the way we hold ourselves hostage to inaccurate and unfair conclusions that we drew about ourselves as kids—these are the things that haunt us all of our lives and mire us down in self-doubt and self-hate. That is, unless we take conscious steps to change our minds about our innate worth and who we really are. When we change the way we see or identify ourselves from within, we will automatically change the way we see ourselves in our world.

There is a caveat here, however, about opting for a new point of view. True choice has no judgment. It only has options.

You know the bumper sticker that reads "Horn Broken, Watch for Finger." I swear, Maxine McMahon could have been sporting that one on her car the afternoon I sat across from her in a session as she simmered with barely contained anger. What I knew and she did not yet accept was that she was using anger as a tool to cover a stabbing pain.

I had been in private practice for almost eighteen years when Maxine first came to see me. She was a still stunning forty-five-year-old woman, who twenty-three years earlier had worn her state's crown into the Miss

America contest. That alone had created a certain set of hang-ups for her, but beauty contests were not the problem we'd been trying to tackle for several weeks. This was a cut to the core of the issue day, and Maxine wasn't pleased.

"Remember," I said to Maxine, "the only way out of this emotional quagmire you're in is to look your fear of guilt straight in the eye and find another way of seeing yourself. How many more years are you going to spend hating and brutalizing yourself for that one horrible, horrible day? In the secret recesses of your mind you've identified yourself as an unforgivable monster. Even if you had been found guilty, no judge in the country would have given you a life sentence without the possibility of parole."

"I don't want to talk about it," she snapped.

"How is not talking about it working so far?" I asked.

"Fuck you!"

I laughed, and she actually cracked a smile with me.

The subject Maxine so dearly wanted to avoid had occurred on an otherwise average, balmy Saturday evening in the summer of her sixteenth year. She was already a debutante-in-training and a beauty pageant junkie, but that hadn't kept her from wanting to be a normal teen. So, she partied with her friends, then decided to take the new convertible her daddy had given her as a sweet-sixteen/keep-the-crowns-coming present out for a spin. Three short minutes later Maxine blew past a stop sign and plowed into a rust-stained, faded green sedan driven by another sixteen-year-old whose name she later learned was Joey. Maxine came out of the accident with nothing more than a bruised knee and a two-inch gash on her right forearm; Joey was dead at the scene.

This was the ghastly secret that had been chasing Maxine for close to thirty years. As a child, the accident was never discussed with her by her family. Instead, her wealthy and influential father sent Maxine, her mom, and sister to the Hamptons for several weeks to "forget about it."

Maxine returned home in time for the hearing. Her daddy said everything would be fine. And it was, but not before she sat in the courtroom with a grief-ravaged face and heard the tearful, desolate voice of Joey's mom. The crying voice on the stand, the dead child at the scene of the accident, her own deep remorse—those were the sights, sounds, and feelings that still haunted Maxine.

"Honey, you can stay pissed at me or anybody else as long as you want," I said lightly, "but in the end you're going to have to forgive yourself."

"How the hell am I supposed to that? The girl's dead!" Maxine's voice was caught in some gray area between a wail and a cry.

"The first thing you need to do is understand what forgiveness is. It isn't looking at yourself or anyone else and saying, 'You're a miserable excuse for a human being, and I forgive you anyway.'"

Maxine listened with narrowed, wary eyes. But at least she was listening.

"The blame game just doesn't work here, Maxine. Forgiveness is about letting go in peace. It's turning toward the part of you that probably did screw up and having compassion for your mistakes and for whomever it is you were when you made them. It's not about abdicating responsibility. But at some point in time, you have to let the self-judgment—the part of you that has been operating as a relentless tyrant—you have to let it go. You have to pull those self-inflicted spikes out of the palms of your hands and jump down off the cross to which you've been nailing yourself all these years.

"And ultimately, Max, forgiveness is about understanding that from a spiritual point of view, there's nothing to forgive."

I was thirty-seven and trying not to curse the fact that my body was so damned attuned to the annual calendar. It was nearing the end of the first week of February, and in spite of my intentions not to have this happen again, I felt the familiar heaviness building in my chest. I tried to relax and breathe deeply. But the heaviness intensified, and I struggled for breath.

I barely managed to get dinner on the table. I told my family I would be spending the next few days in bed. Three to be exact. Then I trudged up to my bedroom to begin my annual and undesired isolating sabbatical into depression.

It was the anniversary of the birth and death of my first-born. A birth that was not my fault. A death that was.

I put on an old sweatshirt and climbed into bed.

I stared into the darkness and thought about the baby I had delivered as a thirteen-year-old. If I had only left him in his little crib at the maternity home—or whatever the hell it was....

He might still be alive today.

How can I forgive myself for the unforgivable?

My gloom cut more deeply into my chest. I was so disappointed. I thought for sure that I had learned enough to circumvent this debilitating depression this year.

Obviously not.

I pressed my mind to reach for the affirmations with which I had been working.

"I am one with all that is," I said to myself.

Yeah, right.

"I am not a victim of my world and circumstances; I am not my experience. Experiences are not who I am; they're only places I have visited."

Okay, I can accept that. Maybe.

"I am one with Infinite Love; I am the treasured child of a forever God. I am forgiven, for in the eyes of God there was never anything to forgive."

Impossible.

How can I accept forgiveness from anyone or anything when I can't forgive myself? How can I have compassion for myself when my confusion ended in someone's death? What gives *me* the right to be the one who lived? In what world is there "in the end nothing to forgive?"

I wallowed in my story of pain, suffering, and personal badness, riding the surfboard of my transgressions all the way to hell. Regret thou art my stigma. I re-hammered the nails into my palms, attaching myself to the cross of my guilt.

But this time, unlike previous years, instead of just succumbing to the abyss, I struggled to lift myself up.

"I am forgiven...."

Then I'd descend back into hell and have to start over again.

"I am not a victim...."

I went in and out of my morass, affirmations, and sleep during that restless night. The following morning I was propped up against the headboard of my bed. I was in the affirmation stage of my recycling.

"I am forgiven...."

The words seemed less hollow, a little easier to feel. My thoughts turned toward the baby, and my belief system about life got activated. If within the tiniest child there exists a full-grown soul that knows exactly what it's doing, then that has to be true for this child, too. What if he's part of a greater game plan that we both agreed to in another time and on another plane? A place we both existed before we entered these bodies.

A convenient thought? Sure, possibly.

But what if it's true? There's got to be something someplace that can make sense of this madness in my life—make sense of the ticker-tape parade of mental lashings whipping harshly, constantly in my mind.

A Divine Order that creates stars, galaxies, and universes; a Divine Order that creates gravity and keeps things from just constantly banging into each other. It's got to be a part of me, too. Right? I'm not so damn special that, of all the creatures on all the planets in all the solar systems, I'm the one who fell out of the belly of God. Get a grip, girl. I, with all of my chaos, am still a part of that orderly Divineness. I *am* one with the Life Force that created a dandelion seed so filled with the urgency of life that it can ferret out a crack in the sidewalk and force its head through into a bloom with new seeds.

What does the dandelion know about itself that I need to remember about me…?

What if the picture of the lifeless form of this innocent child that has blistered my mind for so many years is actually more than a lousy draw of the cards in the game of life? Is it a part of a greater plan that has a Divinity and a driving Life Force at its core? What if this tiny little baby, with a full-grown soul inside of him, is not a victim at all? Was his life an extraordinary gift that helped me unfold a sanity and a wisdom I might not otherwise have found? Not that anything could change the physical tragedy that my son or I experienced. Not that anything could or should justify his death. But what if I was able to view the experience from a different point of view and incorporate that new perspective into an emotional acceptance? How might that change my current reality?

Is there a way to own both the dark, tragic reality of the past and the potential light of it? Was his short life the pain that drove me to find the ultimate gift of my life?

I already accept that the perception of reality is subjective. It's not carved in stone. It's based on whatever point of view I'm holding as truth about what I'm seeing. I've seen it happen a thousand times—put ten people in a room to witness the same event, and there will be a hodge-podge of interpretations, a hodgepodge of realities all based on individual perspectives of the exact same thing.

Can I let go of my old, old need to be the bad guy? The gray, haggard habit of suffering—what does it serve? Can I release the need to keep falling into the all-too-familiar crevasse of decades-old pain? Can I adopt another possibility—another way of viewing the places I have been, the feelings I have felt? Is it possible for me to quit manipulating myself into being either the good guy or the bad guy?

It exhausts me. *I* exhaust me!

Can I possibly break the cycle of feeling punished and re-punished? Can I let go of my need to self-reprobate time and time again?

Can I?

Will I?

In my mind's eye I was once again the lonely child holding her infant boy. And then I had another vision. I saw my son as a strapping young man, light-hearted and happy, playing a game of touch football with his pals. It was so real I could feel his laughter.

"You, turkey," I said to him. "All these years I've been crying all these tears, and you've been playing football on some heavenly football field!"

His eyes twinkled into mine.

For the first time in my life the pain of love fell away. For the first time in my life I actually felt the joy of love flood through me.

I never again cried for my son. Nor did I ever again see him as a victim. Is he really on some heavenly football field equivalent? Who knows? But I saw his light, and to this day I can feel it. On the morning that I first saw it, I felt forgiven by him, forgiven by me, and in the process I discovered the unified world beyond time and space in which there is ultimately nothing to forgive.

Along the way I became aware of a profound truth. It takes two for war and one for peace. That's true whether the war one is waging is internal or external.

To this day I marvel at the many gifts I received from the most painful time of my life and the long, long sojourn of healing guilt. It's the legacy from the brief time I spent with the soul I knew as my first child. It's a legacy born of endings and beginnings.

As long as I was at war with myself, there was no forgiveness and there was no peace. As long as I was my own enemy—as that which deserved to be hated—my world would find places to reflect war.

This is my truth whether I am reflecting on a personal journey or witnessing a global one.

25

THE SURPRISE

Like kneading, pummeling, and stretching dough so that it can rise in the oven and become a delectable treat, being self-raised is not too dissimilar from baking bread. You have to be willing to mold and shape yourself and, occasionally, when genuinely required, throw in a well-placed punch or two (because self-honesty so often feels brutal), then cover the bowl and let it sit for a while. Let that which you are trying to teach yourself rise to the surface because one of the things about being self-raised is that you also have to be self-taught.

There's no one around to tell you how to mold the dough. Whom can you trust to tell you which colors go together, how to style your hair, how to clean your body? Who teaches you how to face your fears, how to develop integrity, how to be sensitive to others? Who guides you so you stop stretching the truth, stop using manipulation to protect yourself, talk straight and be straight? Who teaches you how to forgive yourself and how to dare to trust again?

There's no one around but you. There was no one around but me.

The vision of my dead son in his light, healed and whole, did wonders for me. It released me from the time warp within which I had been holding myself; it released me from my old identity of pain and suffering. What a growth spurt! Spiraling out into self-assurance and possibilities I had not dreamt of since I was a little girl, I felt a new, amazing excitement, vitality, and potential for my life. And I wasn't tormented by that annual, compelling, self-imposed seclusion!

Awesome. But it also made the place where my life was utterly lacking and little more than a pretense starkly obvious.

Leo and me.

Alone, I flew out to Monterey, California, in the midst of the following winter after my healing experience with the memory of my first born. I needed uninterrupted time to think. It was ocean-front cold, leaving the thick marine layer of fog without a fighting chance of burning off. It suited me perfectly. I could walk less than fifty yards from the hotel before it completely disappeared from view.

For three days I sat on the empty beach of my fog-protected haven and spoke to no one, except for two nightly calls: my kids and room service. From daybreak until dark, I sat at the water's edge, contemplating the hovering clusters of seagulls and wondering how long Richard Bach had observed them before he sat down to write *Jonathan Livingston Seagull*. I looked out at the roiling sea and talked softly to it for hours on end like it was my best friend, like it was my only friend.

Finally, it was Tuesday afternoon an hour before I had to catch a plane home. I looked at my ocean and said, "When I'm here, I know exactly what I need to do. But where will you be when I'm back in Denver?"

I closed my eyes as tears slipped out from under them. The ocean whispered in my head almost immediately: "Take me with you."

And that's what I did. I brought the feel, the sound, the smell, the *pulse* of the ocean back with me to the land-locked city I called home. It gave me the courage to deal with the fact that my marriage had been over for years and to let it go.

But there were obvious complications. I had three children who were now sixteen, fourteen, and six, and I had a husband who worked sporadically and made very little money. He spent a good part of most days hanging around the house. But one of us had to leave, one of us had to work, and one of us could not be at home every day. I chose to be the one who went out into the world.

By removing myself from under the same roof as my children, I created a situation that became the second greatest thing I would ever have to forgive myself for. It would literally take two decades before I would be able to forgive myself.

Oh, I didn't go far. Just a few blocks away. Initially, I returned to the family home every morning and got the children's breakfasts, made their lunches, and saw them off to school. A few months later, after our house sold, Leo and the kids moved into the same apartment complex in which I was living. But it would be two years before the kids were actually residing under my roof again, and by that time my daughter would already be out on her own.

I had a lot of reasons for being the one to leave. The money thing with Leo was no small matter. I needed to go to work and be available for long hours. It was essential that I get to the place where I could support myself and the children. I was also afraid that if I took our children, especially our youngest son, from Leo, my husband would break. We were both still very attached to our "baby." I saw Leo as a weak man, and I feared the consequences of his potential collapse. I was afraid he wouldn't survive it, and I would once again be responsible for another person's death. It was, after all, I who wanted the split, not him. I knew that from his point of view I was shutting down his life.

So that was my rationale for leaving the kids with Leo and for moving out. It was without a doubt one of the best things I ever did for myself and one of the most painful things I ever did to my kids.

I soon realized how desperate I had been for time and space. I had gone from an extremely abusive home to marriage and young motherhood without a pause. Those two years of room to grow and heal, room for long uninterrupted thoughts, room to establish myself in my working world and never have to be afraid about money again, room to date, explore, and find myself as a woman—well, self-serving as they were, they were my break-out years. It was the time that put me on course for the rest of my life. Paradoxically, it was also the time I began to teach myself how to be a better mother and how to start down the long road of self-forgiveness for having been such a flawed parent.

My kids, amazing as they are, managed to weather the storm, not only of the marital split and all its attendant fallout, but also of having spent their early years with such a wounded mom. And yet the upside, they have said, is they got to watch, up close and personal, a woman— that would be me—put herself on a learning curve and evolve. They watched me change dramatically, and, God bless them, they reaped the benefits of that change. So, in spite of my early blindness, lack of wisdom, and oozing ignorance, all three of my children have grown into truly good, kind, and delightful individuals. They are loving, resilient souls so delicately housed in the flesh by a mere layer of skin. Today I have a close, mutually caring and supportive relationship with each of them that overflows with love, laughter, and ease. The very thought of them triggers joy in my heart and love in my soul. And visa versa I'm told.

An unexpected, lasting freedom arrived in my thirty-ninth year, when I experienced perhaps the greatest miracle of my life—the greatest shock. A mind-blowing surprise. Six years after I vowed to look at the pain of my past one more time and then never, ever again, that deep, wrenching pain, which had always shadowed me at some level, vanished.

In the words of Jack Paar, "I kid you not."

All those daily mental exercises I had put myself through for all those years—I am not a victim; I am one with a forever God; I am one with a peace that surpasses all duality—finally paid off in a way I had never thought possible.

Through the constant discipline of changing my point of view, I truly was not a victim anymore. And it didn't hurt anymore. I no longer even cared about it. Amazing. What I had carried as a wounded badge to justify my existence and identity was suddenly not even important.

I accepted that it took two for war and one for peace, and if I wanted peace, it was an inside job that I could choose. The pain and torturous thoughts of my past were blessedly and unexpectedly over. I had begun this journey just hoping to find a way to live with the pain. Now it wasn't even there.

It was a Hallelujah chorus moment!

It is just a few months after my realization that it doesn't hurt inside of me anymore! It's still a wonder. I am settling into a meditation with no expectation of what is going to happen. I go deeper and am surprised to feel and "see" with my inside senses that my parents are sitting around me in a circle. My father is on my left, my mother on my right. I haven't seen either one of them in sixteen years, not since the day I estranged myself from them at the age of twenty-three. Now, in this meditation, I pause to look at each of them. Then, in my mind's

awareness, I reach out with each hand to touch my mother and father, which would have been a total anathema just a short time ago. Prior to this, I would rather have put my bare hands in the rotting guts of road kill than touch either one of them. But here I am, hand in hand with them in this deep inner space talking with them.

"Whatever each of you still needs to finish with each other," I say, "that is between the two of you. But between thee and me now, there is peace."

I was forty-two when my father died. He had taken a life of real potential and devolved it into…what can I say? There's no denying that as a personality he was one distorted, twisted, incredibly selfish character. A sick fuck. But he also served me. He provided me with a friction that drove me and pierced me and created in me a determination never to give up. The pearl in my oyster.

Shortly after his seventieth birthday, he caused a head-on collision, and just like that he was gone. A candle that had burned so dimly and then, in the blink of a second, blew itself out.

I was living near the East Coast when I got the news of his death. I left the house and, alone, spent a few hours in the depth of our heavily wooded property. I didn't feel any pain or longing or regret. I no longer needed anything from him. He had become an impersonal figure in my life. But he had been such an intense part of my younger years, I desired to find some way I could healthily relate to him. I finally thought of him as a little boy. I wondered what he must have been like as a six-year-old, what his dreams and hopes were. And in that moment I found compassion for the child he had once been. I was sure no little boy ever dreams of becoming what my father became. I looked through the eyes of the boy and the shattered dreams of the man he had grown into, and I was able to say a gentle goodbye. I stood under the trees in those lush, dense woods and, without resentment, grief, or regret, wished his soul Godspeed.

My mother died several years later—a somewhat unpleasant, ignominious death, which was the result of years of alcohol and prescription drug abuse. I acknowledged her passing with a ritual of sorts. A Christmas tree that had dried out ten days before Christmas (and promptly been replaced) had been taken out of the house and temporarily discarded in a fallow garden area about a hundred yards from the side of our home. I gathered up pictures of my mother and my father, along with some spices and herbs, freshly gathered holly and poinsettia leaves, and placed them on top of the fallen tree. I lit dried twigs at the bottom of the tree and stood by solemnly as the flames engulfed my makeshift pyre and the pictures of my parents. My prayer to them was simple. May you find wisdom; may your souls find peace. And may you know that between us there is no debt.

Karma, that cause-and-effect perspective of some cosmic bank account tallying one's rights and wrongs throughout the ages, is done when we're done with it. At least that's my philosophy.

I was done with it.

One of the perspectives that kept motivating me—more like goading me—through the years to come to peace with my parents was the idea that I never wanted to have to deal with them on any plane of reality again. In order to do that, I was going to have to forgive them. I was going to have to let it truly go in peace, have compassion for all three of us, and understand that on the spiritual plane there was never anything to forgive anyway.

The obvious was there, too. I was going to have to let go of my aversion to encountering them again. So, I thought of the "café in the sky," and I just let go of the whole damn thing.

"Go with God," I remember saying aloud at the pyre I was burning in homage to the souls of my parents. "I release you in every way, and I am released. Between us the deal is done."

26

ONE DOWN

Latisha was eleven, and I was nicely into my forty-somethings when we first met. She was a rough, tough inner-city kid from a large urban area in the East. Her social worker called me campaigning for the child to be included in a summer residential program I had founded for abused and traumatized kids. My talented and dedicated staff of professional and lay volunteers expanded to around forty during the summers when we would try to squeeze in three residential sessions each involving about fifty kids (ages eight to sixteen) per group who came from very harsh backgrounds. Word of mouth spread quickly about our program. Case workers reached out to us for two primary reasons. First, they liked us and our program, and, second, we picked up the tab for everything.

"I can't prove it, but I know she's being abused. I think it's her step-father," Latisha's social worker said to me. "It's her last chance. If she doesn't get some kind of help now, I think the window will be shut and there will be no way to reach her."

"I'm sorry, but I'm out of money for this program," I replied, "and we're full."

"*Please* reconsider. My hands are tied as to what I can do for her, and from what I've heard about your program, I really think you can help her. I think you're her last chance."

I thought for a moment. If her social worker was this willing to go to bat for Latisha, then maybe I could, too. I pulled out my credit card and paved the way for Latisha's entrance into our group. She arrived late on a Saturday night, disheveled, mean, defensive. A wounded animal fighting

171

for her life. Her little suitcase held one pair of panties, one toothbrush, and a six-pack of coke.

I almost sent her home that first night. She was a troublemaker, a ring leader, an all-around difficult kid. Mouthy and obnoxious. But I didn't send her back. Instead, I kept looking for what her social worker had seen in her. I found it in those rare moments when she would stop and pet a cat or a dog with a nurturing hand and the even rarer moments when she would sweetly touch a younger girl who was scared and crying. With gentle coaxing and a huge amount of staff support, the real Latisha slowly began to poke through her protective veneer.

It was only a few days before Latisha would have to return home. She had made great progress. Her rough edges were smoothing out; her smile beamed with little coaxing. But there was still nothing forthcoming about abuse. She knew her time with us was drawing to a close. She came to me and told me she was scared. I hugged her and said, "Honey, we're all here for you. We'll help you in any way we can. It'll help if you can take a chance on trusting us."

That afternoon in a group meeting Latisha broke down. She began to cry and rock her young body. Within minutes a nasty story about her step-father's repeated sexual abuse emerged.

Her social worker was notified. Latisha was allowed to finish her stay with us and then sent from our program into a group home, which in her reality was almost as traumatic as returning home. Plopped into an environment in which she felt so unsafe, she quickly re-laminated herself into the aggressive pain-in-the-ass kid she had been when I first met her.

My staff and I pressed to be allowed to stay in contact with her while she was in temporary residence at the group home. It wasn't easy. Her new caregivers leveraged her need to talk with me into a disciplinary process. If she behaved, she could have contact with me. If she didn't, she would not be allowed to place or receive calls from me that day. Much as it enraged me, I was very aware that I had absolutely no authority in her jurisdiction, so I was fortunate to be allowed any contact at all.

I made a nuisance of myself with the very nice and tolerant detective in charge of her case and was relentless with the social services of her state. Eight weeks later I received a stern, repudiating letter on official state letterhead from the head of the state social services telling me I was unprofessional. And she was right. I'm sure I broke a thousand protocols. She wrote that I was interfering with their process, that Latisha's case was groundless, and that she was recommending the case be closed. Latisha would subsequently be returned to her family home, the one where her step-father, uncensored, still resided. The final court date was in two weeks. Without some kind of a miracle I had no doubt that the recommendation would be followed.

After an intense search, we finally found a sympathetic Assistant D.A. Her name was Katey. She would give me one chance and one chance only.

I arrived in Latisha's home town the following afternoon. Katey had Latisha brought to her office, and the three of us met. At first Latisha was still recalcitrant. I explained to her that if she wanted to tell her story, this would be her very last chance. Katey was patient, giving Latisha the space and time that she needed. Finally, Latisha asked Katey and me to turn and face the wall so no one would look at her while she talked. We complied, and this painfully wounded and very frightened but brave young girl began the tale of what her life at home had been. With our faces still to the wall, Katey asked Latisha a few very specific questions that confirmed for Katey everything Latisha had told us was true. We then sat in a circle, having received permission from Latisha to face her again, and Katey put in a call to the detective and told him she had enough for an arrest. He assured her he would pick up the step-father immediately.

One more hurdle: Could Latisha hold steadfast through the trauma of facing her step-father in court? Would the pressure of that send her back into her defensive cave?

We pressed the system some more, and Latisha became the first child in her state to be allowed to testify against her abuser on closed-circuit television. I was with her that morning with my arm around her, assuring her that she would do fine and that she was safe. She would not get hurt here.

Latisha did great. Her step-father, the predator who had spent years eroding her self-esteem and stealing chunks of her soul, was found guilty and, without being released from jail, would later be sent to prison.

I passed him in the back hall of the courthouse that day—a squat, bulky, powerfully-built individual. I looked him square in the eye and thought with satisfaction and gratitude for Latisha's freedom, "One down."

27

THE ULTIMATE SILENCER

It happened in Paris, but God knows it could have happened anywhere.

It does happen everywhere.

Shame.

The fingers of its dark flame relentlessly scorch the fringes of self-esteem, ultimately breaking through, searing into the core of one's being and blanketing the soul with a black shroud.

Shame: to be or feel dishonored, disgraced, humiliated, mortified. Shame shatters the hearts of the innocent, leaving jagged-edged pieces in painful disrepair.

Shame.

One would think that shame would be the least of Annie Miller's problems. After all, she had just survived a very difficult cancer surgery, chemo so intense that it felled her more than once, and just for good measure, several shots of radiation. She was the proverbial American in Paris, having married a native Frenchman. Her European doctors were aggressive in their protocol with her, and rightly so. The malignant disease she was fighting had killed her mother in her early fifties and shown up in her sister in her late thirties. Annie was forty-six.

Cute, funny, petite, and powerful, Annie had been a force to deal with in her industry of film and editing. Her size was never a deterrent to her bark, and in spite of a sweetness in her heart, when crossed…. Well, you get the picture. She was like a beautiful little Bichon who thinks it's the size of a Great Dane, and it's not long before all the other dogs in the room think so, too. Submissive she was not.

Annie had been a client prior to her move abroad. I had helped her work through the illness and death of her mother, as well as the abuse and abandonment of her father. So, when she called, I assumed she wanted to talk about the fears and challenges of fighting a potentially fatal illness. Initially, that is what we discussed. Then one morning she called from Paris. She began with casual conversation then started to weep.

"What is it, Annie?" I asked gently.

"It's something I have never told anyone, and I thought I could handle it by myself. But I'm starting to have nightmares about it." She paused, almost sputtering, trying to get her tears in check so she could speak.

"I'm so ashamed," she cried. "So ashamed."

"Honey, whatever happened, we'll figure it out. It's okay to talk about it."

So she told me how, after going through what turned out to be a horrendous surgery, she had been pretty much drugged for three days, during which time she wasn't able to do anything for herself. A male attendant had been with her the first day. She didn't like him. Even in her medically-induced fog, something didn't feel right. On the second day, slightly more aware, she managed to ask for a female. The lady showed, but the guy stayed, and when the woman helped Annie out of her bed, the male aide followed Annie closely with his eyes. Her gown fell open. Too foggy and weak to do anything about it, she watched Mr. Ogle Eyes's focus never leave her body. Annie half-walked, half-was-carried into the lavatory by the staunch woman and placed on the toilet. Her gown remained fully open, breasts revealed, genitals exposed.

"The jerk was having a field day," cried Annie. "His eyes bored into me slowly as though he were repeatedly, methodically exploring me. The motherfucker—he had such a sickening smirk on his face. I can't believe it. I can't believe I didn't stop the fucking bastard!"

Annie faltered. Her voice broke as her anger collapsed back into shame. "I felt so violated," she sobbed, "and now all I feel is dirty and wrong. How could I have not reported him immediately? How could I have not closed my robe? How could I have not told the female aide to get him out of there?"

My heart melted for Annie. The fact that this intelligent, courageous, feisty woman was post-surgical, on morphine, and fighting for her life did not soften the emotional reaction of being defiled.

Shame is like that. It's not logical. It's organic. It's a disenfranchise-ment that floods through one's body, organs, and veins like a virulent virus shutting down the healthy cells of self-esteem and self-love, until it feels as though one's very soul is withering.

If you ever wonder why children and others who have been abused don't talk or tell, it is in a large part because shame is the great—the ultimate—silencer.

As a child, I could never have told anybody. I could never have let anyone know what my father was doing, how he kept looking for my pubic hairs to begin to grow, my breasts to start to swell, and how hu-miliated I was when they did. I was certain that I could not have withstood the embarrassment, the disgrace, of letting anyone know how often I had been stripped of my clothes and my dignity. I could not have borne to hear their sniggers and see their disdain. I would rather have died.

But here's the good news: I didn't die, and Annie got it that it wasn't her fault. By the end of our session she had reconnected with her power and made the decision to report this pervert to the head of the hospital. And she did. With the might and bark of a pissed-off Great Dane.

Shame is the scar tissue of sexual abuse. Long after the wound has healed, the scar remains—like an enlarged, puffed-out red worm, snak-ing across one's gut.

Young Latisha knew shame. Lots of it. And none of it was her fault. She had gotten through the abuse of her step-father and the corrosive ugliness of her mother's attitude toward her. She had survived the group home—and they had survived her. The trial, the closed-circuit testimony—all of these things were behind her now. But still, the twelve-year-old was able to keep her history relatively encapsulated. Her name was not pub-lic anywhere. Nor should it have been. It gave her a form of security; it kept a veil between her and her shame.

Latisha was once again in short-term residence with us in our children's program, doing great, actually making—dare I say—peaceful relationships with the other girls. It was quite a victory. I was maybe fifty yards from the girl's dorm on a muggy, sun-drenched morning when I heard a shattering shriek come from within. Blood chilling. Heart pounding, I raced toward the door just as Latisha, still screaming, charged out, closely followed by a staff counselor. Latisha ran into my arms clutching a piece of paper.

"No! No!" was all I could get out of her for several minutes. Finally, she slowed down enough to let me see what was in her hand.

"Fuck," I thought to myself as I read the brief, well-intended note with the newspaper clip attached.

The counselor and I walked with Latisha to a nearby bench and sandwiched her between us. My arm was around the distraught little girl while the counselor held her other hand. We took turns telling Latisha how sorry we were. We held her and rocked her and promised her that she was still safe, that we were outrageously proud of her, and that she could still have a good life.

What had rocked Latisha's world to its very core? Shame. A well-meaning social worker had written a sweet note to Latisha telling her how brave she had been, and then, unfortunately, included the clip from the paper documenting Latisha's closed-circuit testimony and her step-father's subsequent conviction. Latisha's name, of course, was not used, but her step-father's was, and that exposed Latisha to her friends and classmates. It took several days of concentrated effort by a devoted, loving staff to stitch back together Latisha's torn trust and to begin to undo shame's toxic tattoo.

Latisha got through that rough time, as many of us do. But as a society we must be mindful and informed. We must never, ever make the mistake of thinking that sexual assault of any kind or any level—verbal, emotional, voyeuristic, physical—is about sex. It's about power and the horrible theft of innocence that results in shame. It's about people with bigger bodies, more cunning minds, more deadly weapons, stealing the power and dignity of the innocent, because the predators have none of their own. It's about a theft that is never funny and never, ever acceptable whether it happens to the young, the old, or anybody in between.

28

M&MS—MISTAKES AND MIRACLES

Let's do math. Don't worry. No algebra, no calculus, no physics—although technically that's more science than math anyway. And we won't even go near geometry, sacred or otherwise. Nope. We'll keep it very simple. Just plain old basic math. An equation to be exact.

Here we go now. Judgment = guilt = punishment. See? I told you it would be simple. The tricky part is that every component in the equation equals lack. We only judge ourselves because we have decided we have fallen short. We are lacking value, intelligence, beauty, acceptance, right action, discernment, selflessness, courage, awareness, love…. The equation comes full circle rapidly because as soon as we judge ourselves we, of course, find ourselves guilty and must be punished. Sooner rather than later.

Lack.

It is the four-letter word of judgment and doubt.

Love is the four-letter word of creation.

Which will it be today?

Spring 1986

"I saw an amazing property today," my husband said to me over the phone. "A four-hundred-plus-acre cattle-and-horse farm. It has four houses, a large pool, and a small lake. Everything you would want for the children's program and your year-round staff. It also comes with a hefty price tag, but you might like to see it anyway."

"How soon?" I asked. We had opened our children's program for abused and traumatized kids the previous summer and used a vacant, somewhat seedy campsite for our cosmetically inauspicious debut. The kids did great, but my staff nearly bolted. Between the sagging mattresses, clusters of poisonous black widow and brown recluse spiders—well, I don't know if there were actually "clusters," but they did seem to be lurking in every frickin' nook and cranny of the entire place—and the constant plumbing issues, we were definitely hoping for better digs for this year. Four hundred and twenty acres? I practically drooled.

Two days later, my husband, staff, and I tromped through the amazingly pastoral farm mesmerized with the possibilities it held for what we wanted to accomplish. A center that could and would be life-changing. Six weeks later a benefactor loaned us the down payment to get into this $1.1 million property. But it was a loan. This benefactor was not independently wealthy. Naively, stupidly, I signed all the papers that would tie me and several other very good people to our seriously under-funded venture. Had I paused, had I gone within to seek direction, I might have chosen a different route. But I didn't. At least not in a timely fashion.

The morning the property title transfer was being recorded in the county, I lay on my bed in as fetal a position as my adult body could curl itself into. "What have I done?" I thought, "What have I done!" It was as though the impact of my choices had finally shocked me into silence, and I could hear the echoes of my conscience—my intuition—telling me what a boner I had just committed. In that brief moment of clarity I knew this was not going to turn out well. In half an hour, denial—you know, that ancient river in Egypt—was firmly re-ensconced in my head. My fleeting moment of clarity and silence took a back seat.

During the five years we struggled to hang on financially and keep the program intact, we did a lot of good things. Lives were changed. Think Latisha—as well as many others. The children were well taken care of and offered new experiences and opportunities for healing, positive touch, and love. My staff expanded to include a wonderful array of talented, generous volunteers. They were incredible. In many ways all of our lives were changed.

But not all of the changes were easy or, in the moment, positive. Too often, my core staff did as I said because I was the leader; too often, I over-controlled administratively and, worse yet, interfered in their personal lives. Because I was the leader. My ego was such that I thought I knew more than I did. In my arrogance, it never occurred to me that I didn't.

The inevitable happened. We ran out of money way before we ran out of good intentions, and just like that our personal lives were thrown into turmoil. The people in the family trust who had co-signed with us on the farm were thrown into fear. And understandably so. Money can be a scary deal-breaker. Relationships that had been forged in caring, excitement, and trust grew ragged and wary. Some stood with me; some did not. Our weary, tattered little band dispersed, and, for the most part, we all went in our own directions in an effort to reestablish ourselves in our lives. I left having donated $350,000 of our personal income to the program over the five years—which was everything we had. The money wasn't the issue; many of us had put whatever we could into it. But the feeling of betrayal by long-time friends, as two opposing camps surfaced, was tough. Not surprisingly, the others left with their own financial and emotional struggles, several of them feeling equally betrayed by me. Nothing since that horrible depression of my late twenties had shaken or saddened me as much as this did. And yet I didn't know how to fix it because I hadn't yet owned up to how I had contributed to it—how, indeed, I had helped create it.

With my family, I moved back to the West Coast and re-engaged my practice. But daily, in the wee, small hours of the night I sat up alone in the living room, shaken to my core, riddled with a wrenching ache in my gut and deep sorrow in my heart. A book would lie open on my lap as I searched for any passage of inspiration or forgiveness that I might hold onto for dear life.

Nightly, I spent hours trying to balance my anxiety and concerns with contemplation and prayer. I prayed for answers, for guidance, for relief from the pain. How was I going to pay back all that money? How many lives might be seriously compromised? I prayed for those I had hurt, and I prayed for me. "Please, please don't let me stop here," I pleaded. "Please, don't let me get lost in my story of right and wrong. Show me another point of view. Help me understand what I need to see.

"Please."

My hidden agenda of needing to be special because I still didn't feel quite enough was painfully and ferociously playing out in my adult world. Lack triggered the equation. Judgment = guilty = punishment. I judged myself, and through my own ignorance positioned myself to peer through the looking glass and feel judged by others. It wasn't about whether or not they were judging me. In truth, we can only judge ourselves. I saw the reflection of others and through my own lack and residual insecurity named it me. Later, I would come to understand that the domino effect of guilt and punishment was self-imposed until grace ultimately reached out its merciful hand and lifted me up. True love is like that. It forgives without question.

The weeks turned into months. Corporately, we filed a Chapter 11. My nightly sojourns in the living room pressed on. For a year prior to leaving the farm, we had tried to sell the property. The best offer—actually the only offer—we had was from some smarmy little fellow pretending to be our white knight by ponying up $650,000 to take the property off our hands. I said no. So, here we were in court. The bankruptcy judge finally got sick of the whole thing and declared that the property would be sold by sealed bid to the qualified buyer who offered the highest price.

By the time the day had rolled around for the bids to be opened, I was totally distraught. I canceled my appointments and never even considered getting dressed. Around noon I went to the kitchen and heated up a can of vegetable soup. I brought a book to the table with me, hoping I could get past the page I had probably reread twenty times that morning. Not because it held anything of great interest but because I just couldn't focus.

I set my new hardcover next to my soup on the white lace tablecloth, which covered our circular dinette. Knowing my predilection to splatter, I made a concentrated effort not to screw up my book with drippings from my lunch. I finished the soup as carefully as possible, then checked my novel. Nary a drop.

I closed the book and, as I lifted the bowl to take it to the sink, I saw two large splotches of red on the tablecloth. Sighing, I made a half-assed effort to dab at the spots. I looked at the cloth. The spots, undiminished, looked back at me. Too busted to stick with it, I did the Scarlet O'Hara bit. I'll deal with it tomorrow. I left the kitchen, went into my bedroom, and didn't return until the next morning.

The rest of that difficult day passed, the night evaporated into dawn, and amazingly the sun rose again. I had actually slept during the night and went to the kitchen feeling better than I had in weeks. I sat at the table, talking with my husband. Absently, I looked down at the lace cloth. "Oh, John," I said, "you cleaned the spots. Thank you so much!"

"Babe, I don't know what you are talking about."

"No, really," I said, "I spilled soup on it yesterday, and now the spots are not there. I know they were there. I even tried to wipe them off."

The phone rang, interrupting our conversation. It was our lawyer calling from back east. The bids had been opened by the court. Our property, for which we had paid $1.1 million and which had been on the market for well over a year without any viable offers, had sold in a sealed bid auction in bankruptcy court for One Million Five Hundred Thousand Dollars! Every single debt from the center was paid back in full. With interest.

To this day, while I am deeply grateful for the financial windfall, what I truly marvel at is the spots that miraculously disappeared. If I hadn't dabbed at them, I might have thought I made it up. But I didn't. They were real, and the following morning, they were no more.

Life is a mystery rife with grace, forgiveness, and the unexplainable.

Oh, by the way, the purchaser of the farm was a manufacturing company that apparently had decided at the last minute that our property was something it just had to have for its expansion.

Was it the law of attraction? Frequency matching frequency? A miracle? The grace of God? Yes, yes, yes, and yes!

29

MIRROR, MIRROR…

My luscious fourteen-year-old granddaughter got the lead in her school play. I was ecstatic for her. Of course, she comes from a long line of theatrical talent. I, after all, was the Magic Mirror in my school play when I was in the seventh grade.

How ironic, the roles that we pick or that pick us, that shape us. Is it art mimicking life? Or are life, breath, and a point of view born out of our early creative sojourns?

It all depends on how we use it and how we choose it.

During the dress rehearsal for my Magic Mirror role in the school production of Snow White, I twirled out on the stage in my white make-shift, floor-length, tinfoil-studded dress, only to be bombarded by the giggles of the kindergarten kids sitting cross-legged on the gym floor in front of the stage. Apparently, they could see up my costume. How far up I don't know.

But I was impervious to those giggling devils. I had one of the six or seven speaking parts in the play, and I was not about to be undone. I ignored the snickering little plebes and looked the wart-infested wicked witch in the face.

"Your mirror tells you…."

Little did I know how significant the concept of a mirror would become in my life—to say nothing of the importance, yet to be played out in my youth, of confronting the wicked witch. Would I ever get my mother off my back? Would I ever find the Snow White—the purity and innocence—in me?

Life, as it is practiced, is mostly a mirror, because life, as it is frequently lived, is mostly about attachment. To be attached is to need a mirror—an outer reflection that validates something about oneself which can truly only be validated, empowered, and treasured from within. If I use you as a mirror, it's because I want you to be responsible for and make the decision for what I'm thinking or judging about myself.

I'm pretty sure I can do better.

If I am that which has to be right, then I will go to war with the part of me that fears it could be wrong. Right needs wrong to mirror it. Up needs down to mirror or contrast it.

It doesn't mean I'm not ever right or ever wrong. The key here is: How attached am I to needing to be right or wrong? How attached am I to needing a mirror in order to define and validate myself? How many times do I need others to reflect to me what I need to own and reflect in myself?

The reality of consciousness works this way: If I am emotionally attached to being right or being validated by someone or something outside of me or if I am attached to a specific point of view or to a state of war within myself, I will project that point of view into my external world, where, like a boomerang, it will reflect itself back to me and return to bite me in the ass.

That's not to say it doesn't feel good to be heard or isn't lovely to receive accolades. Bouquets are not the problem. It's the attachment to these reflections that is the problem.

There's a Buddhist teaching that, broadly paraphrased, says, "A wise man is swayed by neither praise nor blame." It's a key to freedom.

I learned that one the hard way with my daughter. We had a few rough years together in her teens. Did I say a few? I think it might have been longer than that. At the time it seemed to me it was lasting forever. And for her? I think she felt it was nothing short of eternity. Although she had never been physically or sexually abused, she had been raised by a very wounded mom. So, for a while there, she felt isolated, unheard, and unloved. Me? Initially, I just didn't get it. I wanted her to behave and to watch her mouth. She wanted me to confirm that I loved her and to watch my mouth.

Here's how we played it out: I would go out and do a speech or a class. People would line up afterward and tell me, "You're so wonderful, or you're so this…or you're so that…." I knew they were simply saying thank you, so I said thank you back. I would leave the glow of this fine place and return home, where it often felt my daughter had been lying in wait, although all she really wanted was confirmation that I valued her. So, I'd take the bait, feel attacked, and verbally attack back.

Did I mention that there were times when I could be really, really, *really* wrong?

How could I go so quickly from this bright, serene teacher—which I really was—to this reactive, bitchy mom—which I, obviously, also really was?

I was so troubled by my reactions. Unfortunately for my daughter, it took a while for me to get my own attention. But, once I did, the first thing I did was take permission away from myself to continue this unacceptable behavior on my part. Permission is a uniquely powerful tool, and yet to this day I've never been fully able to put its potential for impact and change adequately into words. There's a frequency shift that happens when we take charge of our behavior, in spite of any emotional conflagration going on in our body. There's a new day that dawns within us when we say, "I don't care how I'm feeling; I take away permission to act this way and give myself permission—demand of myself—that I behave in this other way." It's called leading oneself, and only then do true authority and authorship of self return home to you or to me. It was only when I took away permission to behave inappropriately with my daughter, instead of excusing myself because of her inducements—I mean, really, who was the parent here—it was only then that I could see both sides of the mirror. It became clear to me that my daughter needed the affirmation of love from me that she deserved. She was the kid; I was the mom; she was entitled to that. My agenda became clear, too—embarrassingly clear. I had wanted and unconsciously demanded affirmation from her—affirmation that I was a good mother, a decent person, a good woman. I needed her to confirm for me that I, indeed, was not Ginny.

Like that was my daughter's responsibility…. *Hello!*

I had to become aware of my own inner conflicts and my ability to resolve them. Am I a good woman, or am I Ginny? Do I have the courage to be straight and above board, or am I a thief in the night? Am I Tom? At times, through my younger years, I have been little pieces of both. But I am no more.

So, I learned to be diligent about the polarizing war of opposites. If I become attached to duality, if I need a mirror to validate me, then these petty wars inside of me will show up in my life in some trivial or massive assault. Then, if I'm not careful, I will need to take you down in order to validate and justify me.

No matter how much I profess to love you, I will have made you into my enemy and invited you to make me yours. And whether it involves me or you or all of us, that's what the "war of the worlds"—big or small—is all about.

And, assuming I'm still attached, when I don't feel validated, I will feel re-victimized all over again. I have looked to my world to identify and justify myself, when in reality my world, whatever its size, is at one level only an aspect of me, and I'm an aspect of it. That doesn't mean I can't disagree or stand up for my values. I can and I do, but I have to make sure I stay centered in the process; otherwise, I will once again become polarized, and the point of view of good guys/bad guys will rule me—and that is a very draining way to live.

If I truly integrate myself into the awareness that, right or wrong, I am one with a goodness that has no opposite, would the attachment to needing a mirror or reflection to validate me completely dissolve?

Yes. Just as it did with my daughter.

I first met Justine when she was twenty-six. A wide-eyed, peaches-and-cream complexioned young woman with highlighted auburn hair tightly pulled back into a fashionable bun. I was doing a workshop in Chicago, and she stood out in the sea of faces before me. It was the mixture of innocence on her face and yearning in her large, chestnut-brown eyes that first caught my attention.

She had been homeless at fifteen and somehow had managed to lift herself up and out. But the "inner poverty" remained with her. At twenty-six, with her designer clothes and perfectly made-up face, her past was well masked. Except for those eyes. She married at twenty-seven, divorced a few years later, and at the age of thirty-two she married again. This time to a good-hearted man who was in many ways a better match for her. But her husband, Harrison, had grown up under the auspices of a dad who set the bar so high that his son, a would-be real estate magnate, had no hope of reaching it. Harrison compensated for the fact that no matter what he did his success only met with failure by learning how just to get by. So, brilliant as his mind was, professionally and sometimes personally, Harrison managed just to get by.

The years have flown by, and Justine is now thirty-nine. She has grown into a lovely, consciously evolving woman. Yet, like most of us, she's still working on the mirror thing, and as life would have it, her marriage to Harrison is, not too surprisingly, failing.

"I've had it," she said to me one afternoon. "I'm trying to do this differently than my past. Man, if this were my past, I'd be long gone. For my own sake, I'm wanting to stay this time and work it through instead of running away. But the truth is I don't want Harrison near me. Not even casually. It's not that I'm acting mean to him. I'm being nice to him, and I think I've even been sweet to him. But my stomach is in knots."

"Yeah, right," I replied. "You're channeling your 'nice' through an impenetrable Star Trek force field. It's not *nice*, honey. It's removed and controlled. And if you think he doesn't know that, you're screwing with your own head as well as his.

"Don't divorce him in your mind and stay in the house pretending like you're open to fixing the problem. If you stay, you have to mean it and actually be there for the process. It's not that Harrison didn't break trust with you time after time in withholding what he was doing financially and roping you into it. He did. But you've known for six of the last seven years that was his Achilles heel, and still you never took him to the mat. Why not? What in you kept you from doing that?"

"What do you mean?"

"Look down at the palm of your hand, Justine. In your mind's eye place a round mirror on your palm. Now bring your open hand up to your face. What do you see?"

"Me."

"That's right. Ain't nobody here but you, Babe. So, what about Harrison's lack of responsibility, inability to deal with things head on, or inability to let himself excel and reach for his greatest potential is a mirror to some of your issues with yourself? It isn't that you don't have the right to get mad at him. You need to get mad and work through the anger. But the person you're the angriest with is yourself. It's your job to own the mirror that Harrison reflects for you. It's up to you to care enough about the part of you that sometimes puts her head in the sand, that is just coming out of years of being too scared to reach for all that she can be. You need to quit judging you.

"I don't know if you and Harrison will survive this crisis, because I don't think you've decided yet. But I do know that you have to wedge yourself through this narrow tunnel of self-judgment so that Harrison's insecurities don't constantly reflect your fear of yours. When you do that, the view will change. Then you'll be empowered from within. Instead of being a victim of your circumstances, you'll find that you're in the center of the magnet—the place of your greatest strength, not your divisive polar opposites. It's then that you'll be able to discern whether you and Harrison have enough mutuality and are jointly able to bring enough to the table to make it worth the journey.

"It's all about integration, Sweetie. Whether you're at war with the world or just your little corner of it, you will experience pain and suffering—not just of the body but of the mind. When you are defenseless, when you no longer hold others responsible for your circumstances—even if they are—when you, without blame, see yourself as a co-creator of the condition, when you love enough to quit judging others because you have stopped judging you, that's when you no longer search for love.

"That's when you *are* love."

30

THE FACE OF GOD

Throughout my life, I've done all the usual clichés—lived and learned, loved and lost, gone through trials and tribulations, made some great choices and some really skanky ones. I studied and changed, married and divorced, and began a practice that quickly grew and thrived. And, along the way, I met the indomitable Mary Margaret. A friend of hers had heard me speak at Phipps Auditorium in Denver and gave her my number. I returned her phone call on a Monday night. She was funny, articulate, wonderfully New York, even though she was now living in Denver, and fearless. I liked her immediately.

She asked if we could meet in person. I had a meeting scheduled downtown for Tuesday morning, and I would be practically driving by her place on my way back to my office. I volunteered to drop in and see her first.

The following morning I walked up the steps leading to the front porch of Mary Margaret's Capitol Hill home, admiring the yellow-gold asters in bloom and the lemony-orange leaves on the towering maple that were just starting to turn. I knocked on the screen door, and she called out from someplace deep within the bungalow to "come in." I did so, following the smell of sautéing onions and garlic to the kitchen at the back of the house. There stood Mary Margaret—tall and slender—wearing black leggings, scruffy slippers, teal turtleneck topped by an oversize sweatshirt, and somehow managing to make the whole outfit look totally pulled together. Short, curly brown hair framed her attractive face with its full pre-collagen mouth and wide smile. Four years ago, she had been a hotshot advertising exec in her mid-thirties, living the good life in New York; then, she was diagnosed with an aggressive breast cancer. Any cancer at that time was damn near a death knell. She had done the chemo and all the traditional medical protocols, and after that, she attended the Simonton Institute—a well-known, well-established, alternative care cancer therapeutic treatment center in Texas. She listened to what they had to say, uprooting herself from the chaos of the big city and a high-pressure job, settling in Denver, and studying Zen. Now, that's courage.

She gave me a quick "hi, glad to meet you" hug and turned back to her stove. The assortment of steaming pots and pans demanded her attention. A macrobiotic diet was part of her healing protocol. Her idea was to try to combine the best of western medicine with the best of alternative approaches.

A few minutes later, with everything on the stove under control, we sat across from each other at her kitchen table sipping tea.

"Cancer's back," she said matter-of-factly.

I looked into her large, expressive brown eyes. I didn't see fear there but the brightness of life and curiosity. After trying to say I'm sorry in six different ways, I struggled with what else I could offer her. Birthing always seemed so much easier—so much less scary to me—than dying.

I canceled my first appointment at my office, and Mary Margaret and I talked for over two hours.

"So, what do you think it's all about?" she asked, referring to life.

"I think it's about oneness," I said. "I think it's about embracing the idea that we exist on more than one dimension—more than one plane of awareness. That we are a life force greater than our bodies. I think it's about bringing that perspective or possibility into our everyday world. But I'm not facing a catastrophic illness, Mary Margaret. I'm not dealing with the possibility that what's going on in my body could prematurely end my life.

"I don't know if this will help you, but I'll tell you what I'm working on with myself right now. I'm trying to make my everyday Spirituality become more vibrant and tangible within me. I'm working on *feeling*—not just thinking—the concept that I'm one with a goodness that has no opposite. I want to feel it as though it were flowing through my veins. Because at some level it is."

"Close your eyes, Mary Margaret, and picture yourself embracing someone you love dearly, like your little niece. Feel your heart opening and the love that you are pulsing through your whole body. Now, very gently, take your hand and with the same sweet awareness, lay it against your cheek."

Her open palm rose slowly to her face. Her eyes remained closed.

"Feel the softness and warmth of your hand against your cheek; feel the love that flows through your touch....

"Know that you've just touched the face of God."

And that was the beginning of what turned out to be a beautiful and close friendship. A few months after our first meeting, Mary Margaret came to me and asked if I would facilitate a group of women she was putting together. Their common denominator? They were all in relapse from an original diagnosis of cancer. She wanted to create a forum for hope in the face of death. I agreed to do an eight-week workshop, three hours every Wednesday afternoon.

It wasn't long before Mary Margaret got more bad news. The cancer had now spread to her liver. She cried, and so did I. She asked me if I had any ideas that might help her remember that she lives past death.

"Tonight, go out and look at the night sky," I said. "Hone in on the most brilliant star you can see. Keep looking at it until it blurs out of sight. And when it does, focus on the space between the stars. That deep, dark, all-encompassing midnight blue. It is the womb of all that is—the glue that holds everything together. Every star, every galaxy and planet, every sunrise and sunset, every being that ever was or ever will be exists within the space between the stars.

"Mary Margaret, my dear, we can forget that it exists or we can re-member it, but we can't actually fall out of the belly of God no matter how hard we try."

We talked frequently during the next several days.

"I think there's only a thin veil," she said to me one afternoon, refer-ring to what death might be like, "a change of perception. Maybe a speeding up of my frequency. Like a fan spinning on high speed instead of low. It's still a fan, but you can see more."

"You're right," I said jumping in enthusiastically. "When a fan is set on off or even on slow, you can't see through the blades, and we don't know what's on the other side. But when it's on high we can see right through those babies! Yet, even though separation isn't an ultimate real-ity, while we're in a body, it's a tough experience."

"Still," she reiterated, "all that really separates us is a thin veil." She laughed and added, "A teeny-tiny shift in frequency."

So we added fan metaphors to our growing list of explorations, which now included star watching, macrobiotics, country music, and spiritual glue.

It was after midnight on the night before I was scheduled to begin the cancer workshop Mary Margaret had put together. I took off the reading glasses, to which I had finally caved, rubbed my eyes, and stared blankly at the array of books and blank paper laid out before me. My mind had been churning over and over for at least four hours, searching for a clue. Nada. I simply could not get a handle on how to start tomorrow's session.

An hour and more blank paper later, I laid my head down on my desk in frustration and fatigue and said to my sense of the Spirit within me, "Listen, this is serious. Some of these women may not even be alive when this workshop is over. It's really important that I know where each of them is coming from."

Thankfully, I was exhausted enough to hear. The voice—the echoes of awareness—inside of my head spoke to me and said, "The only one you need to know where she's coming from is you."

I closed my books and went to bed.

"The only one you need to know where she's coming from is you." What a life-affirming teaching I was given that night. It burns as brightly in me today as when I first received it. I am the master of my life, the true captain of my ship, only when I am willing to know myself without defense or judgment. It's the peeling back process of self-honesty, self-awareness, and ultimately self-love.

The cancer workshop went off without a hitch. No one died during those eight weeks. But Millie passed away four weeks after that. Connie died within three months. And beautiful Mary Margaret? She had a colostomy, which bought her a little extra time. Through her courage and love of life, she taught me that death is the process of birthing a new adventure. It's a concept that I embrace fully, but applying it to my own mortality or the potential mortality of those I love so dearly is not always so easy.

Eighteen months after we met, Mary Margaret's body succumbed to the metastasized cancer. On her final day, as she was reaching across the "veil," her eyes lit up with the wonder of what she was seeing.

Her last words were, "Oh, it's so beautiful!" She had re-entered the realm in which she truly was the face of God.

31

SISTERS

Molly died on a Monday. Somehow, I thought she'd make it 'til Thursday. But no, it was a Monday.

Molly was my stepsister, the one who had told my mother about our father abusing her, with the end result being that my mother went berserk, ended up hating me—and, of course, it didn't help poor Molly much either.

Molly was not my sister's real name. But absolute privacy about her past was imperative to her, especially when it came to her second husband and her social status. She adhered to the old-school theory that so many have embraced of not ever airing family secrets, which in effect results in nothing more than a conspiracy of silence. Where my sister was concerned, I had my own slice of silence, too, but it didn't fall under the category of a conspiracy. I never told her how her disclosure to my mother about our father's abusive behavior toward her had caused Ginny to turn on me. That would have been cruel.

But Molly and I did speak at length among ourselves, especially as younger women, about the difficult and abusive pasts we shared, which eventually caused us—each in our own time and own way—to estrange ourselves from the infamous Ginny and Tom. Nevertheless, Molly was stuck in the box of "what will the neighbors think." From her point of view, the abuses that my parents inflicted on her brought shame not only to them, but also to her. I, on the other hand, was more aligned with the "fuck 'em" school of thought and had spoken openly about my life in my work and speeches for decades.

Molly lived in fear that I was going to ruin her life—that some day someone in my audience would cross her path, shed light on the sordid family from which she came, and blow her ugly little secrets right out of the closet. For Molly, "outing" and anathema were synonymous. Without ever realizing the price she paid for it, she preferred the skewed comfort of the dark over the potential of the light. It made her split not only in her inner world, but also in her persona. Molly, so beautiful in her youth, was funny and generous, lonely and difficult, courageous and wounded. She never understood that the way she criticized others was a reflection of the way she judged herself.

The bottom line on my adult relationship with my sister was that it, too, was dualistic. I cared for her; I understood what made her the way she was, and I had compassion for her. Yet there were times I felt illogically responsible for her and times when I went out of my way to avoid her. In a word—or four—she made me crazy.

Like many broken-winged individuals, Molly could, with less than a moment's notice, be teleported from her own good sense to a bit of the mentality of a Nazi. It was a point of pride for her that she could kill in one hundred words or less, and quite frankly, illness and debility had not robbed her of that dubious talent. I, on the other hand, had resolved all my anger issues.

Right. Good for me.

My sister had been diagnosed with a terminal carcinoma. She'd been given six months to live, two years before she actually died. So, when the end came, the expected was somewhat unexpected. It was Saturday, and things were starting to rapidly deteriorate for her, but still I didn't realize how imminent her passing was. I had made the last cross-country trip to be with her only a few weeks earlier. With the critical tyrant part of her at the helm, it was—to put it as politely as possible—tough. She had been needy (which was so understandable), stubborn (which was so normal), in emotional denial, fiercely angry and critical, frightened, and absolutely unwilling to take *any* of the tons of pain relief meds available to her. So she suffered and suffered and suffered.

After that last trip, I left her home with two difficult but clear awarenesses. One was that I was not responsible for her life choices, including her choice to suffer, and I couldn't prevent her from choosing that experience; and the second was that I would not put myself through that ordeal again until it was the end.

So there I was, on a Saturday afternoon, knowing that I had decided to go see her the following week, debating with myself whether to go on Wednesday or Thursday, and feeling the familiar pit in my stomach swell with each passing moment. The anxiety in my nervous system wasn't about not wanting to be with her when she died. It was about an ancient echo that was a part of the dance my body always did at the thought of another visit with Molly. And I knew that the intense flip-flops in my gut predated my trips to see Molly and went straight back to our mutual nemesis, Ginny.

Enough was enough. I could not take this issue back to the East Coast with me again. I put on a CD of Secret Garden and settled into my favorite chair and a deep meditation. I knew that Molly triggered me because, in her biting anger and excessive criticism, she reminded me of my mother. Molly wasn't anywhere nearly as extreme as Ginny had been, but she could give a caustic hell of a ride, and that was more than enough for my brain to cross-reference and make the association.

Part of the prime directive of the brain's function is that it's always cross-referencing, always associating one thing with another. It's part of the organ's brilliance, but when it's busily connecting the dots of today's experience with a chemical memory of yesterday's difficulties, the brain can also be a real pain.

To my emotionally associating brain the stinging energy of Molly equaled the acid burn of my mother. And that's why having to deal with Molly could trigger the anxiety I initially experienced as a two-year-old, when my mother had first turned her rage and contempt on me.

I contemplated this as I went deeper into my meditation. I revisited the total rejection of the toddler I had once been. I brought Molly into my mind's focus and saw how bitterly angry she still was with Ginny and how that anger had controlled and limited her life. But I remained at a loss as to why I couldn't shift my responses to my sister. I understood her anger; I had actually experienced that level of rage. After all, Ginny had tried to destroy every level of my being, too. So, why—all these years later—am I still reacting to Molly?

There's got to be a mirror here. Molly is reflecting something in me, or I wouldn't still be attached to a reaction to her reaction.

Okay. Fine.

And then I saw it. There was still a thread of anger in me connecting me to Ginny and my sister. An anger that tracked all the way back to the first time I felt myself flying through the air on the way to hit a wall. An anger at my mother screaming in my face, "I hate you! I hate you! I hate you!" An anger that any human being should ever have to recover from that level of rejection. An anger and a grief that I had been required to do so.

I stayed deep within myself and watched as the view changed, and I was able to see the landscape of my life from a different angle. I saw my experience with Ginny as the most difficult and certainly lengthiest initiation of my life. An initiation is simply a test, and in spite of Ginny's best shot, I passed the test. My mother, through her abject rejection of me, had given me the opportunity to reject myself. Through the years I have had bouts with self-doubt, depression, self-judgment. But I have bounced back, each time with greater hope and greater promise for what yet could be fulfilled in my life. I never gave up on me, and in the depth of my meditation I realized I had never truly rejected me. How amazing! I felt a burst of blocked energy release inside of me, lifting me up like a helium-filled balloon.

I had indeed passed the test.

I looked at the vision within me of Molly and I said to her, "What has bound us together on this plane is the anger we have shared towards Ginny. That shackle no longer binds us. It no longer exists. There is nothing that holds you here anymore." And then, very gently, I added, "Go home now, Molly. It's time for you to go home now."

I stayed in a meditation with her for a good part of the night, then placed a call to her in the morning. She was unable to speak, but I asked the caregiver, Ruth Ann, to give Molly a message. "Please tell her," I said, "that I love her and that my arms are wrapped around her." Ruth Ann put the phone down for a moment and then came back on the line. "I told her," Ruth Ann said, "and then your sister nodded and smiled."

Sunday I went into a quiet, meditative space again. This time, I thanked Molly for staying in her body long enough for me to get this final lesson—about Ginny and rejection—and its attendant freedom. I thanked her from the depth of my heart for all the times when, in spite of the differences we frequently faced, she had gone way out of her way to be generous with me. The ways in which she was being generous with me in her passing.

Then I said to my sister, as I spoke from within, spirit to spirit, "You're going to be able to do this, Molly, and you won't be alone. It'll be a little scary for you at first, like jumping out of a plane. You'll start to free fall, like a parachutist, but then you'll realize that you have wings. You'll start to fly, and from that point on you're out of your physical body, back into your spiritual body, and home free."

I thought of her in her better days, when she was able to find moments of laughter and joy. I stayed with her in my focus until the early morning hours when she came to me, but not in her physical body. She was a younger version of herself in a light, vibrant, amorphous body, and I knew that Molly was no longer here on earth. She had finally made it to the party that she had always sought but not quite found on this plane.

And so my sister died on a Monday and took with her the completion of an era for both of us.

Godspeed, Molly.

32

FOR THE LOVE OF JOHN

The reason relationships can be so darn hard is because they're based on the relationship we have with ourselves. They're really not designed to be the love/hate torture chambers we often make them into. But it is a truth—at least a truth of mine—we have to become, emotionally and mentally, what we want to manifest. True self-acceptance is the foundation of healthy intimacy. Love can only be given and received within the scope of one's own canvas.

Before I left Leo, I felt like I'd spent years with my shoulder into his mid-back, trying to scoot him forward. It became unbearably confining. Not that it was Leo's fault. We'd married when we were both quite wounded. Then, as my wounds healed, I changed, and we spent the last years of our marriage with little to nothing in common. So, it came as no surprise to me that, after leaving Leo, I was seriously turned off to committed relationships. I wasn't anti-romance or anti-love affairs; I was anti-getting stuck. I thought to myself that if someone were to come up to me and say, "Marry or I'll shoot," I'd look him in the eye and say, "Shoot."

After a while, I softened and began to open my mind and my heart to possibilities. Three extraordinary men helped shape the course of my life as a born-again woman. The first two were "bridge people." They helped me lay the planks that bridged the distance between where I had been and where I wanted to go.

The third man would be the ultimate prize.

Jeremy, middle-aged, craggy-faced attractive, and way above average in charisma, was the first guy. My parents would have been appalled. Except for his success (which would have intimidated them) and the color of his skin—an acceptable tone of white—he was everything they hated. Not only was he Jewish, but he was also a Pole. My God, a Polish Jew! The only thing that could have made him worse in their eyes was if he had also been Black, Brown, Red, or Yellow. Prejudice of any kind, but especially because of skin color, baffled me, but in Ginny and Tom, it downright amazed me. The idea that they could possibly think that anyone was lower on the totem pole of what's acceptable than they were…. Now, that's funny.

I met Jeremy after a symposium I attended in Los Angeles where he had been a featured speaker. Butterflies flapped their wings wildly in my gut when our paths crossed later that day. I was irrationally drawn to him. "Compelled" would be more accurate. Not that he wasn't nice enough. He was always great with a crowd or in public. In private he would prove to be a little trickier.

We chatted and flirted on that sunny afternoon. Then he flew back to his home in Northern California, and I flew back to mine in Denver. We began a correspondence, and with each pulse-raising contact my attraction to him grew.

On my first trip to see him—well, it really wasn't to see *him*. Well, it was, but it wasn't actually a date or anything. He knew I'd be in his area and he would be there, but we didn't have any firm plans. We'd talk. Maybe. Probably. Yeah, I was pretty sure we'd talk.

Talk we did; dine we did. And return to his home? Well, we did that, too.

The attraction was deeply compelling; the relationship, not so much. We were often competitive. When I was with him, I tended to lose myself and my own perspective, and then I'd turn around and fight for it. Nonetheless, I couldn't get him out of my system. He matched me in a composite of opposites. He could be challenging, difficult, remote; warm, charming, personal.

Yet, he helped me in simple but life-altering ways. When I felt needy, instead of ignoring me or putting me down, he stopped what he was doing and paid attention to me. When I started to promote other speakers, Jeremy fixed his penetrating brown eyes on my blue ones and said, "You're an extraordinary speaker. Why aren't you promoting yourself?"

I took his words to heart and realized that whether I was standing behind Leo, trying to push him into his success, losing myself to Jeremy, or trying to propel some speaker I'd never met onto center stage, it was basically all the same thing. I was willing to stand behind people and cheer them on from there, but I needed to get in front of my own line. And that's exactly what I did.

Several months later I was in New York for a speaking engagement of my own. The sponsoring organization rented Alice Tully Hall in Lincoln Center on Sundays, and I was the guest speaker that week. I was staying at the Essex House, across from Central Park. I arrived late on a Friday afternoon and stopped off at the hotel's packed lounge. Rush hour!

I snaked my way through the crowd, finally nabbing a just-vacated stool at the bar. "Absolut, rocks, double—no make that triple—olives," I said to the hatchet-faced, harried bartender. The blending of accents, languages, and voices merged into a dull roar. Contentedly, I drank in both the atmosphere and the vodka.

Two well-dressed men engrossed in conversation were leaning against the far end of the bar at the waitress station. I was too far away to hear them, but the younger of the two had a hell of a profile. He must have felt my gaze on him, because Mr. Profile turned to look at me. He raised his glass, nodded, and smiled. I smiled back and returned to my own reverie. A few minutes later I was vaguely aware of movement on my right. I looked up. The fabulous profile with the laughing eyes was seated next to me.

His name was Gustav, Americanized to Gus, and he would become the second significant man in my new life. The second piece of the bridge I was forging to help myself get to where I wanted to be as a woman.

Born in Sweden, Gus spoke excellent English, but with a give-away accent. Unlike Jeremy, there was no intensity here. Gus was bright, warm, funny, and instantly intimate. We had dinner in the hotel where wine and laughter flowed freely. He returned with me to my room, holding hands and nuzzling in the elevator. We talked for hours, made love, and talked some more. Then he had to go. He dressed without turning the lights on, bent over the bed to kiss me goodbye, and exited through the first door on his left, closing it gently behind him.

"Gus," I called out in the dark.

"Yes?"

"You're in the closet."

Gus, with his light heart and open admiration of me, was a balm for my soul from which I garnered confidence and an opportunity to practice not being ashamed of my background. I explained to Gus that I grew up in a home with a complete lack of morality, including ridiculous ethnic prejudices—a sociological sty; he told me about the long line of Swedish aristocracy from which he hailed. I shared with him how life was my biggest teacher, that I was primarily self-educated, and that, although I did a very good job with the English language, my language skills began and ended there. He regaled me with stories about earning his two masters degrees, learning to speak five languages fluently, and two others modestly. I had trouble remembering high-school Spanish. I had never seen an ocean until I was thirty-six; he had traveled the world all his life. Nevertheless, he loved my mind, the places I had traveled within it, my insights into life, and my ability to express them. And he made it quite clear to me that he thought I was the sophisticated one. We had fun together and learned from each other, but like Jeremy, we were not a perfect match. He loved the corporate world, its power structure and socializing. For me, a little went a long way. He liked to stay over-busy; I liked to walk in the woods. But when we parted, we were friends.

I went back to the drawing board in my quest to find my true partner. I believed absolutely that it would happen—that I would marry one more time and that he would be my life partner. My last piece of an unknown bridge.

To help me visualize and focus my thoughts, I made a list of everything I wanted in a relationship. Then I double-checked the list to be sure everything I wanted my partner to bring to the table I had already accepted in myself. How could I manifest something if I was not emotionally integrated with the essence of it?

I wanted someone who had a great sense of humor, knew himself, had a passion for his inner nature and for life, was spiritual without being dogmatic, was attractive and sexy to me, was kind to the core.

And my list went on....

I knew I needed to be clear on the picture of what I wanted to create. I also had to accept that I was an equal with it and that I could align it with a congruent feeling. A picture and a passion: That became my credo. I set about looking for a model—something that would help me relate to and feel with my dream. And then one night, *voila*, there it was right in front of my face. Robert Wagner and Stephanie Powers. *Hart to Hart*. I watched this show like a convert clutching a new-found religion. The characters of Jonathan and Jennifer Hart come to life on my Sony. The way Jonathan was filled by his lovely wife, how he drank her in—I soaked it up. I would say to myself, "Yep, that's how my guy will look at me. That's how we will delight each other." The Harts laughed together, loved together, adventured together. On screen, they treasured each other. They brought to life the themes and ideas I had been forming in my head for years. I turned back to the metaphoric modeling clay of ideas from which I sculpted my intention for my personal life. A picture and a passion.

Heart to heart.

I checked within myself to make sure I didn't have any hidden agendas. Did I need to be validated by a man, taken care of by a man, made whole or complete by a man, made okay because I had a man? You know the litany.

I was clean. I wanted him just because I wanted him, and because I desired to experience a part of life I had not yet known.

A new mantra formulated in my mind. I was already a convert to the quantum field, which basically says the building blocks of form—particles, waves, molecules—morph according to the point of view of that which is observing them. Cause and effect at its finest. So, I began to think and repeat and repeat: For every thought there *is* a corresponding factor; that which I am seeking is seeking me. That is now, and always has been, the law of attraction in action.

It was a wonder: The idea that someplace in the world an unknown man that I was seeking was consciously or unconsciously seeking me. He was looking for exactly who and what I am, and I was looking for him— not as he could be or would but exactly as he already is. I had married potential for the last time! The thought of us finding our way to each other, like giant magnets being inexorably drawn together, flowed through my body like a current of energy, a frequency, exciting me and lifting my heart. My guy was actually looking for *me*!

That which I am seeking *is* seeking me.

I almost canceled.

I hadn't dated anyone in close to three months. On purpose. All year long, I had felt so strongly inside of me that I would marry my true life partner by the time I was forty—a mere six months away—so who knows? Maybe I was wrong. But I was beyond bored with casual dates and casual sex. So now I sat with focus narrowed on my perfect partner list, perched with telescope in hand, looking for Mr. Right.

Why I had accepted this invitation tonight I couldn't fathom.

Not that John wasn't a great guy. Tall—as in very—and attractive with dynamite blue eyes, he was a genuinely nice fellow. One of the good guys. We had met over a year ago, and while there was definite chemistry between us initially, we were both involved with other people at the time. We had channeled our interest in each other into a casual and respectful friendship.

"And you agreed to go out with him tonight because…?" I chastised myself irritably. It was the night before Thanksgiving; I was cooking for the kids and a few friends the next day. I had plenty to do tonight. I didn't want to go anywhere.

"Go, for God's sake," my good friend Diana said when I called her kvetching. "You've always liked him. Jeez, he finally got away from that toxic ex of his. He's probably lookin' to have some fun.

"Don't think of it as a date," she added. "Think of it as a night with a friend."

So, I put away my attitude and went with John on our first non-date date to see *An Officer and a Gentleman*. That certainly was apropos to John. He'd been an officer—captain in the Air Force—and as far as a gentleman goes, he'd always been chivalrous and kind to me.

After the movie, we decided to have a bite to eat and returned to my condo, presumably to drop off my car. Getting a bite to eat always meant a restaurant to me. But John suggested he cook. He escorted me to the door, then left with the words, "I'll be back soon."

I shook my head as I closed the door behind him. Were we light years away or what? Cooking! Except for Thanksgiving and Christmas, gross.

Twenty minutes later, John returned with a bottle of wine, two great-looking steaks, salad fixings, and some fabulous crunchy bread. *And* flowers. I poured the wine and sat on the kitchen counter, bantering playfully while he made the salad and cooked the steaks. He called me a peanut gallery, but he was laughing when he said it. I set the table; he lit the logs in the fireplace and the candles on the table. I was aware that my interest was palpably perking up. When our late-night dinner was ready, I lowered the lights. He held my chair, then he went over to the stereo to select music. He put on Beethoven.

I was getting more impressed by the moment.

We talked, teased, laughed, and opened another bottle of wine. When the Maestro's second movement of the Fifth Symphony played, John was visibly moved. I observed him in the soft glow of the candlelight. I was seeing facets of this lovely man I hadn't known were there. The differences in our styles, instead of creating disharmony, were actually complementing each other. At the end of the evening, I invited him to join us for Thanksgiving dinner.

John encircled me with his long arms, smiled down at me, and said yes. Then he kissed me. Warmly, sweetly, sexily.

Well, that was the beginning of an almost instant and very passionate love affair. But it was about to be interrupted. Weeks ago I had decided I couldn't wait around for Mr. Wonderful. I had to live my life. The kids would be with Leo this Christmas, and I had never had a real vacation. I booked first-class tickets to Hawaii and, with Diana, rented a condo right on the beach. Mr. Wonderful was just going to have to find me.

As connected as I suddenly felt to John, I was not going to bail on Diana or change my plans. On December 23rd I celebrated an early Christmas with my children. We went to dinner—as in *out* to dinner—came back, and opened piles of presents. As they were leaving to go to their dad's house, snowflakes were starting to fall.

John came over later that night. He had met my kids, but it was too soon to introduce him as a "sleep-over" friend. The game plan was that I would have special time with my children; he would arrive afterward and spend the night, then drive Diana and me to the airport in the morning.

I turned the alarm off minutes before it rang, slipped quietly out of bed, took a shower, then looked out the window. Or tried to. Every window of my first-floor condo had mounds of snow piled high against it. The doors, too.

It was the Christmas Blizzard of 1982. Nobody was going anywhere. Overnight, traffic in the entire city had vanished. Stapleton Airport was closed and would not be reopening soon. Passengers on the last flights to land during the night had been stuck for hours on the tarmac; pilots couldn't locate the gates. Cars were abandoned on the road, emergency vehicles lodged precariously in small mountains of snow. Neighbors, who had barely known each other, spent Christmas together instead of with their families.

The great city of Denver had ground to a halt.

John and I were magically cubby-holed for the next few days, endlessly talking and laughing, keeping the fire aglow both in the fireplace and in ourselves. Music played softly in the background. We split a pork chop for Christmas dinner—that was all I had in the freezer. It was enough. New love was filling both of us. I snuggled deeper into the wonderful plush robe John had given me for Christmas and sighed. It was the most romantic two days I had ever known.

"Put away your telescope," my inner senses said to me. "Mr. Wonderful—Mister All-that-you-had-ever-hoped-for—is right before your eyes."

Days after we dug ourselves out of the snow banks, John was still there. Then he chose not to leave, ever. We married in May, nine days after my fortieth birthday.

And just like in the storybooks, we lived—and continue to live—happily ever after.

The love of John—his innate kindness, loyalty, and laughter; his integrity, unfailing caring, and his beauty—for the love of John my life has been transformed. Not because he healed me. He did not. I did that. But through my life with him I have had the opportunity to experience life and love the way it was always meant to be.

For the love of John, my heart sings forever with gratitude.

33

MY SONG

Stella, a close friend of mine, called me early one morning several years ago. She told me about a lucid dream she had just had and asked for my take on it. I closed my eyes, as I always do when asked to interpret a dream, and listened closely to my friend's story. A gypsy woman with a long red scarf was the main character in her dream. In my mind, the elderly, gray-haired gypsy sprang to life. It was as though I could actually feel her. She was seated, as if on a bench. The long red scarf that was looped around her neck draped down into her lap. Her skirt touched the ground. I could see her so vividly. I looked into her soft, blue-gray eyes and realized with surprise that the garb and heritage with which she presented herself were just window-dressing. She was actually a shaman.

I was explaining this to Stella, when all of a sudden, in my head, the gypsy woman/shaman of my friend's dream turned to me and said, "You think your life has been about pain and suffering. You are wrong. It's been about resurrection."

What a profound teaching. It rang inside of me with such truth that I was blown away. It helped me own and release attachments to duality and pain that I had still been holding onto. My need to use my world as a reflection of me—which I had been working to eradicate for so many years—was cracking and chipping away right before my eyes. Her words registered within me in a way that none had before. They brought me closer to owning and valuing the different aspects inside of me that are me. I didn't have to be at war with any parts of me anymore. It's the pieces of the whole and the whole of the pieces.

A merging was forming inside of me. A oneness that was beginning to hum in harmony within me.

The different parts of me were no longer segmented in private, disjointed compartments. They were just aspects of me that I could take out and express and experience at any time. Like outfits in my closet. But they were no longer separate from each other. They were part of the whole. I could be funny, smart, the teacher, the student. I could be technologically challenged, never able to remember my zip code, bull-headed, stubborn, and on occasion just plain stupid, and still not be separated from the all of me. I realized that life is not about yin and yang. It's about yin in yang, yang in yin. It's the gentleness of strength and the strength of gentleness. It's about the flow that is the song of the spirit of me, moving through all of its segments. Moving through me.

I looked at the shaman and felt as though an orchestra were tuning up inside of me....

My life had not been about pain and suffering. I *lived* for God's sake. It's been a celebration, a symphony—a resurrection unfolding. It's been an opportunity to experience in this lifetime a soul's truth so much greater than pain and isolation and aloneness.

To be resurrected, I reflected to myself. To breathe life into that which I thought was dead.

My sojourn is to remember that the darkness is a part of the light, but it can never fully obscure it. To search out that light every day—and if I don't find it today, to be doubly determined to discover it tomorrow. To let the wisdom of the laughing Buddha have voice in me.

And that's my song. The cracking open of a once-wounded heart, the experience of love. The journey of rising from the ashes of that within me which I once felt was surely dead. The discovery of the light in the midst of darkness, the resurrection of hope, the healing of pain, and the promise of a new day.

For with each dawn comes the light.

ABOUT THE AUTHOR

Sandy Brewer is an author, speaker, therapist, coach, and humanitarian. For over thirty years she has helped and inspired thousands of people to move beyond their own personal tragedies in order to explore and embrace the possibilities in their own lives. Her work has been featured on NBC's *Nightly News* with Tom Brokaw and a nationally televised documentary.

The abuse Sandy endured as a child was so horrific that many would not have survived it. But she did survive it and more. As Sandy examined her abuse, along with the resulting crippling depression, she began the work to untangle and dismantle the pain of her past, bringing light and hope into it and emerging a victor over it. Along the way, she developed seminal techniques that enabled her not only to overcome, but also literally to gain strength from these experiences. Enlightened and empowered by her journey, Sandy began to share what she had learned with others. She has worked with countless individuals, leading them out of the darkness and into the light. Over the last thirty years Sandy has taught her vision and techniques through workshops, seminars, counseling, and speaking engagements across the nation.

Now Sandy has memorialized her innovative work and techniques in her memoir *Pursuit of Light*, an entertaining, frank, soul-gripping, inspirational book that gives her own personal account of abuse and how she came to "find the light" and how you, too, can look at your life from a new perspective and create new choices.

Sandy Brewer is an exceptional woman whose time has finally come to get this story told. She has a loving husband, John, three children, and five grandchildren. She recently retired from her counseling practice of thirty years and moved to Carlsbad, California, to focus on her writing and speaking.

You can learn about her current appearances, programs, and other product offerings by contacting her at: Sandy@PursuitOfLight.com or through her publisher at: www.PeachTreeHouse.com.

"A stunning, inspiring, powerful book. It stayed with me. I couldn't put it down"
—**Paul Antonelli, Two-time Emmy winner**

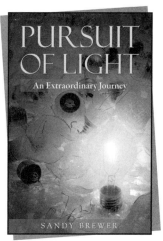

PURSUIT OF LIGHT
An Extraordinary Journey

Sandy Brewer
Transcending the Past

Pursuit of Light: An Extraordinary Journey, by Sandy Brewer, 224-page hardcover, ISBN 978-0-9796554-4-9, $24.95 plus $6.95 shipping and handling (CA residents add $1.93 sales tax per book). Order online at **www.PursuitOfLight.com**, or send order to publisher PeachTreeHouse, Inc, P.O. Box 1008, Carlsbad, CA 92008, or phone order at (760) 230-8123.

Special offer: Order 2 or more copies and pay no shipping and handling fees (minimum savings of $13.90). CA taxes still apply.

ORDER YOUR COPY TODAY
A GREAT GIFT FOR ANYONE SEEKING INNER TRANSFORMATION

– –

YES, I want to order this inspiring book. Go now to **www.PursuitOfLight.com** to order or complete and mail this form to the publisher as noted below or call (760) 230-8123.

Send me _____copies of *Pursuit of Light: An Extraordinary Journey* at $24.95 plus $6.95 each for shipping and handling (CA residents add $1.93 sales tax per book). *Special offer:* Order 2 or more copies and pay no shipping & handling fees (minimum savings of $13.90)

Name_____Phone _____

Organization_____Email _____

Address _____

City/State/Zip _____

Please contact me regarding Sandy speaking to our organization at phone # _____

My check or money order for $_____is enclosed

Charge to my ❑ VISA   ❑ MasterCard   ❑ AMEX

Card number _____

Exp_____   Signature _____

Mail to: PeachTreeHouse, Inc • P.O. Box 1008 • Carlsbad, CA 92008
Or call your credit card order to (760) 230-8123

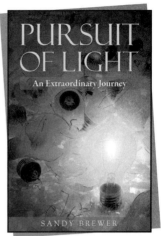